The New Northwest Passage

# THE NEW
# NORTHWEST
# PASSAGE

## A Voyage to the Front Line
## of Climate Change

### CAMERON DUECK

GREAT PLAINS
PUBLICATIONS

Great Plains Publications
345-955 Portage Avenue
Winnipeg, MB  R3G OP9
www.greatplains.mb.ca

Great Plains Publications gratefully acknowledges the financial support provided
for its publishing program by the Government of Canada through the Canada
Book Fund; the Canada Council for the Arts; the Province of Manitoba through
the Book Publishing Tax Credit and the Book Publisher Marketing Assistance
Program; and the Manitoba Arts Council.

Design & typography by Relish Design Studio Inc.
Printed in Canada by Friesens

LIBRARY AND ARCHIVES CANADA CATALOGUING IN PUBLICATION

Dueck, Cameron
    The New Northwest Passage: a voyage to the front line of climate change /
Cameron Dueck.

Includes bibliographical references.
Issued also in electronic formats.
ISBN 978-1-926531-36-6

    1. Dueck, Cameron--Travel--Northwest Passage. 2. Sailing--Northwest
Passage. 3. Climatic changes--Northwest Passage. 4. Climatic changes--Arctic
regions. 5. Inuit--Canada--Social conditions. 6. Northwest Passage--Description
and travel. I. Title.

FC3963.D83 2012 910.9163'27 C2011-907038-3

ENVIRONMENTAL BENEFITS STATEMENT

**Great Plains Publications** saved the following
resources by printing the pages of this book on
chlorine free paper made with 100% post-consumer
waste.

| TREES | WATER | ENERGY | SOLID WASTE | GREENHOUSE GASES |
|---|---|---|---|---|
| 23 | 10,520 | 10 | 667 | 2,333 |
| FULLY GROWN | GALLONS | MILLION BTUs | POUNDS | POUNDS |

Environmental impact estimates were made using the Environmental Paper Network
Paper Calculator. For more information visit www.papercalculator.org.

FSC
www.fsc.org
MIX
Paper from
responsible sources
FSC® C016245

*For Linda Dueck—*
*my mother, who was graceful and brave*

# TABLE OF CONTENTS

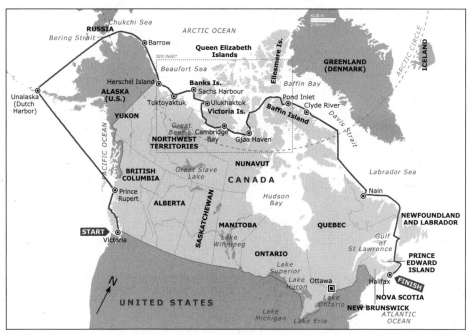

The 8,000 nautical mile (15,000km) voyage of the *Silent Sound* in the summer of 2009.

map/Troy Dunkley

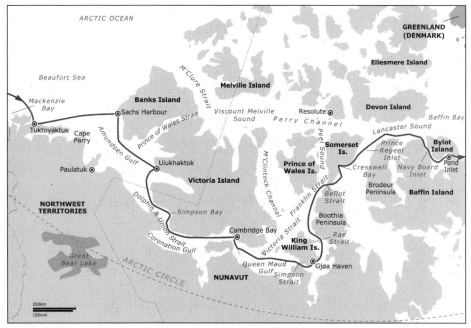

map/Troy Dunkley

# AUTHOR'S NOTE

*The Inuit*

The term Inuit refers to a group of culturally similar indigenous peoples living in the Arctic regions of Canada, Greenland, Russia and the United States. Inuit means "the people" in Inuktitut, the language of the Inuit. An Inuit person is called an *Inuk*.

The Inuit are the descendants of the Thule culture, which emerged from Alaska around 1000 AD and spread eastwards across the Arctic. The Inuit displaced the related Dorset culture. Today there are more than 50,000 Inuit living in Canada, with about 80 percent living in Nunavut, the Northwest Territories, Northern Quebec, and Labrador.

In the US the term Eskimo is used to describe the Yupik and Iñupiat peoples that live in Alaska. The Iñupiat are an Inuit people in northwestern Alaska and the Bering Strait region who share similar ethnic heritage with the Chukchi people of Russia. The Yupik are closely related but are not Inuit, creating a reason for the use of the term Eskimo in Alaska as it includes both the Yupik and Iñupiat. The term Eskimo has fallen out of favour outside of Alaska and is considered derogatory by many natives. The Inuit say that the name was given to them by the Cree Indians, one of their traditional enemies, and that it means "eater of raw meat." Most academic linguists do not agree with this theory, but "Eskimo" remains a derogatory term in Canada.

I have used the term Eskimo to describe the native peoples in Alaska, while using Inuit to refer to Canadian natives. However, for sake of simplicity, I use the term Inuit, inclusive of Alaskan Eskimos, when discussing pan-Arctic issues that involve both the Inuit and Eskimos.

In many cases Inuit and Eskimos choose to identify themselves by their own distinct cultural group, such as the Iñupiat of Northern Alaska or the Inuvialuit in the Western Canadian Arctic. I have used these more specific names where suitable.

*Distances*

Distances at sea are measured in nautical miles. One nautical mile equals 1.852 kilometres, or 1.151 statutory miles. Similarly, wind, current and boat speed are expressed in knots. One knot of speed equals 1.852 kilometres per hour, or 1.151 miles per hour.

Distances on land are expressed in kilometres with a few exceptions, such as within quotations. Canada officially uses the metric system, but the imperial system (miles, gallons, etc) is still in common colloquial use.

*Place Names*
Many places in the Arctic have undergone several name changes in recent centuries. For example, Ulukhaktok, a small community on Victoria Island, was named Holman by early European Arctic explorers and it went by that name until 2006 when it switched back to its native name. I have tried to use the names most often used by the people that live in these communities, and when in doubt have chosen the traditional Inuit, and official, names. In most cases I have tried to mention alternative names if the place is known by more than one name.

Some towns are commonly called by their abbreviated names. For example, Tuktoyaktuk is widely referred to as Tuk. I have used these abbreviations where suitable after providing the full name.

*Let us raise a monument to them, more enduring than stone:*
*the recognition that they were the first discoverers of the Passage.*
—Roald Amundsen, 1908

# INTRODUCTION

**S**houts and whistles filled the air as the other sailors pointed at my yacht, dockside in the crowded marina, and congratulated me on the lucky omen. I had only hours earlier signed the papers to make *Silent Sound* mine and had just returned to port when a bald eagle gracefully alighted on her masthead. "She's mine! I bought her this morning!" I shouted back, craning my neck to look at the giant bird balancing at the top of my mast.

I needed all the luck I could get. I was about to set off on the greatest voyage of my life. And my planned route through the Arctic was littered with tales of failure. When Sir John Franklin's Arctic expedition set sail from the Thames on the morning of May 19, 1845, his daughter Eleanor spotted a dove in the rigging of one of the ships. "Everyone was pleased with the good omen, and if it had been an omen of peace and harmony, I think there is every reason of it being true," she wrote to her aunt. Franklin died on that voyage, trying to find the very passage I was preparing to sail, and I could only hope that an eagle on my masthead would bring me more luck than that dove brought Franklin.

My plan to navigate the Northwest Passage began five years earlier on the deck of a yacht in the blistering sun of coastal Brazil—about as far away from polar adventure as I could get. I had crossed the Atlantic Ocean from South Africa and was nearing the end of a year of travel and sailing. It had been a splendid year, but I missed the intellectual challenge of my journalism career. I wanted to find a way to combine my passion for sailing with my career in writing. It didn't take me long to realize that the Northwest Passage, which was fast becoming more navigable due to climate change, offered the sailing challenge *and* the story I was looking for. I let the idea brew for a couple of years before I began to lay my plans.

Since the discovery of the New World, the fabled Northwest Passage through the Canadian Arctic had been an elusive dream for explorers and mariners alike. Throughout the grand age of exploration, it remained the ocean's one unattainable prize, luring young men seeking wealth and fame. They were looking for a sailing route over the top of North America, which would give the Old World quicker access to the spice and silk markets of Asia. It was a route to the northwest of Europe, and thus the name. It would replace the tedious overland journey and the long and dangerous southern routes around Cape Horn or Cape of Good Hope. Men were eager to fill in this mysterious void on the maps of the known world.

Wealthy patrons poured fortunes into the quest, gaining little more than their names on distant, frozen spots on the map that few would ever see. In 1745 a Parliamentary Act in Britain created a £20,000 reward for the discovery of the Northwest Passage. The potential Arctic short-cut from Europe to Asia subsequently became an icy graveyard for the hundreds of sailors who, trapped in the shifting sea ice, died from starvation, scurvy and the bitter cold. They died wandering, lost, through a maze of Arctic islands and rocky waters, not knowing if there really was a passage between the Atlantic and Pacific Oceans. Wooden sailing ships were crushed in the ice and sank, leaving scant clues to the suffering of their men. The most famous of those ships were Sir John Franklin's *HMS Erebus* and *HMS Terror*. His two ships sank without a trace and their 129 men succumbed to cannibalism before perishing on the ice.

In 1906 Roald Amundsen became the first man to sail through the passage. This "shortcut" took him three years to complete. Despite his success, the ice-choked passage never became the commercial shipping route that early explorers hoped for, and few people could boast of sailing its entire length.

Since Amundsen made it through the Northwest Passage it has been traversed many times by icebreakers and small working ships. However, most of these voyages happened in the last 25 years. There were only 11 full transits of the Northwest Passage between 1906 and 1984. Increasingly, small private yachts have been making the trip, and by the end of 2008 about 35 boats comparable in size and design to *Silent Sound* had made it through. But the area's remoteness and a lack of marine facilities and support continue to make this a difficult journey for smaller vessels. Charting of these waters remains scant, relying in some instances on data collected a hundred years earlier. The pull of the magnetic North Pole renders compasses useless and poor satellite coverage over the polar region means global positioning systems are unreliable. The window of opportunity, when there is enough open water to sail in the passage, is only a few weeks long. Even then the ice is a constant danger and ships may be forced to wait for ice to melt in crucial parts of the passage. Add to this strong currents and shallow reefs, and the Northwest Passage remains an epic yachting challenge. Far fewer people have sailed a yacht through the Northwest Passage than climbed Mount Everest.

The Northern Sea Route, or Northeast Passage, above Russia, is a more travelled route by comparison. This passage, from Murmansk on the Barents Sea to the Bering Strait and the markets of the Far East, was first sailed from end to end in 1878, by Finnish-Swedish explorer Nils A.E. Nordenskjöld and Lieutenant Louis Palander of the Swedish Royal Navy. Since then, Russia has developed an extensive fleet of icebreakers and navy ships that have sailed these Arctic waters. By some estimates there have been 3,000 transits of the passage since it was first discovered. These waters are generally deeper, better charted and contain less ice than the Northwest Passage, and it is the Northeast Passage that shipping companies see becoming the first commercial Arctic shipping route.

Climate change is causing temperatures in the Arctic to rise much faster than elsewhere on the globe. Average global temperatures have risen 0.6°C in the last two centuries, while in Alaska and northern Canada winter temperatures have risen as much as 3 to 4°C in the past 50 years. Sea ice plays an important role in reducing the transfer of heat from the ocean to the atmosphere, and therefore winter temperatures are increasing more rapidly than summer temperatures. As the extent of sea ice is reduced, solar heat absorbed by the sea in the summer is more easily transferred to the atmosphere in the winter, raising air temperatures.

Each summer there is more and more open water as the sea ice melts, making it easier to sail through the Arctic. Ice absorbs only 10 to 20 percent of solar energy reaching it, while open ocean water absorbs 80 to 90 percent. The less ice there is, the faster the ocean warms, and the faster the ocean warms the faster the ice melts, creating a vicious cycle.

From 1979 to 2000 the Arctic had about 7.7 million square kilometres of sea ice, about the same area as that of the Australian continent. By September 2005 that had shrunk to 5.3 million square kilometres, and by 2007 the ice area was down to 4.4 million square kilometres. An ice area equal to one third of Canada's landmass had melted and disappeared in the summer sunshine. The giant melt of sea ice has brought a renewed urgency to the discussions over the Arctic's future. Instead of a frontier luring explorers and adventures in search of riches and fame, the Arctic is now seen as a melting ice pan with far reaching implications for the entire globe. The warming climate is forcing Arctic communities and wildlife to adjust to survive, and highlighting Arctic issues of sovereignty and resource management.

Stories about the effects of climate change in the Arctic were appearing in newspapers on a daily occurrence as I made my plans. They spelled out how many thousands of square kilometres of ice was lost, which species were in danger, and which navy or shipping company was preparing to break its way through the weakened sea ice that remained. But the story of the people that lived in the Arctic, the Inuit, was missing. The Inuit and other northerners had become the first people in the world to feel the day-to-day impact of climate change. I knew practically nothing about modern Inuit even though I'd grown up in the same country as them. I was curious to learn more about them.

Although climate change would make it easier for me to realize my dream, there were still plenty of challenges left for me to solve. I was on a tight budget and was living in Hong Kong, from where the Arctic and the Northwest Passage seemed rather distant goals. Nor did I own a boat. I started saving and borrowing while reading every book I could find about the Northwest Passage. In the spring of 2008 I flew to Victoria, British Columbia, to look at yachts and meet some Arctic experts. *Silent Sound*, a heavy 40-foot sloop only a few years younger than me, seemed right for the job and priced right for me. In buying her I had committed to making a west-to-east transit of the passage, which was the reverse of the classical Northwest Passage voyage. My decision had been subconscious, influenced by my greater familiarity of Vancouver and Victoria compared with East Coast cities. I also had family on the West Coast so I would be leaving a port that I knew nominally to sail east and to a side of Canada I'd never even seen. It was the way that felt most natural to me.

A few months later I left my reporting job at the *South China Morning Post* and signed on as a desk editor at the *Financial Times*, without informing my new employer of my plans. I reasoned that my Arctic plans could still fall apart, so I better take the job opportunity as a back-up plan. The more prestigious *Financial Times* offered a slightly higher salary, which would help pay for my plans, and instead of running around town as a reporter I'd have more time at my desk to coordinate preparations. The break in between jobs also gave me time to return to Victoria and complete the purchase of *Silent Sound*, the moment crowned by the bald eagle. Suddenly, what had been a far-fetched dream had become a plan. I spent the next few weeks sailing *Silent Sound* in the Gulf Islands off the west coast of Canada, naively basking in the glow of my ambition.

The following months were spent mastering my new editing job while secretly surfing the internet in search of willing crew and using the office fax machine to send off equipment order forms. Tom Mitchell, the friend who had recommended me for the job, was the only one in the newsroom who knew of my plans. He took great pleasure in stopping at my desk with a smirk on his face to ask obscure yachting questions that left the rest of the co-workers with quizzical looks on their faces while I worried that he'd blow my cover. Nearly every person I needed to communicate with, from the coast guard to the shipwrights, was based in Canada. I began to spend most nights at my computer or on the phone, arriving at my new job bleary-eyed and tired in the morning.

My friend Troy Dunkley began designing a website while I was chasing potential sponsors. By now my dream had a name: The Open Passage Expedition. Because of the global credit crisis it was difficult to find sponsors willing to back an inexperienced adventurer sailing through the Arctic on an aged yacht. But, slowly, I began to cajole discounts from sail and chart makers until I had most of the essential gear. All of this was done in virtual secrecy, as I was afraid of announcing my plans at work before my probationary period had ended. Finally, on November 15, the website went live and the secret was out, with friends and family coming to a launch party on the roof of my apartment. Two of my brothers were visiting Hong Kong, adding to the festive air. Exposing my wildest and most impractical dream to the world was a dangerous thrill. I felt like I'd stepped off the edge of a cliff.

Six days after the launch party my mother passed away, following years of illness. I had told her about my dream a year earlier, during one of our last proper conversations, and she gave me her blessing. My brothers and I, in Yunnan Province preparing to go hiking, hurriedly booked flights home. I returned to Canada and spent time with my family on our turkey farm on the Manitoba prairies. From there, still feeling raw and disoriented, I went to *Silent Sound*, where she was moored in Esquimalt, near Victoria. It was cold and rainy winter weather, and I got very little work done towards the goal of getting the boat ready to sail. I was paralyzed by grief and the enormity of the task ahead. Instead I spent hours sitting alone in the saloon, questioning my plans while I nursed a bottle of rum and wondered what my mother would make of it all. Waking up alone in my frigid boat, huddled in my sleeping bag and watching my breath turn the air white was a vivid reminder of what I was planning to do.

From *Silent Sound*'s cockpit at her pontoon I could see the Fisgard Lighthouse, Canada's oldest and most famous west coast beacon, as well as the Esquimalt shipyards. I was far from the first sailor to use this harbour to prepare for an Arctic voyage. Vilhjalmur Stefansson launched his rebuilt *Karluk* from here nearly a century earlier before setting off on his cursed Arctic expedition. Stefansson, perhaps the most intrepid and infamous Arctic explorer of his time, was born near my family home in Manitoba and I would cross his path again before my journey was over. We were from vastly different eras, and my challenges appeared paltry compared to those he had faced, but I took some small pleasure in knowing he had probably asked himself similar questions while preparing nearby.

I set a goal of leaving on June 6, 2009, but the preparations felt endless. I was still looking for crew, for funding and in general felt woefully inadequate for the job. I contacted as many people as I could find who had done the passage before, but much of their advice was contradictory. I decided to take the most conservative line of advice and buy all the safety equipment I could afford, and then hope I wouldn't need it. New sails, a life raft, survival suits in case we had to abandon ship ... the list seemed endless. The walls of my Hong Kong flat were papered with Arctic sea charts. When I did find time to go out and meet my friends I would spend much of the time babbling on about ice predictions and century-old tales of a place they had barely heard of. I had never skippered my own boat on a long voyage or been responsible for keeping one mechanically sound. I read diesel mechanic guides, trying to remember what little about engines my father had taught me while I was growing up on the farm.

My three-person crew started falling apart about six months before departure, with the last of the original crew leaving the project in late March, about two months before our planned departure. I scrambled to replace members as fast as they resigned due to other commitments and illness. By early April I once again had a full team, and I prayed they would stick with me. Hanns Bergman, a professional sailor from Germany, was recommended by a friend. We had never met. He was keen, but I could sense he was wary that the expedition might never leave harbour. I tried to assure him otherwise and felt relieved that at least I had another sailor aboard, and one that had far more experience than I did. Anna Woch was a filmmaker from Montreal who had never sailed but was confident she'd find her sea legs. I spoke to her family and friends, trying to get a sense of whether or not she was up for the challenge. I warned Anna of the dangers and discomfort the voyage would involve, then signed her on, sight unseen. The fourth member was Tobias Neuberger, a German medical doctor who had left medicine to work for a Chinese cosmetics company. I'd met Tobias in South Africa in 2004. I was driving across the country to Cape Town to join a trans-Atlantic yacht delivery, and he was on a driving holiday from his job as doctor in Cape Town. He saw me stopped beside the road, looking at a map, and pulled over to chat. We'd been friends ever since. Although he too had never sailed, he had a broad mix of outdoor adventure experience and I was confident he would learn quickly. His photography and medical skills were a welcome addition to the team.

I quit my job at the *Financial Times* one month before I was scheduled to set sail, thanking my employer and co-workers for kindly ignoring the fact my mind had been miles away from my desk for the nine months I'd worked there. It was a good place to work, and leaving the paper tested my resolve to realize my dream. I put my possessions into storage, rented out my flat and moved to Victoria for the final preparations. My mind swirled with fundraising plans and modifications I had yet to make to *Silent Sound*, but by now I had an army of volunteers, friends and family pitching in. They even shared my gnawing worry that I would become yet another victim of the Arctic ice.

# CHAPTER 1
# Silent Sound

*How then am I so different from the first men through this way?*
*Like them, I left a settled life, I threw it all away.*
*To seek a Northwest Passage at the call of many men*
*To find there but the road back home again.*
—Stan Rogers, "Northwest Passage," 1981

**M**y eyes were tired of seeing so little. The sea was flat and grey. The sky was overcast. The land was low, featureless and dun coloured, and had been so for hundreds of miles. There'd been little to see, to note or point at, for days.

It was just after midnight on July 17, 2009 and a light rain was falling through fog. *Silent Sound* was well out to sea, off Franklin Point, where Alaska's north coast is carved into shallow swooping bays and sandbars. There was little wind, and we were under engine power.

A white smudge appeared in the distance. I squinted at the blurry outline in the dusk. It was hardly the dramatic encounter I had been imagining. I turned towards it, sailing a mile off course to get a closer look. Distances are deceiving in the eternal light of the Arctic summer, so I turned on the radar to double-check what I was seeing with the naked eye. The radar showed something in shallow water about half a mile off the coast. It was our first ice.

By morning the wind had filled from the northeast and we raised sails. It was still drizzling, but visibility was improving and we began to see a few small ice floes near the boat, this time to the north. Then, as morning wore on, a white line materialized on the horizon. Now we were sailing between the ice pack and the land. It was time to shake off the stupor caused by the tedious grind of making miles and instead feel the excitement and nervousness of danger.

A change in wind direction could push the ice ashore, taking *Silent Sound* with it, just as it had done to so many ships in the past. We were nearing Point Barrow, the far northern tip of Alaska, which has been a graveyard for ships for as long as ships have sailed here. Most of the ships caught by the ice were whalers or had come north to collect furs from trappers.

One of the most famous Arctic shipping catastrophes happened right here between September 12th and 14th of 1871 when 32 of 41 whaling ships in the Point Barrow area were driven ashore and crushed by ice near Wainwright. Five years later at least ten ships were caught in ice northeast of Point Barrow, again surprised by an early September freeze. Some accounts say up to 12 ships were lost in the ice this time as the ships drifted north with the ice, unable to break free. The 60 men aboard the ships were never heard from again.

Point Barrow's ice has also claimed its share of ships during the spring break-up in July and August, with maritime records tersely describing ship after ship that was "stove in by ice and sank" in these waters. Others were pushed ashore by ice when the wind direction changed, giving crews little choice but to rescue what possessions they could and jump across the ice floes for a long hike to safety. *Silent Sound* was far more fragile than those sturdy whalers, and if the ice turned against us we would be in deep trouble.

As the first pieces of ice bumped against her hull I realized I'd found the challenge and adventure I'd come looking for, and wondered if all my preparation had been enough.

*Silent Sound* was far from ready to challenge the Arctic when I bought her. The family who owned her before me had lived on her for more than a decade and spent five years cruising the South Pacific. She was in good condition, but her electronics were outdated, her sails floppy and I wanted to strengthen her bow for the ice that lay ahead. I arrived in Victoria one month before departure, faced with an overwhelming amount of work left to do, from finishing the installation of the new electronics and long distance radio to planning our provisioning and buying charts.

Tobias was the first to join me, stepping off the ferry from the mainland weighed down with suitcases full of medical supplies for the first aid kit, wet weather gear for the entire crew, and his own personal equipment. Tobias was tall and wiry, with a mop of curly reddish hair, an ear-to-ear grin and a corny sense of humour. He was lean and fit, a long-distance runner and hiker. Our friendship, which had begun on the side of a highway in South Africa, had developed during his visits to Hong Kong for business, when we'd troll the city's bars and embark on raucous pranks together with Troy. Tobias was a late addition to the crew, and had to negotiate a sabbatical from his job in order to join. As soon as he'd confirmed his plans he threw himself into planning and fundraising with an enthusiasm that came just at the right time as I had started to wear down with exhaustion. Although my friends around the globe had rallied as much support as they could, they all had jobs and lives far removed from my adventure. It was a huge relief to finally have another person working with me to share ideas and concerns with.

Tobias and I spent the next two weeks working on the *Silent Sound*. We installed instruments and built a computer workstation. Much of the time was spent driving a borrowed truck around Victoria searching for parts and equipment. One of our biggest jobs was installing a single side-band radio, which required that we lay hundreds of square feet of metal into the hull in order to give the radio signal more range. The exact amount, placement and type of grounding plate needed are hotly debated questions among experienced installers, and we were trying to produce a remedy on a tight budget and without any experience. Tobias and I shuttled from one radio expert to the next seeking advice, and we finally we settled on the most cost-effective solution. We drove to the hardware store and stocked up on rolls of galvanized tin, along with a long coil of heavy copper wire. We lined the inside of the hull with tin, cutting and bending it to fit the boat's cramped lockers and engine space. Then we stitched it all together with a long winding strap of copper. Our antenna was a copper cable hung from the mast and tied to a wooden dowel fastened across the backstays. Our installation looked a mess, but we crossed our fingers and hoped for the best. It would be another month before we'd find out if our unconventional installation would do the job.

Hanns, my first mate, arrived two weeks before our planned departure. I drove to the ferry terminal and scanned the crowd spilling down the gangplank. I'd only seen a small photo of him and wasn't sure I'd recognize him. But I knew it was him as soon as he stepped off the ferry. Hanns was tall, broad shouldered, with a close-cropped head of blond hair and an impish smile. And he was carrying a rucksack so enormous he could only be a sailor setting off on a long voyage.

"Finally we meet," he said, extending his hand giving me a firm handshake. It was the most confident I would feel all day.

I introduced him to *Silent Sound*. Hanns, Tobias and I had coffee in the cockpit, going over our plans. Then we got ready to move the boat from the dock where she had been living for the past year to a boatyard where we planned to lift her from the water to work on the hull. But before leaving we needed to load our new life raft, a heavy, unwieldy plastic box sitting on the dock. Hanns was settling in below deck, so Tobias and I tried to lift the raft to the deck of the boat and over the lifelines. As if in a slapstick movie, our efforts pushed the boat away from the dock, and slowly we found ourselves reaching farther and farther to close the gap between the boat and the dock. We were red-faced and gritting our teeth with the weight of the raft above the widening gap. Eventually physics took over, and we dropped the raft into the water with a splash. Tobias managed to stagger back onto the dock while I dropped to my knees and ducked into the water after the raft. With horror I remembered that the raft was designed to deploy automatically when submerged. The lid would pop off, allowing the orange six-man boat to explode from its case with a hiss. The potential embarrassment of the raft deploying under the dock was not lost on me, and I tried to hang on to it as it hit the water. The boat was now drifting back against the dock, where my entire upper body was hanging over the edge as I tried to keep my head above water while hanging on to the heavy, submerged raft. Tobias jumped onto my legs to keep me from going under water altogether. And there we were, waiting for an explosion of orange rubber. Hanns had heard the splash and in his understated way—which I would come to appreciate over the next few months—came to our assistance. We pulled the raft from the water and I sat back, rubbing my chin where I'd banged it on the dock in my attempted rescue dive. My jaw would remain sore for weeks, but now it was my ego that hurt the most. Hanns quietly took one of the halyards, clipped it to the raft, and used a winch to lift the load onto the deck.

*Silent Sound* slipped her lines and we steered north towards the Canoe Cove boatyard near Sidney. We planned to spend the night at anchor on nearby Sidney Spit and then enter harbour early in the morning for our lift out. We had already removed the old depth sounder but had not yet installed the new one, so we approached the shallow anchorage with caution. We found what looked like a good spot to drop our anchor, but soon we'd drifted back too far, too close to another boat, so we tried again. Then, as I tried to manoeuvre *Silent Sound* into a better spot, I caught the line of a crab pot around the rudder. The current was strong, and the pot quickly became a dragging anchor. With the line near our propeller I couldn't use the engine to help us fight the current. I was seething with embarrassment, and wondered how I would manage to skipper the yacht through the Arctic if I couldn't even make it to the boatyard without event. Eventually we got rid of the crab pot, set our anchor and settled down for the night.

Lifting the boat the next day began a hectic week of itchy, dusty fibreglass work. We were two weeks from departure, with the boat sitting high and dry and a big job ahead of us. Rod, my oldest brother, had driven 2,500 kilometres from Manitoba to help apply a sheath of Kevlar to *Silent Sound*'s prow to protect her in the ice. Kevlar is a strong, light material used to make bulletproof vests. It is applied in much the same way as fibreglass, with cloth and resin. But before we could start applying the Kevlar we had to grind away the gelcoat, or outside layer, of the fibreglass hull. Clouds of glittering dust rose from the boat despite our attempts to build a tent around it so the tiny glass slivers wouldn't drift onto other boats. Boat owners nearby were giving their yachts a spring coat of varnish, and they complained loudly and petitioned the yard manger to stop us. We sweet-talked and bullied our way forward, worried about any delay.

It was slow, agonizing work, and none of us knew if we were doing things correctly. I was grinding away the hull of the boat I hoped would carry me to the Arctic, and I wasn't sure if I knew how to rebuild it. Rod, who had built steel fishing boats on Lake Winnipeg as a young man, had done the research on applying Kevlar, and that was enough to make him the foreman of our motley crew. My 80-year-old father stood by, shaking his head at his son's folly. Those days were reminiscent of my childhood on the farm, stubbornly pushing on with an unpleasant job, just getting on with it. Each day the yard workers, experts in this work but too expensive for my meagre budget, would generously drop by and offer advice.

It was in the midst of this that I met Ian Hansen. He had found my website and had sent me emails from his home near Victoria while I was still in Hong Kong. His writing was confused, and I wasn't sure what he wanted, so I largely ignored his messages. Then one day as I worked on the boat he telephoned me; his speech was as unclear as his writing. He said he wanted to come see the *Silent Sound* and her crew. Soon he was in the boatyard, and he brought along his lovely wife Jo and his friend Ben Gray, who had transited the Northwest Passage aboard his self-designed motor yacht *Idlewild* in 2005. We soon had an invitation to dinner at Ian and Jo's nearby home.

There I heard Ian's story. He was a retired commercial airline pilot who had spent years flying in the Arctic, and upon retirement he set out to realize his dream of sailing the Northwest Passage. He bought a sturdy yet elegant expedition yacht, renamed her *Yonder*, and began to lay his plans. But then, only months after buying the yacht, he suffered an aortic dissection. He was lucky to live through it, but the medical complications left him with brain damage. Now Ian was fighting to regain his health, driven by his dream to sail through the Arctic. In the meantime he was cruising *Yonder* in waters closer to home and feeding his dream by keeping in contact with others who were setting sail for the north.

Meeting Ian erased any doubts I had over whether or not I should be chasing my dream. I had encountered many boats and expeditions that were much better funded, prepared and equipped than my own and I knew that with a few more years of saving and experience I'd be able to set off in better style. But I wanted to do it now in fear that if I put it off it would never happen. *Silent Sound* looked small, raggedy and poorly equipped next to the gleaming *Yonder*, and I asked Ian what he thought of my plan.

"You should go now. Don't wait," he responded in his slow, stuttering speech.

Ian's generosity, joy and sense of humour, in spite of his bad fortune, humbled me. The day after having dinner at his home I was walking across the boatyard, once again downcast after a discouraging telephone call with an equipment supplier. I looked up to see a bicycle speeding across the dusty yard, its rider hunched over the handlebars, helmet askew. It was Ian. There was a fresh breeze blowing across the yard, and the dust he'd kicked up arrived before he did. He slammed on the brakes beside me, breathless and wearing his usual wide smile.

"I have something to give you," he said, even before we had exchanged greetings. Then he reached into the pocket of his windbreaker and pulled out a messy fistful of cash, the wind tugging at the notes.

"Here," Ian said, pushing the cash towards me. "The bank is giving it away today."

I was speechless, and just as well, as the lump in my throat wouldn't let me speak anyway.

Soon we were frantically applying layers of Kevlar and rolling on the sticky resin. We kept one eye on the clock, knowing that we had a strict deadline to meet if *Silent Sound* was to be back in the water by the end of the week. I had booked a lift time for Saturday, planned to match the tides and busy schedule of a boatyard at the start of the sailing season. If we couldn't make our scheduled time we'd have to wait until Monday for our next chance. Rod muttered that we wouldn't be ready in time. I insisted we would be, but worried that he would be right.

It was agonizing to stand by and wait for the sun to dry the new protective layer so we could begin painting. *Silent Sound* was standing on steel supports high above the ground in a parking lot of land-bound yachts, and she had become a spectacle in the boatyard with the ugly yellow wound on her bow and her amateur crew of workmen. We were living aboard, covered in dust and surrounded by tools. Soon everyone in the boatyard knew our story. One after another boat owners dropped by to encourage, advise and disparage our plans. We began painting the rebuilt hull the day before she was supposed to go back in the water, working until late in the evening and praying the paint would be dry by morning. Surely this time I'd pushed the schedule too far.

On the morning of May 31st, exactly one week from our planned departure for the Arctic, I rolled from my bunk and crawled on deck. I climbed down the ladder to the ground and reached up to touch the freshly painted hull. My fingers were expecting soft, sticky paint. It was dry. We would make our lift time. At high tide we lowered *Silent Sound* into the water with her shiny new bow and set off for Victoria, where the harbour authority had donated a berth in the Inner Harbour for our last week. It was a prime position, in front of the sprawling Empress Hotel and in the midst of Victoria's summer tourist crowds. As we docked *Silent Sound* in the centre of the city, our friends and family began to arrive from around the world to help us with the last week of preparations.

Victoria was a popular port for ships sailing for the Arctic, and it was also the base for many of Canada's icebreakers. Unlike people in Hong Kong, those in Victoria understood the danger of my planned voyage, and there was a look of surprise on people's faces when I told them about my plans. Most of my friends in Hong Kong saw my journey as just another fun sailing voyage. In Victoria, I was met with low whistles and pointed questions about my boat and plans. But it also meant that there were people in Victoria who could offer me advice.

Earlier that spring I met with Captain David "Duke" Snider, director for the Pacific Region Coast Guard fleet and an experienced Arctic icebreaker pilot. He was burly, with a trim grey beard and twinkling eyes. His office walls were covered with pictures of icebreakers and Coast Guard souvenirs. Captain Duke struck me as the kind of man who read sailing adventure stories as a boy and never got over the romance of the sea, even after spending years rescuing men from its icy grip. I stuttered my way through an introduction and the short version of my plans, and then came to my point. "I'm here to give you a chance to talk me out of it," I told him.

Captain Duke told me that the Arctic changes and surprises mariners all the time, and especially when they think they have it figured out.

"We've had a couple of good years [good ice years, from a sailing per-spective] and often that's followed by a bad year. What happens when you have a few years of melting ice is that the big blocks of multi-year ice in McClure Strait melt, and that is what has been holding back all that bad pack ice. This can then come rushing into the passage. That's what got Franklin."

That wasn't very comforting to hear. Captain Duke then gave me a quick navigational lesson on how to duck and run through Arctic ice, hug-ging the shallows along the shore to avoid the pack ice, which becomes grounded before reaching the shore, like the first piece of ice we would eventually see. He sketched out the roughest parts of the passage, where to watch for "razor-sharp rock piles" and the stretches of water where strong currents were most likely to grab the *Silent Sound* and refuse to let go. I listened, wide-eyed and nervous.

"You have an advantage, and, well, I guess it's a liability as well. Your vessel is pretty small, so you can hug the shore and escape the pack ice. But then again, if you get caught, well, you're in big trouble," he said with a chuckle. I didn't really see the humour in that. But in the end Captain Duke gave me confidence. He said I wasn't the craziest, least prepared Northwest Passage dreamer he'd ever seen, and to me that was as good as a blessing.

"I've seen some mad, insane people up there. They're not prepared and they haven't registered with the authorities. Our icebreakers can be more than two days away if they need help."

I described the precautionary measures I was taking and the safety gear I had bought, and he seemed to approve. *Silent Sound* would have numerous GPS and satellite communication systems, as well as radios and live online tracking of our progress. With the coast guard contacts he had given me and my plans to register with them once in the Arctic, I felt I'd built the best safety net possible.

"It's about layers of information and support, that's what you need to protect yourself," Captain Duke advised. "If we have that, we know where to watch for you and we have an idea if you're having trouble." He had sailed the length of the Northwest Passage aboard ships twice, plied both ends of the passage countless times and lived in the Arctic. I liked knowing that Captain Duke would be watching.

"There's no reason why you don't have a reasonable chance, actual-ly a very good chance, of making it through in one season. I've looked at your website; you seem to be taking the right steps in preparation." Now

I was beaming. But then he added a dose of reality. "But don't forget the Arctic is about variables, nothing can be assumed. And it's too early to know what the ice will be like this year."

The Canadian Ice Service issued its annual ice forecast on June 1, one week before our departure. Earlier ice reports had indicated that summer 2009 might see higher ice levels than in the recent past. Rapid ice development in late November, 2008 had made up for the warm previous summer. However, the new report predicted warmer than usual temperatures along the coast of Alaska, Yukon and Northwest Territories for much of the summer, which was encouraging for us. The opening of a water route to Point Barrow, the most northerly point of Alaska and our first major bottleneck in terms of ice, was predicted to be about one week earlier than normal.

However, as Captain Duke had predicted, more extensive melting of first-year ice had removed the barrier holding back the multi-year ice that lived in the Arctic Ocean to the north. Older ice was predicted to drift down into the waters we wanted to sail through. Multi-year ice is harder and generally comes in larger chunks than first-year ice, creating a greater danger for yachts.

"Of concern for the western Arctic region for this summer is the unusual amount of old ice described earlier in Franklin Strait and M'Clintock Channel. This will most certainly prevent the clearing of the Northwest Passage for a fourth consecutive year and affect transit through the Victoria Strait region during late August and early September period," the report said.

Our last week in port was a frenzy of trips to the hardware store, sorting out problems with our email and satellite systems, and hauling truck-loads of provisions from the supermarket. Each load of food and gear was repackaged and stowed in *Silent Sound*'s lockers. The stress of readying the boat, finding financing and making time to spend with family and friends was causing clumps of my hair to fall out. But there was no turning back now.

Anna Woch arrived from Montreal during our last week of preparations. I met her at the bus station, scanning the disembarking passengers for a face that matched the photo she had sent me. The woman that stepped off the bus was unassuming, unadorned and a bit reserved. She was carrying enormous bags stuffed with the camera gear I'd had her buy for the expedition

Anna was a Polish immigrant who had given up her science career to work in film, and had spent considerable time teaching film in northern communities. I admired her audacity, joining three strange men on a four-month Arctic voyage when she did not know how to sail. Despite her commitment to the trip, it wasn't long after our first meeting that I began to wonder how well she and I would work together. We were creatively mismatched, and I felt she was struggling to fit in with the crew from the very start. But we were days from departure, and I convinced myself that once we were underway everything would fall into place.

I was no longer the only person with something at stake in the expedition. As my improbable dream to sail through the Arctic developed, more and more people joined to help to bring the pieces together, both those who would sail aboard *Silent Sound* and those left ashore. The expedition had grown into a team of 40 or more people around the world who had no obligation to commit time and money to the project, but who were supporting me nonetheless. There was a constant flow of volunteers coming and going from the boat as they ran errands, organized our departure party, brought hot food to feed the crew or helped us sort out our remaining equipment problems. Some of them were living vicariously through my dream, unwilling to take the risks themselves but enjoying some of the thrill by becoming part of the team. Others probably saw that without their help I would never succeed, and they helped me in order to prevent a disaster.

Friends and family had flown in from overseas and across the continent to help send us on our way. Tobias's family had arrived from Germany. Troy, who was running the website, and my girlfriend Jackie had both travelled from Hong Kong, and several members of my family had come from across Canada to help. Complete strangers became integral parts of our preparations, lending time, vehicles, homes, expertise and connections, or donating equipment and money. At times I felt bewildered by the energy and emotion my dream had sparked in others when busyness had forced me to push my own feelings aside. It was gratifying to be in the centre of this storm of activity and see how my dream had been adopted by so many. Passersby would stop at the boat and ask a few questions, then donate money without giving us a chance to properly thank them.

On the night before our departure the crew, our families and many of our new friends met at a dockside restaurant for dinner. It was a blur of speculation, excitement, and for me, a sense of worry that I would disappoint all of these people. Jackie repeatedly reminded me that friends and family were there because of my dream, but I felt distant from it all. *Silent Sound* was just outside the restaurant doors, tugging at her mooring lines, eager to go to sea, and in my mind I was already aboard her. I was desperate to cast off and begin the journey, if only to put an end to the preparations. My brother Bryan had sent along a parting gift that was presented to me at the dinner. It was a photo of my mother and I, taken during the visit when I'd first shared my plans with her. She was the bravest, most stoic person I'd ever known—traits I'd need in large measures in the months to come. I'd felt her spirit in this adventure from the very start, and I hung the picture on my cabin wall to remind me of that spirit every time I rolled out of my bunk to begin another watch.

The memory of my mother, and the life she'd provided me, also reminded me of why I had worked to make this dream come true. In Hong Kong I was surrounded by friends and colleagues who also enjoyed immense family and financial success and security. We were among the wealthiest and luckiest people in the world, born on the right side of the world's widening wealth divide. We were not wealthy by modern middle-class standards, but few of us faced any real risk in life. If we lost our jobs, our money or homes, we had professional skills and degrees that meant we could earn it all back. In addition, most of us came from financially stable families with ample resources to offer us at least basic support if things really took a turn for the worse. We enjoyed extensive safety nets that protected our privileged lives. Yet, even with all of this security, it was rare for us to take real risks and do something that could drastically alter our lives. I felt that all of our security was a waste if we didn't leverage it and push ourselves out of our comfort zones. "You don't keep your money in the bank, do you?" I asked friends working in finance. "You leverage it, you risk it, so that you can earn even more. Why would we do differently with other kinds of security we have in our lives?" It was something I believed strongly in, and the time had come to put it into practice.

I'd also long had a niggling worry that I was missing out on life in some way, and it created a restlessness that no amount of travel seemed to cure. I had enjoyed my journalism career and the international lifestyle it afforded me, but I was also bored by it. I needed to add some zest to my life. I wasn't particularly brave—I had given up rock climbing because I was afraid of heights—and while I enjoyed travelling rough and sailing across oceans, I had never tasted the kind of adventure that intentionally put me into life or death situations. I would never ski to the North Pole or walk, unaided, across a desert, if for no other reason than that I wasn't fit enough to do it, and too lazy to become that fit. In fact, knowing that I'd never put myself up for a real challenge left a gaping hole in my self-confidence. Maybe this voyage, tough but not life-threatening, would address that. If not, at least I'd have a good story to tell. Adventures are only as good as the story they produce, and I reckoned this journey could produce a yarn that would give me interesting pub stories for years to come.

On June 6 *Silent Sound* was as ready as she'd ever be, loaded for her journey with fuel, water and provisions. Friends and family, and a few curious onlookers, gathered on the dock to send us off. Norman Prelypchan, who with his wife Trudi had offered me considerable support in Victoria, arranged for Father Edward Lewis and Robert MacRae to officiate at our send-off. Robert was a distant relative of John Rae, the first man to sight the Northwest Passage and discover the fate of Franklin and his men. A bagpiper played as we boarded *Silent Sound*, and Father Lewis read a blessing written by Robert.

> *Bless Anna, Hanns, Tobias and Cameron*
> *May God and Columba and Donan, bless this craft*
> *May Angels dance above its deck*
> *To ward off dangers fore and aft*
> *From wind and wave and sunken wreck*
> *All who sail it may they protect*
> *And may all who sail the mighty Arctic*
> *Treat it always with respect*
> *And no foolish risks ever take.*
> *Amen.*

We hoisted our mainsail and sailed out of Victoria Harbour at noon. I had set the departure time more than a month earlier, and we left on time, nearly to the minute. But while everyone on the dock thought we'd finally set off on our voyage north, we only sailed about five miles before stopping. Bits of equipment and provisions lay strewn about the boat, needing to be repacked. We were tired, excited and needed a good night's rest before properly setting off. Soon *Silent Sound* was once again at anchor on Sidney Spit, but this time the preparations were over and our journey had begun.

CHAPTER 2
# Early Trouble

*The mountains said I could find you here*
*They whispered the snow and the leaves in my ear*
*I traced my finger along your trails*
*Your body was the map, I was lost in it.*
*Floating over your rocky spine*
*The glaciers made you, and now you're mine*
—Great Lake Swimmers, "Your Rocky Spine," 2007

Our first week was spent sailing north through the Inside Passage, which winds its way between Vancouver Island and the mainland before ducking into a maze of islands along the coast of Alaska. Dark green forests stretched from the water's edge up distant mountains, which were crowned with snow caps. Small bays offered quiet and protected anchorages, and there were plenty of logging and fishing towns for reprovisioning and fuel. It was a good place for *Silent Sound* and her crew to get to know each other and slip into a seafaring rhythm.

The crew was slowly settling into the boat and making it their home. Finding a place for their glasses. Getting comfortable in all their new gear and clothing. Remembering in which pocket they hid their candy for the midnight watch. It was a ritual Hanns and I had undergone many times, each time we went to sea, but this time we had two landlubbers aboard.

But Tobias and Anna were both doing well as they adjusted to life at sea. They made themselves at home in the galley, mastering the art of cooking aboard a small yacht at sea, which requires flexibility and creativity with a limited larder as well as efficiency in a cramped, unstable work area. Anna learned how to work the windlass to raise the anchor on her own and she was slowly becoming steadier on the helm. I saw a look of surprise cross her face as we started to pitch and heave through the ocean rollers in Queen Charlotte Sound, but she soon seemed to get the rhythm of it. She started to shoot video and worked on a system to monitor our provisions. On a boat, food is scattered amongst many different cupboards and hideaways, making it hard to know how much you actually have aboard unless you keep track of what you are using and subtract it from the list of supplies you started with. I tasked her with monitoring our inventory.

Tobias was great at wandering around the boat fixing small things. He'd make a good farmer I thought, always fiddling with bits to make them fit and work better. He was also working to sort out issues with our email systems, which relied on satellite connections. As for Hanns, I barely noticed him. He puttered about on deck, testing different sail configurations and makings sure we had the deck gear we'd need. He was a much more experienced sailor than I but also gracious enough to recognize that I was the captain. Although he didn't speak much, I was beginning to appreciate his dry sense of humour and was confident we'd get along fine.

Our first port of call was Comox, a Canadian air force base on the east coast of Vancouver Island. One of the first people I'd met when I started planning this voyage was E.C. (Chris) Pielou, a mathematical ecologist whose book, *A Naturalist's Guide to the Arctic,* has become the bible of many Arctic scientists. When I started reading books by Arctic climate change experts and Arctic adventurers I noticed her book often appeared in the bibliographies. I bought it for myself and found out why. Written in an accessible and interesting way and illustrated with her own exquisite ink drawings, it soon became a regular reference for me as I did my research. Then I began looking at yachts on Vancouver Island, and knowing Chris lived on the island, I arranged a visit. I'd also found out that Chris and I shared a birthday, exactly 50 years apart.

Our first encounter was meant to be a short coffee meeting but it went on for the better part of a day as Chris hauled out book after book to point out interesting places in the Arctic. Soon her living room was a mess of maps and open books as she gave me a personal tour of Arctic ecology. Chris is the grand dame of Arctic scientists. She has made more than 20 trips to the Arctic in the past 30 years and over the years has become a keen trekker, rafter and kayaker. She exuded a sense of adventure and confidence that immediately made me feel this Arctic trip was not only possible, but that it was the best plan I'd ever had. As I left, she hugged me and wished me luck, adding that she wished she could come on the expedition. I soon realized that the expedition would do much better with her as our scientific advisor, and she gladly accepted the job of explaining Arctic climate change to us as we sailed the passage. Now, a day after our departure, we stopped in Comox so the whole crew could meet our scientific advisor and have her aboard *Silent Sound* for tea.

Within a week of leaving Victoria we had crossed Queen Charlotte Sound and arrived in Prince Rupert, near the border with Alaska. It was cool and rainy when we arrived, but soon the skies cleared and the sun came out. We had to wait for several pieces of last-minute equipment to catch up with us, so we spent the next five days pretending we were just another cruising boat.

The crew was in high spirits. *Silent Sound* had made good progress in her first week at sea and Prince Rupert was celebrating Sea Fest, its annual summer fair. Arm wrestling, vintage car show, beer garden, hot dogs and bouncy castles—it was an old-style town fair. I entered *Silent Sound* in the boat parade, earning us an introduction to the entire town on the public address system. We also joined the survival suit swimming race. It took some convincing to get Anna to jump into the chilly water wearing a survival suit, but eventually she consented and we entered as a team. We didn't win, but it was a sobering lesson of how cumbersome and difficult it was to move in the suits. At least now we'd know what to expect if we'd ever have to put them on in an emergency.

Prince Rupert is a fishing port in transition from working town to tourist town. The streets were full of big men wearing floppy rubber boots, hoodies and denim. I watched as boats came up to the fuel docks and were expertly spun around and parked by their teenaged drivers, their grizzled fathers slinging plastic crates of fish and ice on the aft deck as the diesel engines sputtered in the oily harbour water. Everyone sported tattoos, big ones smeared across the meaty backs of the women, across the beef-slab biceps of the men. People were friendly, helpful and proud of who they were and what they did.

We were moored at The Prince Rupert Rowing and Yacht Club, a tiny but busy marina full of sport fishing boats with names like *Salty Bastard* and *Asylum*. I watched as a boat was loaded for a fishing trip … in went two 40-ounce bottles of vodka, three 24-can cases of lager and a shopping bag of beef jerky and pepperoni sticks. Three men jumped aboard and headed off to sea. This wasn't the kind of club where yachties spent hours polishing boats. It was for real boats that leave port. There was the sound of saws ripping through hardwood, the whine of drills and shouted curses as boats jostled for dock space and provisions rumbled down the ramp in steel trolleys. Cranes swung buckets of ice into holds and cases of beer onto decks. Men stood about, arms crossed as they swapped advice on bilge pumps and engines, or explained how they converted a tractor transmission to fit their fishing boat.

We had barely left Prince Rupert when it became clear that all was not well. *Silent Sound* was working her way through Dixon Entrance, at the top of the Queen Charlotte Islands. These waters have a reputation for sudden squalls, but now there was no wind to be found and we were becalmed and motoring. But the big Pacific Ocean swell was still there to remind us that we were no longer in the protected waters of the Inside Passage. While Hanns and I were excited to be back in the open sea, Anna was not feeling well. She had already voiced her concerns in Prince Rupert, based on how she'd felt as we'd made the short crossing of Queen Charlotte Sound and Hecate Strait on our way into the port. The open sea frightened her and she was no longer sure she wanted to make this journey. I'd encouraged her to stick with it and give her body some time to adjust. It was far too early to give up, I told her. Now Anna was spending most of the day in her bunk, becoming more depressed by the hour as we sailed away from land.

Our next port of call was at least 1,200 nautical miles away across the Gulf of Alaska, and likely more because we'd have to tack and accommodate the wind shifts. Hanns and I discussed our options. It wasn't too late to turn back to the Queen Charlotte Islands to let Anna get off the boat, but it seemed absurd for her to drop out after only a few days at sea. She had given up her job and spent weeks preparing for this journey. My instinct was to give her more time to adjust. I also balked at the idea of letting my crew fall apart this early in the expedition. Yet Anna's discomfort and dislike of being on the boat was obvious, and it was clear she'd underestimated the challenge she had undertaken. I remained hopeful that with some time Anna would regain her enthusiasm and become more involved in daily life aboard *Silent Sound*. I coaxed her to stand her watches and Tobias administered medication as we tried to rally her spirits.

Soon we began seeing whales. Our first sighting was along the coast when two orcas surfaced near the boat. Now that we were out to sea we saw larger whales daily. Early one morning Hanns and I were standing in the cockpit chatting when I spotted a grey whale several hundred metres off our port bow. Hanns and I watched it blow, dive and then resurface, this time slightly closer to us. The whale was on a collision course with *Silent Sound*. What if the whale surfaced underneath us? We were under sail, moving at about six knots, and rapidly closing in on each other. The whale looked to be at least as long as *Silent Sound*, and each time it surfaced it shot a plume of spray high into the air. Finally it surfaced and then dove only 10 or 15 metres from our port bow, and we held our breath as we cruised over the submersed whale. A minute later the whale broke the surface again, this time off our starboard quarter, 50 metres clear of the yacht.

Above us wheeled an assortment of sea birds, but the fulmars in particular caught my attention. The Northern Fulmar stays at sea, flying or swimming, its entire life except during breeding season. They drink seawater and excrete the salt through tubes on their beak. They will puke on you if you scare them. They can vomit stinking oil from their stomachs that is capable of killing other birds by destroying the water repellency of their feathers, damaging their buoyancy. But they don't look that dangerous from afar. They flew past the *Silent Sound* solo or in small flocks, saving their vomit for something more threatening.

This was my first real test of *Silent Sound*. I had sailed her in protected waters in the Gulf Islands, but had never sailed her at open sea before, although the previous owners had proven her worth by sailing her to the South Pacific and back. She was one of 26 Amor 40s built in the late 1970s and early 1980s. Each were rigged and finished differently, with Fred Amor of British Columbia doing all of the design. *Silent Sound* was a fairly standard cutter rig sloop for her time, with a thick fibreglass hull, sturdy rigging and an interior designed for life at sea, rather than the more open and spacious cabin designs of modern cruising yachts.

Her pretty lines were lost in the clutter that covered her deck. At the stern were lashed a series of 20 litre fuel and water cans, giving us extra carrying capacity as well as ensuring we'd still have clean supplies if the main tanks became fouled. Our rough, homemade radio antenna snaked up one of the double backstays, further marring her appearance. I'd considered replacing the canvas dodger, which offered shelter over the companionway and the front of the cockpit, but I had run out of time and money for cosmetic repairs. Now we sailed with a badly faded and rotting dodger that required repairs throughout the summer. Filling the entire deck space between the dodger and the mast was our rowing dinghy, sitting upside down on a wooden rack. We lashed our wooden boarding ladder to the frame and crammed as much gear as we could under the overturned boat. Just forward of the mast was our life raft, in a hard canister with an automatic release mechanism should *Silent Sound* sink before we could manually deploy the raft. Lashed to the port bow rail was an extra rudder, salvaged from a self-steering system, which I'd left aboard at the last minute. Forward of this the bows were relatively open save for the inner forestay, windlass and a heavy mooring bitt.

*Silent Sound* had a beam of 12'6", giving her a considerable amount of cabin space for a boat of her length. Immediately to port as one descended the companionway steps was a door into the cramped owner's cabin, which had a double bunk and a small desk with fold-down bench. On the starboard side was narrow single berth, with a large top-loading refrigerator just forward of it. The single sideband radio was mounted on the cabin ceiling above the refrigerator—low enough for Tobias to repeatedly hit his head on it when he opened the refrigerator. Forward of this to starboard stood a large navigation table, with an additional GPS plotter and the VHF radio. The L-shaped galley was to port across from the navigation station, and it also contained the diesel-burning heater. The galley had a double sink, a stainless steel three-burner gas stove and oven, cupboards and drawers and a gas-fired water heater. Just forward of the galley, across a low partition, was the main settee, which became Tobias's bunk. Across from him on the starboard side, with the folding table in between them, was another settee, which became Hanns's bunk. A spacious head and shower was forward of the main saloon, with an access door into the sail and anchor locker in the bow.

Although comfortable, *Silent Sound* was slower than I'd expected when I bought her. Heavily built, with a nearly full keel and loaded with more than 1,000 litres of fuel and about 1,000 litres of water, she needed a stiff breeze to get moving. When I'd first lifted her she had weighed in at nearly 17 tonnes, a figure I was doubtful of but that the lift operator maintained was accurate. But she had a seakindly motion, and her overhanging bow cut through the waves cleanly. She was relatively dry on deck, and her deep, narrow cockpit felt safe. She was difficult to balance off the wind, and I found her wheel a bit small compared to the racing yachts I normally sailed on. Over the coming months her lack of speed would sometimes frustrate me, but in exchange she always felt solid and secure regardless of the conditions.

We were also still learning how to use the electronics I had installed for the voyage. We'd fiddled with the single sideband radio before leaving to make sure it worked, and had spoken to coast guard stations on shore, but now that we were at sea we could properly test its range. We were about 200 miles from Kodiak, Alaska when we raised their coast guard station for the first time. The operator had a rich southern drawl and answered using every flourish of airwave etiquette, yet he did not know what time zone he was in or at what times or frequencies his station would broadcast weather. Then we tuned in to Prince Rupert, with whom we'd spoken several times since leaving Victoria. Tobias had met one of their operators at the Sea Fest parade in Prince Rupert, and when he mentioned he'd arrived on a yacht they asked him if he was aboard *Silent Sound*. We'd raised them on our way up the Inside Passage and they were tracking our progress. As folksy and casual as they were, they had all the information we needed, and we spoke to them regularly as we sailed west toward the Aleutian Islands.

We started many of the live-aboard habits that would stick with us for the remainder of the summer. Everything from hot oatmeal porridge breakfasts to the way we woke each other up for watches would become a comfortable pattern. The crew were also getting used to deck showers. We were carrying about 1,000 litres of fresh water—a large amount for a boat our size—but we didn't know when we would be able to refill our tanks, so I decided to save the water for cooking and drinking and use seawater for bathing. I'd taken many deck showers with seawater in tropical seas, but doing it in the chilly waters of the Gulf of Alaska was a different challenge altogether. I would warn Anna, strip down and go on deck with a bucket and soap. Standing on the bow, I dipped a bucket of water to get wet, then lathered up and rinsed off with some more seawater. Tobias preferred to swim, and if we were under engine power we would throw a line out behind the boat as he would dive over the rail for a quick scrub. In the gulf the water was a relatively warm 11°C, but in the Arctic we would go through the same exercise at temperatures hovering near or below 0°C. The other option was a stack of baby wipes kept in the head, but this wasn't nearly as refreshing as a deck shower. Anna, for understandable reasons, wasn't keen on joining us on deck, and I told her to use the shower and fresh water if she liked. Her spirits had fallen so low even that effort was too much for her.

We had started the expedition on a four-hour watch system, with the crew split into two watches of two people each. This meant each crew was on duty for four hours and then had four hours off. Helming during the watch was divided between the two crew sharing the watch, as were the cooking and cleaning duties that came with being off watch. Anna and I were the first watch, with Hanns and Tobias on the second watch. This system gave each crewmember about six hours per day on the helm.

*Silent Sound* had no autopilot. While this would not have been unusual 20 years ago, today most yachts have an autopilot. But as I planned the voyage I realized that we would be sailing with a small crew in difficult waters. Instead of long ocean crossings where there's little traffic to worry about, *Silent Sound* would be cruising coastlines for much of the summer, and a large portion of our miles would be through poorly marked Arctic waters where ice was a constant threat. With autopilot there is always the temptation to leave the deck and go below to use the head or make a cup of tea. One minute quickly becomes five or 10, and by then the yacht could be in trouble. So I didn't install an autopilot. The other reason we had no autopilot was that I was hard pressed for cash and I couldn't afford the extra equipment.

Now Anna was out of the watch cycle, often refusing to leave her bunk for several cycles in a row, so I was helming for four hours straight on each of my watches. This wasn't a problem in light winds, but as we got farther out to sea we picked up a stiff southerly wind and the seas began to build slightly. With the wind abeam or on the quarter *Silent Sound* became harder to helm, and four hours left me exhausted with aching arms. The long solo night watches were particularly tiring.

Hanns and I again discussed our options. Tobias was also seasick, but was stoically fighting it off and standing his watches. The more active he remained, and the more time he spent on the helm, the better he felt, and we tried to convince Anna to do the same. She was eating and drinking very little despite our prodding and she spent increasingly long periods burrowed in her sleeping bag. I was losing hope that Anna would come out of her slump and regain her interest in the expedition, so teaching her to helm in all conditions was becoming moot. She was still willing to helm when the sails were down and we were motoring, which was a help, but we needed to rework the watch cycle for a three-person crew. Tobias had already picked up the basics of sailing and helming in moderate conditions. He had been peppering Hanns with questions, and I would often lie in my bunk listening to Hanns on the deck, giving Tobias sailing lessons in German. Tobias still struggled to keep the yacht from gybing when we were running downwind, but I felt comfortable with him alone at the helm as long as Hanns or I were ready to go up and help at moment's notice. So we cut the watches to three hours each. Hanns and I split the duty of being Tobias's "lazy watch," standing by in our oilskins and harness to help if needed. Now the three of us were on the helm an average of eight hours a day, and we'd live by this schedule for the rest of the summer.

A week into the Gulf of Alaska I sat down and discussed the options with Anna. So far the voyage had been relatively easy, but we had more than three months of hard travel ahead of us. I was worried that in her weakened state she could get hurt and I doubted that she would be able to contribute much to the expedition if she stayed aboard. She was no longer shooting video and she was only taking her turn in the galley in the calmest of weather. While I didn't doubt that she felt seasick, I also suspected that she had lost her enthusiasm for the voyage. We decided she would book a flight home from Dutch Harbor while I would try to find a replacement crewmember. It was a setback, but we'd already proven we could sail the boat with three people. I was more worried about how we would film the expedition without Anna aboard.

Despite these problems and our slow progress, I was in high spirits. I was busier than I'd ever imagined I could be while at sea, and I remained tense and on edge with concern over how the voyage would unfold, but I was enjoying myself. Tobias and I had a few arguments over provisioning and the way I was running the ship, but I assured myself that crew conflicts were to be expected. However, I was exhausted. I'd worn myself out during the months of intense preparations and began the journey in poor physical condition. Now the odd sleeping patterns and the stress of keeping the expedition moving forward had me knackered. But it was a small price to pay for the beauty of open ocean sailing.

The Gulf of Alaska was empty. We did not see a ship or an airplane in the first week after leaving Dixon Entrance. But the sea was far from featureless. We sailed over underwater mountains that rose several kilometres from the sea floor. Bowie Seamount rises to within 23 metres of the surface of the sea, while nearby the chart showed a water depth of 3091 metres. The Patton Seamounts south of Kodiak were just off to starboard, rising from a depth of 4123 metres to only 168 metres beneath the surface. They top most Rocky Mountain peaks in prominence, but are seen by no one.

The colour of the sea was constantly changing as well. Dull, metal grey waves barrelled towards us from the south. The top of each wave stuck out its chest and slapped our hull as *Silent Sound* climbed up and over it. As the waves raced away from us to starboard, the sunshine on their backs turned them a bright blue until they found another ship to bully.

Although we'd lost precious time waiting for a new storm jib in Prince Rupert, expecting we'd need it crossing the Gulf of Alaska, we'd experienced very little wind so far. During the first three days at sea we fitfully raised and dropped our sails as wisps of westerly breeze teased us. Westerlies were unfavourable given we were travelling straight into them, but we were eager for any breeze we could get. A sailing yacht loses her spirit when she's under engine power and she tends to wander when you leave the helm, while full, well-trimmed sails keep her balanced and on course. The engine, which we named Miss Perkins, kept us moving steadily towards our goal, but there was no sense of life to the boat. The flop of an empty mainsail, back and forth, back and forth, is the ultimate sound of futility. Hearing it hour after hour made me want to gnash my teeth.

Finally the winds started to build, but after two days of reasonable conditions the southerly breeze began veering to the west again, pushing us north and off our intended course. For the next week we alternated between southwesterlies that gave us good speed but slowly carried us north and periods of no wind when we were forced to start the engine. At one point our volunteer shore crew sent us a message asking if we were lost. They were watching our progress via the satellite tracker, and they were mystified by our steady northward track when Dutch Harbor was due west. I was determined to sail whenever we could, even if it meant a few extra miles in order to make the most of unfavourable wind. Running the diesel engine was noisy and expensive and contrary to my sailor's instinct. One of our sponsors had purchased carbon offset credits on our behalf, making up for the emissions we produced as we chugged across the sea, but I still much preferred the silence and speed of sailing. The crossing we'd hoped to make in 10 or 12 days took us two full weeks, with plenty of extra miles sailed in between.

Late on June 30th the green mountains of the Aleutian Islands came into view. The slopes were bare except for a thick green carpet that followed each contour, giving the landscape a clean, sculpted look. Every dip and ridge stood out in stark relief, covered in bright green foliage that was unbroken except for the occasional scar left by a landslide. By midnight we were slipping through Unalga Pass as dark clouds signalled a storm approaching from the west. The shoreline was shrouded in fog, and the southern sky was low and black. The current picked us up as soon as we entered the pass, and soon we were cruising along at nine knots with the wind behind us, blowing at over 20 knots. Even though it was near midnight we were at a high enough latitude that there was plenty of light to see the land. We gybed back and forth down the middle of the one-mile wide passage, avoiding the weather over the land and the rocks that guarded the shore. As we rounded Cape Kalekta to turn south into Unalaska Bay the storm hit us with 30-knot winds. We dropped sails, awoke Miss Perkins from her cold slumber and motored into Dutch Harbor. The fishing harbour was bustling with activity despite the hour, with loaded trawlers coming home and empty ones heading out to sea. After two weeks of empty ocean sailing the brightly lit trawlers and steady radio chatter was a shock to our senses. It was just before dawn when we tied up at the Spit Dock among hulking fishing boats and a fleet of motor cruisers bound for Japan. The first big leg of the voyage was over. *Silent Sound* had sailed nearly 2000 miles since leaving Victoria three weeks earlier.

Anna flew home the day after we arrived. I called Drew Fellman, an American photographer and film producer who had initially been part of the team but then pulled out due to other commitments. Anna had been his replacement. Now Drew agreed to fly out from Los Angeles to join us. But he was only available at the start of August, still one month away, and he had to return home a month before the planned end of the voyage. Unless we could find another crewmember on short notice we would be down to three crew for two of the remaining three months of the expedition.

The town of Dutch Harbor is rather ugly until you raise your eyes to the stunning green hills around it. This is the home of the *Deadliest Catch* television series and it lives up to its rough working-man reputation. It looked like most northern towns, but we didn't know that yet. The roads were mostly unpaved, with 4×4 trucks splashing their way through the potholes. The buildings were thin-walled and blocky, sheathed in tin and plastic with pokey little windows. The newer buildings, the civic centres, libraries, recreational centres, were so uniform in appearance I could only tell them apart by the colour of their tin roofing. The tin-sided Grand Aleutian Hotel, the town's best lodging, could at first glance be confused with one of the fish canneries. The "Grand" referred to the kaleidoscope carpeting and bits of wood trim that set it apart from its neighbours.

Much of Dutch Harbor's population was transient, with barracks full of fish factory workers who came from around the world for high wages. Some of them had been there for several years, and a few had put down roots. Even those who had lived there for many years gave off a restless air that made me wonder if they would disappear if I looked away for a moment. But they were hospitable without exception. Stranger after stranger quickly became friends. They were all keen to help, offer us a ride, point us in the right direction or lend us a tool. Everyone seemed to have time to chat. And the town was rich in talented artists, musicians and people who had carved their own unique path through life. For all its dusty drabness, the main bar in the Grand Aleutian hosted fantastic jam nights with the likes of Vinnie James, a self-made sailor, odd-jobber and musician whose song became a theme song for *Deadliest Catch*. One night we were in the bar and an Egyptian flute player arrived in town, adding an exotic trill to the blue-collar beer-drinking crowd.

Everyone was in "Dutch" to earn money, but many of them had trouble holding on to it. I met Langston Holmberg walking down a muddy road between the fish cannery and one of the town's harbours, and as he told me his story it began to blend in with the common refrain amongst Dutch's hard-working crowd. Many people told me they'd come here to work on the ships and processing plants to make some money, and then they were going home. Some had been caught in a tough spot in their lives down south, with bills to pay and no job, or a marriage on the rocks. Others, often the younger ones, were trying to build up a bank account to start their own business, buy a house or go travelling. But everyone came for the money.

"There's nothing to do in Dutch," Langston said. "Once you've been to the bar and up and down this road, well, that's about it. That's why we work so many hours. You can do pretty well earning $10,000 a month as a deckhand. Most everyone makes anywhere from $60,000 to $120,000 a year."

But higher living costs were starting to eat into Langston's earnings. A two bedroom apartment in a company housing complex was costing him $1200 a month. He had come to Dutch four years ago, but he'd spent a decade fishing other parts of the Alaskan coast before that.

"It's not all like you see on *Deadliest Catch*. Not that glamorous really, look at my hands," he said, showing me his calloused, salt-corroded palms. "Pain is free here, man. But it still beats doing the nine to five somewhere, and doing that all year long to get your few days off. Here we really have to bust our ass when we're out there, but then you can come in and we chill for three or four months a year sometimes."

Langston described himself as 'Afro-Eskimo', and he sported a wild mane of frizzy black hair. He had just stepped off a fishing boat after doing two back-to-back 14-day trips out to sea. His last had been a stormy one, with day after day of heavy winds. The fish had been hard to find, and he came home with only $600 in his pocket. The exhaustion was written across his face, his shoulders slumping, but he was still smiling.

"It's bad fishing now, the currents in June are no good for going after pollock," he explained. "I can spend that much in my first weekend back in the bar. So I'm leaving that boat. A buddy of mine got me another gig on a different boat, we'll try that. They're going after black cod."

Langston had a week's break before he shipped out on his new boat. He swept his arms out wide and did a turn, taking in the desolate working town around him. Should he stay here for the next week, and likely blow most of his earnings in the bar, or fly out to see family?

"There are not many women here. My wife calls me and asks. 'What are you up to? What are doing? Who you hanging out with?' She's asking to see if I'm getting in trouble. With whom? Where are the women? I don't see many women that could tempt me here. It's all dudes in this town. I'm missing my family. They're in California, doing some travelling, having some fun. I'm kinda blue up here, but I don't want to let on when I'm on the phone with them and ruin their good time."

All he could think about now was his wife and five-month-old baby, but Langston planned to stick it out in Dutch Harbor for a few more years, hopeful he would eventually get his captain's licence. But being a fishing captain isn't what it used to be. Consolidation within the industry has squeezed small operators while wavering fish stocks make their future less certain.

Not long after Langston waved goodbye Byron Singley came splashing by in a beat up, mud-splattered car. I waved him down to ask for directions and then invited him to join me for a drink at the bar. He was the captain of the 24-tonne *Nancy Allen*, a small coastal fishing boat based in Dutch Harbor. The kind of fish the boats rely on to pay their bills changes from year to year, depending on what they can catch. Longliners, which go after halibut and black cod, were having a tough time at the moment. The halibut have been getting smaller and smaller over the years, even though Alaska's fishery is heavily regulated. The big mature halibut, the ones the fishermen call "barn doors," are the ones that keep the stock going, and they're becoming harder to find.

"If I can catch a big 300- or 400-pounder it's pretty hard to let that go for the good of the stocks when it's worth $1500 to $2000," Byron said, now bellied up to the bar and waving to other captains clustered in small groups, drinking and swapping stories. He wore a baseball cap with a curled bill, pulled low. Stubbly cheeks, jeans, work shirt and boots completed the Dutch Harbor uniform.

Along with years of overfishing, Byron said the weather had changed the industry. As temperatures have risen, cod fishing has improved. Opilio crab has become harder to find in recent years, although stocks are slowly rebuilding. Opilios, also called snow crabs, have long been one of the mainstays of the Dutch Harbor fleet.

"The warming conditions have got to play some kind of role in all this," Byron said. "Fifteen years ago there was a lot of crab but back then there wasn't as much cod. Now that's changed. With a bit warmer water the cod have rebounded, but the snow crab like it cold, right by the edge of the ice. Some species are doing better, others worse."

The docks behind the fish processing plant were lined with 150-foot fishing boats, their engines gently rumbling as they unloaded their catch. Crews hopped on and off the ships, arms laden with gear bags and equipment. Some boats had repair men crawling over their engines and machinery, the fishermen idly leaning on the gunwales, smoking and watching the work. Occasionally the doors to the fish plant would open and workers in blue coveralls came outside, pushing carts and trolleys or carrying tools over their shoulders. The men were all part of a highly orchestrated business, with buyers, processors and quotas. But Byron was wistful for the days when Dutch Harbor was a fishing town, not a factory town. He missed the days of smaller fishing boats, when owner-operators brought their families north for the season, helping to keep the town alive.

"Those were the guys that come to stay, people that buy homes and move their family here," Byron said. "But it's expensive to live here, and you need half a million or a million dollars to get started with a boat. I got in early enough that I can keep going."

"Those were the days, in the mid-80s," he said. "There was booze, drugs, partying. You had lines of coke going down the bar and no one said anything. People were making big money and spending it as fast as it came in. I earned $78,000 as a deckhand the first year I was here but I can't remember where it went. Those days are long gone."

The bartender was eavesdropping on our conversation, and when she heard a reference Dutch Harbor's heydays, she chimed in. "You used to have guys come into the bar and slap $100 tips down."

"That used to happen twice a night," another woman behind the bar said, adding that the tips were often followed by impromptu marriage proposals from fishermen drunk with success.

Halibut and other longline fisheries have come under new quota systems that encourage industry consolidation, cutting the fleet from thousands of vessels to hundreds. The crab fisheries in the Bering Sea and Aleutian Islands have undergone a similar trend, with less than a hundred boats remaining in the fleet. Even though the wild days of fishing the cold northern waters are history, the stories continue to draw a steady trickle of hopeful young men to Dutch Harbor. They wander the docks, asking captains if they need help. They will usually earn their sea legs on smaller, poorly managed boats, where danger is high and pay is low, and hope to work their way up to better ships.

Alaska's remoteness has attracted waves of oddballs over the centuries, and they all have their own stories. Often they live by a simple philosophy that is refreshingly practical to a city dweller. Jeff Juahfa would find himself glaringly out of place in most of America's southern cities, but in Alaska his raw character fit right in with the swashbuckling fishermen and impossibly rugged terrain.

Jeff lives aboard *Hooligan Lady*, a wooden motor cruiser designed and built during World War II to rescue pilots shot down over the Pacific Ocean. Although her long, clean lines still hint at the glamorous intentions of the designers, *Hooligan Lady* has become a cluttered and decrepit houseboat, with cats and dogs scampering about underneath the helm and down the companionway. The scene suits Jeff perfectly. Jeff is, by his own definition, a hillbilly. He invited Tobias and I aboard his home and settled into an armchair, clearly enjoying the audience.

"I'm a boat propologist," he tells me when I first meet him. I'm confused. Proctologist? No, a propologist. He explains that he is a machinist. He fixes boat propellers and propeller shafts.

Jeff starts telling his life story, from the beginning when he grew up "land rich and dirt poor" and eating racoons, to delivering babies in the countryside and serving in Vietnam, then returning to the US to earn a college degree. It's a meandering tale where dates, place names and hard facts criss-cross and become just bothersome details. The point is that now he's here, and this is the land of men. Real men.

"I'm the closest guy in 2,000 miles that does what I do," he says, pausing to light another cigarette. "It pays off being a hillbilly." Then he's off again, chortling as launches into a story about building his first go-cart out of scrap metal when he was only eight years old. But I want to hear more about the men of Dutch Harbor.

"The level of craftsmanship here in Dutch Harbor is far beyond what you'd find elsewhere in the US," he explains. "Guys who work on the boats that are floating out on Bering Sea, those lives depend on their workmanship. They have more pride. They have no time to screw around. In this place you lose two friends to the Bering Sea every year, sometimes as high as seven. Living here gives me an exhilarating lifestyle. I don't need to play video games."

Before we say leave I ask Jeff to play a song he mentioned earlier in our conversation. He picks up a banjo and growls his way through a few verses of "Redheaded Like the Dick on a Dog," a song he wrote about a cheating ginger-haired man he encountered in some obscure chapter of his life. When he runs out of improvised verses the song ends and he makes it clear it's time for us to leave. Jeff is off to the bar to have his regular afternoon whiskey with the fishing captains.

The storm we dodged sailing into Dutch Harbor has been raging ever since, with 35-knot winds coming off the Bering Sea to rake across the harbour. Two nights after we arrived we were invited to a house party, and it was late when we returned to *Silent Sound*. She was pitching violently in the waves and rolling against her mooring lines so we put out extra lines before crawling into our bunks. I have a well-deserved reputation for being a light and easily disturbed sleeper on a boat, at sea or tied up to a dock. This time I had just fallen asleep when I felt the yank and then snap of the stern line as the waves pulled at *Silent Sound*. I dashed up on deck to see the stern of the boat drifting away from the dock, the remaining mooring lines stretched bar tight. In minutes Hanns and Tobias joined me in the cold rain to run fresh mooring lines. We returned to our bunks, uneasily listening for further trouble on deck.

Morning after morning we would listen to the forecasts of 35 knots of wind and steep seas, and then decide to stay in port for another day. Five days after arriving in Dutch Harbor the forecast began to clear. I went to the fishing docks, where a fleet of trawlers rumbled and belched smoke as they prepared to head out to sea. Crews paced the decks and waited for captains who were off having one last drink at the pub, where they swapped the latest weather and fishing rumours with other captains. I found Byron, the fishing captain, in the bar and he assured me the winds would begin to die that afternoon. He was right. By early evening *Silent Sound* was slipping her lines and returning to sea. The Arctic Circle lay 900 miles to the north, and beyond that awaited the ice.

# CHAPTER 3
## Into the Arctic

*Ice is stone—a floating rock in a stream.*
—Sir John Ross (1777–1856)

The Arctic was opening up for another year of sailing thanks to climate change. While ribbons of ice remained each summer, drifting with the wind and tide, much of the Northwest Passage had been open water for the past three summers. September is the peak of the melt, when the Arctic has absorbed an entire summer of sunshine and the new freeze has not yet begun. The first time the passage opened from west to east was in September 2007. This does not mean there was no ice, but that there was open, navigable water from end to end. In 2008 there was slightly more ice, but a new record of six yachts made it through. The extent of the summer ice depends on the conditions in the previous summer, the temperatures of the winter in between, as well as wind and current. All this is applied to different ages of ice, which play different roles in the overall ice condition. At the end of the summer of 2008 the extent of old, multi-year ice was much lower than normal in parts of the Western Arctic and freeze-up occurred between two to six weeks later than normal in some areas. Much of the Beaufort Sea remained depleted of multi-year ice, which takes longer to break up in spring than the thinner year-old ice.

For the last few weeks I had thought of little else other than ice. Was it breaking up? Where would we hit our first floes? Had any ships made it past Point Barrow, the first big chokepoint? I did not want *Silent Sound* to arrive in the Arctic too early, and then have to wait for the ice to break up in order to continue. Yet I also did not want to sail across the Bering Sea when ice conditions would have allowed us to be much farther along our planned route. My goal was to spend as much time as possible in the heart of the Northwest Passage. I wanted to enter this zone as soon as the western end was open, and exit the eastern end as late as was safely possible.

The spring break-up was happening faster than usual as we made our way north. Before setting off on the expedition I had contacted the Canadian Coast Guard, speaking with their icebreaker captains and ice experts to learn as much as I could. Tobias and I had gone to the Institute of Ocean Sciences outside of Victoria, where scientists study the ocean currents and ice movements of the Arctic. We studied their ice charts, listened to stories of their many summers in the North and tried to glean any information that would help us during our coming voyage. Humfrey Melling, the institute's ice expert, would be in the Arctic at the same time as us, working aboard an icebreaker. He offered to stay in contact throughout the summer, feeding us ice analysis. Now, as we set off across the Bering Sea, I emailed Humfrey in search of insights.

"The present extent of northern sea ice is very similar to the extents at this time in 2008 and in 2007," Humfrey wrote back. "It is close to values seen also in 1995 and 1990. It is about five percent below the long-term average of 12.2 million square kilometres. The regions with dramatically less ice presence than average at this time are the western Chukchi Sea, the Beaufort north of Alaska, northern Baffin Bay, Eastern Greenland and the northern Barents Sea. Other areas are relatively normal in terms of ice coverage."

The Canadian Ice Service had just issued their July ice report showing a faster than normal break-up in many parts of the Arctic even though temperatures were normal for late June. The break-up for the western Arctic was running one to three weeks ahead of schedule in many areas, and as much as one month faster than average in isolated regions. The key choke points in the western Arctic, where we had the greatest chance of having to wait for the ice to melt, appeared to be clearing well on time. Ice often stalls northbound traffic at Point Barrow, about one week's sail north of Dutch Harbor. We had expected we would be forced to stop here and wait for the ice to clear, and had identified a few safe, nearby anchorages on our charts just in case. Instead, the doors to the Arctic were open, and we were in a rush to get through.

In Amundsen Gulf, still a month's sailing from our current position, ice was fracturing more than a week early. A 60 to 100-mile wide strip of open water was developing along the southern Beaufort Sea between Banks Island and Point Barrow. The way to Tuktoyaktuk, our next port after Barrow, would soon be open. Better still, at least from a sailing perspective, the Bering Strait ice pack was expected to remain well offshore, allowing us easy sailing to Point Barrow. And by late July the ice was expected to clear from the western portion of Barrow Strait through Peel Sound, across Victoria Strait to the Queen Maud and Coronation Gulfs. Climate change was hard at work.

A steady southeasterly wind was blowing at 20 to 25 knots as we steered *Silent Sound* out of Dutch Harbor and raised our sails. A few of our new friends waved from the breakwater as we sailed by on a downwind run. It was overcast and chilly, but we were in high spirits and well rested after our time in port. Soon we had two reefs in the mainsail and were making good progress to the north. We set a northeasterly course towards Kvichak Bay in order to avoid the bad weather that continued to boil farther west. But one day after leaving Dutch Harbor the winds died and we were back to motoring. The next few days would bring only listless winds from the north, along with fog and overcast skies.

It was steadily becoming cooler as we sailed north. The sea temperature was about 8°C leaving Dutch Harbor, compared to 10°C or 11°C in the Gulf of Alaska. During the day the air temperature hovered around 10°C on deck. It wasn't cold, but it was damp and the chill was continuous. We craved fat to keep our bodies warm. I had tried stocking *Silent Sound* with fattier foods, but shopping for high-fat food showed us how much of food in North America comes fat free, low fat or low calorie. Even potato chips, candy and other junk foods were trimmed of fat, making them truly empty calories. We had walked the isles of Dutch Harbor's grocery stores searching for lard and full-fat foods. We found butter, but pure pork lard was scarce. None of the stores carried it, and when I asked for it I got only quizzical looks in return. I began to add dollops of butter to our stews, soups and anything else that would carry the extra calories to our bellies.

We had brought along a stack of German tinned processed meat. Each tin was topped by a thick layer of lard. Tobias had introduced me to this delicacy while I was in Hong Kong, and I had to confess to him now that it had not appealed to me. I had saved the tins he brought me on each visit to Hong Kong and took them along on the voyage. Now, shivering at sea, the fat was a treat. I watched as Tobias would butter his bread and then smear the fatty sausage on top, and then risk cutting his tongue trying to lick the last morsels from the can. Despite my earlier reservations it now seemed a grand idea. Peanut butter was another delicacy, globbed onto biscuits or dry granola bars on top of a coating of butter. Nor could I pour enough hot cocoa, sugary tea and coffee down my throat. But we were still losing weight. The long hours wrestling with the helm and cold weather melted away our body fat. I was hardly concerned about this as I had brought plenty of extra weight along to lose, but Tobias was already rake-thin when he stepped aboard and he struggled to stay warm at sea.

Forecasts called for southeasterly winds of 10 knots, building to 25 knots. We eagerly prepared for the fresh breeze, but it never came. Instead we continued motoring across the Bering Sea with only fitful puffs of wind from the north. When we left Dutch Harbor there were several low pressure systems lurking in the south, with predictions that they would move north and bring wind. Instead we were becalmed. It was calm enough to stop *Silent Sound* and let Tobias dive off into 7°C water while Hanns and I kept to the more traditional deck showers. On July 11th, with cold grey skies overhead and the crew feeling chilled after our seawater baths, I lit the cabin stove for the first time. Condensation was becoming a problem below decks, turning our bunks clammy and thwarting our attempts at drying our clothes. With the heater lit the saloon turned into a scene of chaotic domestic bliss. Leather sailing boots, socks, towels and other gear were hung to dry above the stove. During the day, sleeping bags were slung across the cabin like bright bunting. Wedged into a corner of the galley to counter the roll of the sea, we would stir a pot on the stove while dodging a pair of wet boots that swung from the ceiling.

When a rare beam of sunshine did appear, Hanns would dash up on deck with sextant in hand to hone his celestial navigational skills. But most of the time the sea and the sky were the same dull grey, a barely visible line separating the two. The glassy swell continued to gently rise and fall, as if the sea were breathing with long, slow breaths. The scene resembled a computer-generated image, with glassy reflections and unreal uniformity stretching off in all directions. The emptiness was disorienting, leaving me blinking and squinting as I tried to focus my eyes on something, anything. Occasionally a sea bird skimmed over the water, chased by its reflection. I began to wonder if I was floating on the sea or in the air.

We had motored almost half of the miles we had travelled since leaving Victoria, and each mile under engine power was a slower mile than one sailed. Add to that the irritation of the engine noise, the added fuel cost and the extra fumes we belched into the atmosphere. I had used what I thought was a wide margin of error when I predicted our fuel consumption in order to calculate our carbon offset credits. Now my prediction was becoming more accurate by the hour. But if we wanted to make it through the passage in one summer, we had to use the engine when the wind died.

Weeks of open water sailing can slip by without event as the crew moves from watch to watch, barely aware another 24 hours passed, another 100 miles sailed. We were five days out of Dutch Harbor and spirits were lagging due to the poor weather. On July 12th, a Sunday, we broke the spell. I baked banana bread and for a few hours the sweet smell of baking replaced the normal reek of diesel and wet clothes in the cabin. Then the skies began to clear, and with the sun came some a southerly breeze. We put Miss Perkins to sleep, raised sail and *Silent Sound* sped up to six and seven knots on a beam reach. We sat on deck, eating fresh banana bread with our afternoon coffee, watching the sea glide by.

That afternoon we made our first radio contact with Peter Semotiuk, call sign XNR79. Peter lives in Cambridge Bay, where he has a civilian job with the Canadian military. He's well known among Arctic sailors as a friendly voice on the radio as he relays ice and weather information. Peter's daily radio calls have become less crucial since he started them more than 20 years ago because most boats today carry satellite communications and receive regular weather and ice updates. But our daily chats with him still formed a crucial part of our route-planning as he passed on information and observations from boats elsewhere in the Arctic.

We were still about 1,700 miles to the southwest of Peter when we tuned in to 6224 MHz. Although we'd tested the radio in the Gulf of Alaska, and had picked up weather stations several hundred miles away, Tobias and I were still unsure our rough installation job would give us the signal range we needed. We fiddled with the radio, spending as much time learning its functions as actually tuning it, when Peter's voice came crackling over the speaker "…Very good, very good … alright let's see if *Silent Sound* is listening today … *Silent Sound, Silent Sound, Silent Sound,* this XNR79, do you copy?" Tobias and I were so excited we nearly forgot to reply. Peter's voice came through clearly, and he was able to hear us as well. We tried a few more frequencies before proclaiming the radio test a success and promising to tune in again the next day. For the next several months we would speak to Peter nearly every day, cherishing this little chat with someone on land.

The sunny break in the weather and chat with Peter had our spirits running high as we approached Bering Strait. Tobias began work on a potato soup for dinner and everyone gathered in the sunshine of the cockpit for an afternoon gin and tonic. I finished my watch at 2100 and went straight to bed, hoping to get a good sleep in before my next turn at the helm at 0300. Standing watch alone at night can be tedious. It's cold, there's not much to look at and if the winds are light the three hours can be boring, frustrating and slow. But on other nights there is solitude and beauty.

The first job after coming off watch was to fill in the logbook. Latitude, longitude, speed over ground, course over ground, heading, total log, distance to next waypoint, wind and weather conditions. A month into the journey we hung a thermometer in the cockpit to track the air temperature, while a device in the hull constantly measured the water temperature along with our speed through the water. Once I'd filled in the logbook I'd putter around the galley, make a cup of tea and turn on my computer. Maybe I'd write, edit a few photos, or read weather and other administrative emails that had been downloaded earlier. I tried to write letters to my family, girlfriend and close friends while at sea, and have a bundle of them ready to send off at every port.

Before crawling into my bunk I would normally slide open the hatch and check on things one last time. "How's it going?" I'd ask Tobias. He would give a quick report of how the boat felt, if the sails needed trimming, or if he could see anything on the horizon that wasn't there when I handed over the watch.

Finally I'd prepare for my bunk, stripping off oilskins and boots. I took out my boot liners so they could dry and hung my socks over the tops of my boots. I peeled off one fleece top and my fleece trousers, leaving a layer of long underwear top and bottom and a T-shirt. Then I crawled into my bunk, zipped up my sleeping bag and read for a few minutes before falling asleep.

As I drifted off to sleep I'd hear the cacophony of sound that accompanies a yacht at sea. The creak of rigging, the steady swish and burble of water slipping past the hull, the squeak of the helm. If the engine was running it filled my ears with a dull drone, loud but unnoticeable after a few hours. When *Silent Sound* hit a wave her contents gave a rattle, the pots and pans clinking and her stores settling deeper into their cupboards. These are the ordinary sounds of a boat at sea. All these noises blended and became white background noise, and they did not interrupt my sleep. But should a winch handle drop on the deck, should the sails flog untrimmed or should a saucer fall to the floor, I would be awake instantly. My mind recorded each sound, and registered which were those of a yacht travelling safely and smoothly through the sea, and which ones signalled that something was amiss.

I am a light sleeper and a sleepwalker, an affliction that affected my crew more than me. On past voyages my nocturnal wanderings concerned skippers so much they insisted I tie myself to my bunk. As we sailed towards the Arctic I regularly shouted out warnings and curses from my bunk, imagining a grounding, a loss of rigging, or some other sailing catas-trophe in my sleep. Hanns was usually the one to respond from his bunk. "Cameron, everything is okay, you're asleep." I would sit up in my bunk for a few befuddled moments before burrowing back into my sleeping bag, grudgingly conceding that all was still well.

At one point the crew expressed their nervousness over the fact that the rifle and ammunition was kept in my cabin, next to their sleepwalk-ing captain. I also had a nasty habit of groggily sliding open the hatch to interrogate the helmsman with "How's it going? What's our speed? What's the wind speed?" without waiting for responses in between questions. One dark night Tobias had enough of my nocturnal activity and snapped back with. "Can't you first ask how I am, instead of just 'What's our speed?'"

July 13, 0240hrs

Hanns is at the foot of my bunk in a glow of red light from his fil-tered headlamp. The red filter protects everyone's night vision while pro-viding enough light to work. "Good morning Cameron." Hanns said the exact same three words in the exact same tone every time he had to wake me—about 200 times over the course of the summer. As soon as Hanns is sure I'm awake he darts back to the helm. I'm awake instant-ly, but allow myself an extra minute or two of warmth before climbing out of my sleeping bag. Everyone likes, and needs, different amounts of time to prepare for their watch. Tobias and Hanns prefer an earlier wake-up call, but I like the extra sleep and need only 20 minutes to get ready for my watch. In the Bering Sea it is a damp 8°C or 10°C in the cabin at night, but by the end of summer it will be much colder. I scoot to the end of my bunk, where there's enough headroom to sit up. First I put on my sea boots. With the boat heeling and rolling in the waves it is too slippery to walk around in the saloon in stocking feet. I slip on my headlamp and stumble to the head, grabbing at rails and counters along the way to steady myself. It has become brighter as we sail north and no longer truly dark at night, but it's still dark enough below decks to use a torch. In the head I hang onto the boat with one hand while struggling with my clothes as the boat pitches and rolls.

I walk back to my cabin, swinging from handhold to handhold like a chimpanzee. I try to keep quiet and focus my lamp on the floor to avoid waking Tobias, who, along with Hanns, has a bunk in the main saloon area. Tobias is curled up with his back into his lee cloth, a piece of canvas strung between his bunk and the cabin ceiling to secure him as the boat heels over. I go to the galley where Hanns has put the kettle on for me. It's just beginning to whistle as I grab it, make a cup of hot chocolate and put my mug in the sink to cool. I check my wristwatch.

Ten minutes until my watch starts. I like to be in the cockpit five minutes early to get a feeling for the helm and the seas before taking over.
I return to my bunk to pull on the rest of my clothes. A pair of fleece
salopettes, a fleece top, a fleece hat. Next I do an awkward one-legged
hop and dance as I struggle into my waterproof bib trousers. I wrap
the Velcro closures around my sea boots so that water won't go up
my pant legs if I have to go up to the bow, where waves often wash
over the deck. On top of this I add my heavy waterproof jacket, which
already has an extra fleece zipped into it. I have resisted pulling out
more warm clothes so far, such as gloves, as I'd rather get used to the
cold and save them for when the mercury really drops. Finally I put on
my harness, which inflates automatically to become a life vest should
I, God forbid, fall into the water. I fasten the metal D-rings of the harness with a stainless steel carabineer. This is attached to a tether which
will be clipped to the deck to keep me on the boat should I stumble
and fall or should a wave sweep over the deck.

More times than not the last thing I do before leaving my cabin
to stand my watch is look at the picture of my mother and me which
hangs on the bulkhead. It is in the middle of the night, when I am
cold, sleepy and in no mood for adventure, when her image encour-
ages and inspires me.

Good snacks are crucial when standing night watch. We are carrying some 1,200 cellophane-wrapped granola bars, thanks to a generous granola-bar factory that became sympathetic after hearing my
sister describe my fundraising woes. The peanut butter ones in a brown
wrapper are okay, but I always search for a blue one with cinnamon. If
you find a red one, with fruit in it, you know you're on a lucky streak.
We are also carrying about 12 kilograms of turkey jerky, made by my
brother Terry on the family farm. Each kilogram of dried jerky requires
three kilograms of fresh turkey. That's a lot of protein, and much of it
is eaten as a snack while on watch.

I stuff a few chocolates into my pocket for good measure before
retrieving my mug of hot chocolate from the sink. I climb up the companionway and slide open the heavy wooden hatch. Again, Hanns
and I exchange greetings. I sit down in the cockpit as Hanns tells me
what I need to know before taking the helm. Has the wind shifted or
is it steady? How's our speed? Any current? Any traffic? Did you see
any whales? Any storms on the horizon? What heading have you been
steering? Once I am caught up on our progress I reach down to unclip
Hanns and clip myself into the steel tether points in the cockpit. I slip
behind the wheel as he steps away and try to get a feel for the boat
and the wind. He waits for a minute or two, and we discuss possible

changes to the sails. Then he wishes me a good watch and I wish him a good sleep, and he crawls down the companionway.

I'm alone on deck. I play the wheel to see how the boat is balanced. It's chillier than I expected, so I pull on my jacket's neon yellow storm hood, muffling the sounds of the boat. If we're under engine power I'll look at the gauges for the engine temperature, the engine speed and oil pressure. All okay. The steady drone of the engine becomes a white noise after a few hours. If we're sailing I'll flick on my headlamp and crane my neck to check the trim of the sails.

It is overcast and the grey of the sea bleeds into the dull sky with only a hint of a line separating the two. The sky, never completely dark during the summer at this latitude, is already beginning to lighten with the start of another long Arctic day. In front of me the chart plotter glows blue, with a crimson line showing our planned course and a tiny black dot marking our position. Islands stand out in pink. This is one piece of equipment I have splurged on, buying the biggest screen I could find. All of the data of our progress is on the screen, the numbers slowly ticking over as we creep across the sea. Below the chart plotter on the binnacle is the compass, its card wobbling back and forth in its green-lit bubble. If we're sailing, the loudest noise is that of water hissing by the hull and the wind in my hood. A halyard taps at the mast every few seconds. Somewhere on the boat a bit of canvas flaps in the wind. The mainsail telltales, which indicate if the sail is in trim, rustle in the breeze. The boat is heeled over at a comfortable angle, and if we are close-hauled I can lean on the mainsheet, which is attached to a track aft of the cockpit, leaving me relaxed with one hand on the helm, the other kept warm in my pocket. The wind shifts slightly and I move forward and ease the genoa. The sheet groans as it slides over the winch and the whole boat shudders with the release of pressure. The mainsheet also complains with a high-pitched squeal every time it is eased. With every move I make the carbineer on my tether rattles on its hook, a sound I know is amplified below deck but, like the noise of the engine, has become white noise. When crew walk forward, clipped to the jack lines on deck, their tether drags on the deck and makes a sound like the upstairs neighbours moving furniture.

With the boat well-balanced I let my mind wander. Past adventures, old loves, stories I've heard, tales I'd like to tell. I think about my friends, family and girlfriend. I picture all the different changes I could make to *Silent Sound* and what I need to do to make her look better. I think about what I may write in my next blog, or plan some of the million small tasks involved in running a boat and an expedition with sponsors and media obligations. Mostly I just daydream, letting the smooth motion of the boat and the open sky carry my mind away. Many a time I wrack my brain for songs to sing, wishing I knew a few sea shanties, but besides some tuneless humming, I remain quiet.

By 0500 hours I start to check the time at 10-minute intervals. My hot cocoa is long gone and I've eaten all of my snacks. I'm stiff with chill and desperately need to use the head, but I'll wait until the next watch comes up on deck. The sky is filling with light, so I go below to the control board and turn off the masthead and instrument lights. The cockpit of the boat begins to glow a dirty bluish white as the sky lightens. The crumbs dropped on deck while eating midnight snacks appear in the growing light, along with a splash of spilled coffee. At 0530 I make sure *Silent Sound* is properly balanced and holding her course and then get ready to wake Tobias. I unclip my harness, slide open the hatch and drop down the companionway, turning on the red bulb of my headlamp as I do so. I push my way past the swinging oilskins hung up to dry and find Tobias's bunk. I give him a shake and greet him with "Good morning. Your watch." He stares up at me blurry-eyed and I make sure he's awake before making my way to the galley, where I put the kettle on for him. Under ideal conditions the boat remains steady on her course without my hand on the helm, but when reaching off the wind she starts to wander by the time I climb back up on deck. I tidy up the cockpit while I wait for Tobias, coiling sheets and draping them around winches, collecting my mug and anything else I've brought on deck during my watch. At 0555 I peer down through the hatch. Tobias is putting on his harness and he'll be up in a minute. When he crawls into the cockpit I go through the briefing, the same as Hanns did with me. Then I dash down below, shucking off oilskins in my rush to get to the head. My watch for the night is over.

The Alaskan mainland came into view early on July 13th. We had crossed the Gulf of Alaska and Bering Sea, two of the biggest crossings of our voyage, without incident. This is the far western tip of continental North America, a rocky headland named Cape Prince of Wales reaching out to sea just below the Arctic Circle. Siberia was only 45 miles away, faintly visible across the Bering Strait. Few boats sail through this strait, and I felt as if we were approaching unknown lands. The shore rose into the sharp peaks of the Brooks Range that march east across the top of Alaska and the Yukon. We dropped sails half a mile from Tin City and I looked through binoculars for a harbour, a landing beach, any place to get ashore. I could see a small landing for barges, but the coast was exposed and didn't look very welcoming. Tin City is now a military radar station.

The name comes from the tin ore found in Cape Mountain in 1902. The mine is long abandoned and its buildings are derelict except for the ones used by the small group of radar staff.

Tobias had been in contact with a German Arctic expedition that recommended we visit Dan Richard, an American war veteran who had worked at the Tin City radar station when he came back from Vietnam. He'd fallen in love with an Eskimo woman in Wales, a settlement about five miles up the coast from Tin City. They got married and started a family, and Dan had lived here ever since. We sailed along the coast to Wales, which was just as exposed as Tin City, still looking for a place to anchor and go ashore. The onshore wind and heavy surf made it a risky move and we were about to raise our sails and continue north into the Chukchi Sea without meeting Dan when we spotted a beach that offered some protection. I called Dan on the satellite phone and told him where we were. Once the anchor was set I made a breakfast of bacon and eggs and waited for him to arrive.

Hanns chose to stay aboard and watch the boat while Tobias and I went ashore. We were off an exposed beach, the waves pulling at *Silent Sound*'s anchor chain. Dark clouds were building in the southern sky and there was a risk we would drag anchor.

But I also knew Hanns wanted some time alone. He was the quietest and most reflective of the crew. I had misinterpreted his silence as dourness at first, but now I was starting it appreciate it. Day after day at sea made me more introspective as well, and I appreciated not having to speak to him for the sake of speaking. We'd already had some long, rambling chats about boats, religion and women, but on most days he said little other than the occasional joke or discussion on navigation or sail trim. Hanns was the quintessential sailor as described in Joseph Conrad's *Heart of Darkness*: "Their minds are of the stay-at-home order, and their home is always with them—the ship; and so is their country—the sea."

Soon three ATVs appeared on the beach, with one of the machines towing a trailer. Tobias and I loaded a few empty fuel cans into the dinghy along with a bag of camera gear and started for shore. I wanted to buy extra fuel after our many hours of motoring across the Bering Sea. This was our first landing with the tiny dinghy, and now I realized how small it was, loaded with two men and a heap of fuel cans. But it was surprisingly seaworthy, gamely bobbing through the waves as I pulled at the oars. We splashed ashore and Dan and his friends helped us drag the dinghy up the beach and lash our fuel cans to Dan's trailer. Dan was tall, broad-shouldered and ample-bellied. He had a booming voice that was in constant use. A long grey beard and ponytail, flying about in the wind, completed his look. Tobias climbed on with Dan while I rode with a hunter named Frank Oxereok Jr. Frank wore a baseball cap and glasses, showing only a bristling moustache and wide smile. He proudly told me he was the grandfather of two "even though I have hardly any grey hairs."

Frank was driving a borrowed quad with a new style of transmission. The transmission didn't work. He rocked the machine back and forth trying to get it into neutral so he could start it, all the while muttering under his breath. "Piece of junk. What a piece of junk. I'd take an old machine to this any day." Dan didn't miss the chance to rib his friend, and they kept up the friendly banter the whole time we were with them. Dan was one of the few Caucasians living in Wales, and the only one who was a permanent resident. Most of the others were contract teachers or nurses that flew in for a year or two of high-paying government work before returning to the south. He was accepted as one of the local hunters, and many of the people I met referred to him as a brother or brother-in-law.

Finally Frank got his machine started and we set off across the sand towards Wales, about 15 kilometres away. The shoreline was a narrow sand strip protecting a long ribbon of lagoon. Beyond the lagoon lay the mainland, a flat grassland rising to mountains in the distance. A three-peaked mountain separates Wales from the military installation at Tin City. On our charts it was named Cape Mountain, but to locals it was the Three Widows, named after a tale of three old women looking out to sea for their husbands who disappeared while hunting. We raced along the empty beach towards the Three Widows, the air filled with blowing sand and mist from the waves crashing on the beach. The ATVs weaved and passed each other, with the wind snatching at the shouted conversation between the riders.

As we sped over the beach a herd of frightened reindeer galloped over the sand dunes. Reindeer are domesticated caribou, which roam the Arctic by the tens of thousands. In 1894 a reindeer station was established in Wales to feed the local population. Frank said that in the 1960s they discovered that Koreans would pay a lot of money for antlers. "They use it like Viagra," he said with a laugh. So the herders stopped killing the animals for meat and became rich selling just the antlers. Then in the 1980s the Koreans discovered other antlers that were cheaper but were capable of the same tricks in the bedroom, and the market for reindeer antlers collapsed. "So now we eat them again," Frank said.

Frank pointed out the low grey outline of Siberia on the other side of the Bering Strait. In the middle of the Bering Strait are Russia's Big Diomede Island and the USA's Little Diomede Island, less than two and a half miles apart from each other. We had been advised against trying to visit the Russian island without prior permission, while the Eskimos living on Little Diomede charged visiting yachts exorbitant landing fees.

Eighteen thousand years ago, during the last Ice Age, sea levels here were so low that Alaska, the Yukon and Siberia were joined by a broad land bridge called Beringia, connecting northeast Asia and northwest North America. The bridge remained ice-free because there was not enough snowfall to form an ice sheet. The arid steppe was a pastureland for mammoths and mastodons and now-extinct species of horses, camels and bison. It provided a path for plants, animals and humans to migrate from Asia to North America. Scientists think this is the route taken by the first humans to migrate from Asia to North America thousands of years ago. Carnivores included now-extinct dire wolves, American lions, sabre-tooth cats, and giant short-faced bears. As tall as moose, the bears were fast runners with powerful jaws. Humans used the bridge as well, and the tools they made from mammoth and mastodon tusks have been found near Old Crow, Yukon. Beringia disappeared under the water as the glaciers thawed.

This now submerged landmass, as well as Bering Strait and Sea, were named after Vitus Jonassen Bering, a Danish captain and navigator who served in the Russian navy. Bering led two Arctic expeditions in the 1720s, exploring the waters of the North Pacific between Asia and North America, including the strait that lies between Chukotka Peninsula and Seward Peninsula.

In 1725, Bering was selected by Peter the Great to explore northeastern Siberia and seek a North East Passage. This was a blank spot on maps of the day, and navigators were unsure if Asia and North America were connected by land. Bering set off in the summer of 1728, sailing north through the strait that now bears his name. He followed the Siberian coast northeast, turning back when he determined that the two continents were not linked by a land bridge. The curve of the land to the northeast suggested he had found the entrance to the long sought after Northeast Passage. However, due to heavy fog, Bering was unable to even see the Alaskan coast, and upon his return to St. Petersburg he was admonished for not making a greater effort to explore the North American coast as well. A few years later he once again set out, this time exploring the Aleutian Islands and the mainland coast.

A burial mound from the prehistoric Inuit Birnirk civilization dating back to perhaps 900 AD was discovered near Wales. Frank said the hill-sides hemming Wales against the sea used to be littered with graves and burial offerings until European relic hunters came and stole them. "Now there's just trash up there," he said.

Most of the 150 people living in Wales are subsistence hunters and beneficiaries of state aid. The town looked less permanent than its long history would suggest. It had an airplane landing strip, a school and a nursing station. Dan managed the airport with his son as assistant. His son was the postmaster and Dan in turn acted as his assistant. A dirt road ran through the town, tracing the shore. On the other side lay tundra and the mountains beyond. A row of grey ramshackle homes lined the road. The village was littered with old snowmobiles and the rusting remains of heavy machinery abandoned by the US military. Sand and salt scoured our faces as we walked through the town. In winter, 100-knot winds and -58°C temperatures blister the paint on the houses. Winter snowstorms are so vicious that people remain huddled in their homes, afraid of los-ing their way in the whiteout. "My daughter was walking home from school, and she stopped in at that house over there," one of the hunters said, pointing to a building about 100 metres from his own. "They called us and said she could stay the night. It was blowing too hard for her to find her way home."

Dan took us to his house, built on sand dunes at the edge of the sea. His home was a mix of trailers, shacks and sheds cobbled together to form a cozy compound for his extended family. One small building was connected to the next through a maze of doorways and rooms. The walls in Dan's living room were plastered with photos and clippings from Alaskan newspapers and family photo albums. On the dining room table, a scattering of family photos were preserved under a thick layer of lac-quer. As we sat around the table drinking coffee and chatting, our plates and cups were occasionally pushed aside to find a photo to support the story being told.

Dan's wife Ellen, a slim, smiling woman, as small and silent as Dan was large and loud, asked if we were hungry. We'd eat if there were food, we said, trying to be polite. Perhaps they had some traditional foods we could try? The suggestion went unheeded as Ellen pulled burritos from the freezer and popped them into the microwave while a large television played the Saturday soap operas. The shows, and a hundred other chan-nels, were pulled in by a giant satellite dish in the middle of the town.

Their house had satellite television and broadband internet, but no flushing toilet. While we ate the burritos, Ellen sorted through bowls of wild greens picked from the tundra. Once she had picked out the bugs and weeds she tossed the leaves in fresh seal oil to preserve them. "Better than any salad dressing you can buy," she said. The oil had a faint fishy taste to it, and went well with the slightly bitter tang of the greens. A squeeze of fresh lemon would have been a nice addition.

Despite the modern conveniences in their home Ellen and Dan still relied heavily on wild food. And harvesting from the land year after year had made Ellen aware of minute changes taking place.

"Salmon berries are ripening earlier and earlier every year," Ellen told me in her quiet voice. "A lot of berries are ripening early like that. Normally they'd take a few more weeks. Now it's late July and early August, when it used to be August and September. It started to change about four years ago. If my kids can't catch fish, hunt and gather berries, what are they gonna eat?"

A steady flow of people had begun to arrive at Dan's house, eager to meet the visitors. They did not knock, but rather shouted out a greeting as they entered the house, and were in return greeted with a boisterous hello. With each new visitor Ellen would point to the coffee pot on the kitchen counter, welcoming them to help themselves while she continued to sort through her wild greens.

Ruben "Soup" Ozenna, a thin, wiry hunter who had met us on the beach, sat on the floor beside the dining table. He had long straight black hair and a sparse goatee. His dark eyes looked straight into mine as he spoke, which wasn't often. The others told a story about how he once stabbed a polar bear, and he smiled and nodded, saying nothing. Here, all the stories centred on hunting—and now climate change. "The shore ice is getting thinner and thinner every year," Soup said to me in a low, steady voice. It was an aside to the noisy conversation around the table, as if he had a secret to share. "When we were young we'd go chip a hole in the ice for ice fishing and it would take us a whole day to get down to the water. It used to be deeper than I'm tall, now it's no problem to dig through. The thin ice makes it a lot more dangerous for hunting. You have to work a lot faster now, because the weather can change so fast. You can end up adrift on a floe. My uncle went out hunting and he ended up floating to Point Hope. Then he went there a few more times after that because he found a wife there." I ask a few more questions about this unique Arctic romance. But that's it, that's how the story is remembered and Soup offered no further details.

The hunters said the sea ice now often began to break up in May instead of June, as it once did. Little Diomede did not have an airfield last year because the ice was too thin. In years past they smoothed out the sea ice and planes landed on the sea right in front of the village. But most worrying to them were the changes in the wildlife they relied on for food. Warmer temperatures meant southern species were moving north. "We saw sea otters on the ice this spring," Soup said. "That's unheard of. It's the first year we've seen that. Next thing you know we'll have sharks up here."

Frank, who gave me a ride into the village, is a community elder and the leader of his hunting crew when they go out onto the ice in search of walruses and bowhead whales. These days they only kill a handful of walruses each year. When the village of 150 people was much larger and relied more heavily on the land they took many more. "We're starting to see warmer climate animals here, like porcupines. I'd never seen one in my life before. That was 11 years ago or so," Frank said. He sat at the table wearing a black T-shirt emblazoned with "Proud to be American." He complained to me about how his people were duped into selling their oil rights by the Alaskan government, so I asked him how that resentment against the US government squared with the message on his T-shirt. "I'm Iñupiat-American," he said with a laugh. "I'm proud of both."

The only topic that got them as excited as hunting was the state of their youth. The local school had about 35 students and eight teachers. The previous year they had only two graduates. "They don't teach them what they need," Frank complained. "They teach them what they need to live in Colorado or in Seattle, not the skills they need to live here. I'd like to see more kids grow up the way I did; hunting, berry-picking and camping out. We are living in two cultures, the Eskimo culture and the western culture. We saw our culture die fast as we tried to become more like the white man. Now we start to see what we lost."

Everyone around the table agreed that young people got too much aid from the government. It was taking away their incentive to work. But there were few if any jobs available to those who did want to work. Their choices were to stay in their traditional home and rely on government aid while eking out a living as a hunter, or get an education and leave their culture behind. "The school system took some of the culture away," Frank said. "After some time they wanted to put it back in, but the state can't really give us our culture back. The state can't put back what it took. It's up to us."

Jason, Dan's 30-year-old adopted son, was busy getting ready for a flight to Anchorage while we'd been chatting. He had a thin beard and long hair tied up under a baseball cap. His face was distinctly Asian, with high cheekbones and narrow eyes. Jason wanted to become a heavy equipment operator and had high hopes for various proposed roads and pipelines in the area. He had already helped build several airfields around Alaska and now dreamed of earning his operator's license. He shared the disappointment of his elders who muttered about the younger generation. "There's always a choice," Jason said. "They sleep all day and stay up all night playing video games and watching movies." He dressed sharp and took pride in it, wiping traces of dust from his shoes and smoothing his shirt as he spoke. He fiddled with his iPod and discussed the advantages of MySpace over Facebook.

In a few hours Jason would fly to Anchorage to escort a medical patient to the hospital—and in exchange enjoy a few days in the big city. He planned to shop for a new mobile phone in Anchorage, but he would also carry Ellen's bowls of seal oil-dressed tundra greens to a city-bound aunt who missed her traditional foods. On the return journey he would carry as much food as he could from McDonald's. Burgers that were not wolfed down upon arrival would be frozen and microwaved back to life for a future treat. Dan put in his order, requesting a mountain of deep-fried simulated meat, a break from the wild, tundra-fed meat they normally ate. Dan and his son were gleeful with anticipation of their first Big Mac in a long while, and Dan made a friendly threat of what would happen to Jason if he ate too many of the burgers on the way home.

Late in the afternoon the pastor of Dan's church arrived and announced that a storm was brewing. This had me worried, as we were miles away from *Silent Sound* and she was anchored in shallow water off an exposed beach. The wind was building and black clouds were rolling over the top of the Three Widows. It was time to go. We drove the ATVs to the general store and searched for the fuel man. Once located, he unlocked the wooden fuel shed to fill our cans. Tobias and I went into the store to pay for the fuel, watched with silent curiosity by the staff of bored teenage girls wearing tight jeans and heavy makeup. They only giggled and looked at the floor when we tried to make conversation. Dan and Frank drove us down the beach to our dinghy. The seas were building, and it was a hard row through the waves back to *Silent Sound*. We clambered aboard with our fuel cans and a sack of meat from the hunters. Seal ribs, a frozen Arctic char and dried whale meat. We waved a final goodbye to our friends on shore and set sail for the Arctic Circle, some 60 miles to the north.

July 14, 0500 hrs

We have just officially entered the Arctic and the western entrance to the Northwest Passage. It is overcast and I am alone on deck. The Arctic Circle, at 66° 32" North, is the latitude marking the northernmost point at which the sun is visible on the northern winter solstice and the southernmost point at which the midnight sun can be seen on the northern summer solstice. By now the longest summer day is already behind us, but the nights remain bright. We have sailed some 2,800 miles since leaving Victoria five weeks ago, travelling as fast as possible to reach this point, and I'm feeling a sense of accomplishment and arrival. From here on in we can expect ice at any time.

I spent much of my first day in the Arctic with my fingers covered in shit. *Silent Sound*'s sewage tank was plugged, creating a dirty, frustrating job that put me in sour mood. The head was in the bow of the boat, and the holding tank under the anchor chain locker. It was a cramped, smelly and dark corner to be working in as the boat climbed up one wave and down the next. That evening, once my job was done, the winds built and we were able to sail again. The forecast called for our light southerly breeze to build to 25 knots, filling us with hope. Tobias barbequed the frozen Arctic char given to us by Dan and served it for dinner; a delicious end to an otherwise frustrating day.

Life aboard *Silent Sound* was filled with mundane tasks even as we passed headlands and bays that are described in countless history books and accounts of Arctic exploration. Each bay, beach and creek promised some mysterious insight if I were only to stop long enough to go ashore and explore it. Our radar gave us an image of the shore through the fog while centuries ago sailors navigated this coast by dead reckoning and the occasional sun sighting. We passed Cape Lisburne, which was first sighted by a European in 1778 when Captain Cook sailed this coast. It was shrouded in clouds while everything around it was dappled in sunshine. There were patches of snow on the dark, treeless land. Low mountain ridges ran west, squeezing the cape's small settlement and airstrip against the shores of the Chukchi Sea. On top of the mountain sat what resembled a giant white golf ball. This was the western end of the Distant Early Warning (DEW) Line of radar stations built during the Cold War to detect Soviet invasion. From here a string of 63 radar stations stretched more than 8,000 kilometres across the top of the continent.

We had started our own cold war aboard *Silent Sound*. I knew when we set off that personality clashes would be one of our main challenges and emotions rose steadily as we sailed north. Now, with a mild flu making me feel less than charitable, we were bickering constantly. Tobias was unhappy with the way I ran the expedition. He felt he was being pushed too hard, without enough personal time, but I reasoned that there was a lot of work to be done. Sailing 24 hours a day, day after day, was tiring enough, but we were also trying to keep up with photography, writing and video editing. Tobias wanted more instruction and guidance, but I was not always sure what the next step would be and my uncertainty showed. I wanted to just keep moving and address problems as they arose, but he wanted things to be more organized than that. My uncertainty was making me sensitive to criticism of how I was running the ship. When I did have a plan in mind I often didn't articulate it very well. Yet, I became impatient when things were not happening as smoothly or quickly as I'd like. The weeks at sea in an unfamiliar environment also made Tobias emotional and sensitive, and he lost his ability to discuss things calmly. I wanted him to buck up and get on with it. I tried to be diplomatic in making decisions aboard, but a boat at sea is a dictatorship not a democracy, with the captain acting as dictator. Still, I needed him to remain on as crew. He had done well learning to sail and stand watch. After every argument we both went back to our corners, no happier for our clashes.

Hanns remained quiet. I wasn't sure if he disapproved or was indifferent to the bickering. I hoped it was because he had a better sense of the day-to-day flexibility that was needed on a journey like this. He had taken on a huge amount of the sailing responsibility and I was learning a lot from him. He was very conservative with the boat, which was a good balance to my more casual, and admittedly amateur, approach. So far Hanns and I were getting along just fine and we had struck a delicate balance where he respected my position as the leader, while I respected and deferred to his sailing experience. I was not sure if this was a good arrangement and I wondered how it would work in an emergency, but for the moment it meant we were making safe progress without conflict.

I tried not to let the disagreements with Tobias discourage me, and focused instead on our goal. I was enjoying the journey but was emotionally, mentally, and physically exhausted. I knew that this began as my dream, not the crew's, so I needed to be the one to carry it through. They looked to me to keep up the energy and enthusiasm. But I had never managed or led people before, and I had I never pushed myself this hard before.

One early morning I burst out laughing as I dragged myself from my warm bunk to go up on the dark, cold deck for my watch. I was tired because my sleep had been interrupted with a sail change. But I began to laugh when I realized I was doing this for amusement, for a challenge. It buoyed my spirits to remember that I chose this because I loved sailing and adventure. I just needed to remind myself of this sometimes.

I revelled in the openness of the sea and looking to the empty horizon. I loved the grey sea and dawn colours. A few fat seals watched us pass by. A bird skimmed the waves as it hunted the sea for food. We had recently seen a large number of dovekies, which need a long runway to get into the air. They're comical, fat little things that propel themselves over the surface of the sea with a loud pattering noise, bouncing off the tops of waves as they build up speed and then finally rise into the air. Then there were the whales, which visited us on a regular basis. They looked like bowheads, but we often got only a short glimpse of them so I couldn't be sure. I had yet to capture one on camera.

We barbequed the seal ribs that Dan gave us. I made some barbeque sauce and Tobias grilled the meat to perfection, and served it with boiled potatoes. The raw meat was dark purple, and once cooked it was nearly black. But it was delicious and tasted like liver, with a slight fishy or oily taste. The ribs were surprisingly lean. Tobias explained that animals with a thick layer of fat under their skin do not have much fat in their meat. Hanns was not a big fan of barbequed seal ribs, but he did taste them. We were eating very little meat, with only the occasional canned sausage or tuna, so the seal ribs were a treat.

Eating while at sea was never a relaxing repast. Whoever was cooking, which was often Tobias, slung the food into large bowls and passed them around. Our bamboo bowls had become beaten, ugly and waterlogged. The helmsman had a choice to make: wolf down scalding food with a giant spoon while trying to steer the boat in what could be rough weather; wait until his watch was over to eat his portion, by which time it would be cold and picked over by the others; or ask someone to eat their food extra fast and take the helm so he could get to the trough. The best meals were during a watch change, when the saloon and cockpit became crowded with men, leaning into bulwarks to stay upright, half dressed in their foul weather gear, sharing a laugh and a meal.

I baked bread for the first time, ever. I'd watched my mother bake bread many times, helped other sailors do it at sea, and I had made my own in a bread machine, but I'd never done it the honest way on my own. I did a simple white "sailor's bread." It came out of the oven looking like a brick, and weighing about the same. But we ate nearly the entire loaf

while it was still warm, so it can't have been that bad. Baking bread at sea
gave me a pleasant feeling of self-reliance and domesticity.

We were nearing Point Barrow, a notorious choke point for ships entering
the Arctic from the Bering Strait. By 1889 so many ships had been sunk
by ice here that whaling owners in New Bedford, Connecticut pushed
through a bill in Washington to pay for a rescue station at Point Barrow.
A year earlier the *Ino*, a flat-bottomed schooner out of San Francisco, had
been blown ashore in a gale. The boat was salvaged and the lumber used
to build the rescue station. However, the cost of running the station was
too high to maintain, and it was closed in 1896.

Charles D. Brower, who ran a whaling station in Barrow, witnessed
more than his share of strife in the seas off this point. In July 1897 Brower
made an overland trip to nearby Icy Cape for business. The trip took him
nearly three weeks, and when the whaling ship *Navarch* offered to carry
him home by sea, he accepted and moved aboard. On July 28, as the ship
waited at anchor, the ice closed in, and then the floe to which the ship
was anchored began to drift north. The captain and crew of the *Navarch*
panicked and did nothing as the ice took the ship with it out to sea. On
August 10, with the *Navarch* getting farther from safety every hour, the
men abandoned ship in several parties. Out of a group of 32 men led by
Brower only 16 survived the 12-day walk across the ice to safety. Many of
the survivors died from their injuries or had their feet amputated. Six men
remained on the drifting boat and were thought lost forever. But weeks
later the ice pushed the ship back towards shipping lanes and they were
rescued. We were in a harsh and mysterious corner of the Arctic.

I spotted our first ice along the shore near Point Barrow during the
night of July 17th, but saw nothing the rest of the night. My next watch
began at 0900 hours, and when I came on deck Hanns warned me that
he had seen more ice to the northwest. About one hour into my watch
I spotted something in the distance and pulled out the binoculars for a
closer look. It was ice, and that wasn't the only piece. As I stood in the
cockpit peering through the binoculars there was a sudden dull thud
and *Silent Sound* shuddered from the impact. A chunk of ice the size of a
refrigerator rolled away from the hull to starboard, streaked red with anti-
fouling paint. The noise below decks was frighteningly loud, and Hanns
and Tobias came scrambling up the companionway to investigate.

There was ice all around us now, so we dropped sails despite the good
wind and restarted the engine in order to give us better manoeuvrability

to zigzag through the floes. By noon we were in the thick of it, with ice blocking our way at every turn. Still, we made slow but steady process. Stopping, reversing, and slowly bumping around floes while we held our breath. At times we were able to push chunks of ice aside, but more times than not the ice stood its ground and the boat would bounce off with a thud and a shudder. The ice floes were hard as rocks and razor sharp. If we were careless, or even just unlucky, the ice could easily crush our fibreglass hull and sink us, leaving us precious little time to board our life raft. Or, the ice could begin drifting and carry us with it, like the *Navarch* more than a century earlier.

I sent Tobias up the mast to look for clear lanes of water through the ice floes. He hung from the top of the rig in a harness, looking through binoculars and calling out directions. Despite all of our technological progress we were still at the mercy of the ice. Hanns was even quieter than usual, moving between the chart table and the cockpit, nervously scanning the horizon. When he spoke it was in clipped, tense sentences.

Soon it was not only ice on the horizon. We were puzzled to see that many of the distant ice floes had dark spots on them. As we drew closer we could see hundreds of walruses sunning their flabby bulks on the ice, bellowing, barking and belching. We sailed so close we could smell their stench and admire their yellowed tusks. For hours we wound our way between the floes as the walruses lazily watched our progress. Some floes supported only two walruses, lying together in what looked suspiciously like postcoital bliss. On other floes the walruses all but hid the ice, their wrinkled mass drooping over the edges and into the water. Some slept, their bodies propping up other beasts who lazily turned their heads to watch our passing.

Walruses prefer shallow waters covered in sea ice, allowing them to feed on the ocean bottom and haul themselves out on the ice floes. They need open leads of water in which to surface after diving to feed on clams and sea cucumbers, but they can use their thick skulls to batter their way through 20 centimetres of ice if they need to. Walrus bulls, which boast the largest baculum, or penis bone, of any mammal, average 1.3 tonnes on the Pacific side of the continent, with tusks more than 60 centimetres long. One bull charged the boat as we passed his ice floe. He snorted loudly as he halted his quivering bulk only a metre short of our hull. We were focused on the walruses when we heard a WOOSH as a bowhead whale surfaced next to the boat, its barnacled head only metres from our fragile hull. The whale surfaced a few times and then gave us a wave of his giant tail before again sinking to the depths.

I was giddy with excitement. We had spent more than a month at sea to get here, putting in day after day of slow progress north. All those miles had become worthwhile within one afternoon. We had arrived at our destination. The ice, walruses and whales, all under a brilliant Arctic sun, gave us a hint of what early explorers must have felt as they sailed these waters.

If I had been paying closer attention to the forecasts I could have avoided our first potentially dangerous encounter with ice. When we plotted the ice forecast on our sea charts we could see that we had strayed too far north and into the main ice pack when we should have been hugging the North American coastline. We began working our way towards where the chart showed the ice ended. After several hours of tense motoring we were back in open water, cruising towards Barrow with the ice a few hundred metres to port, where it formed a glittering white barrier on the sea. Once we were confident that we were in the clear with Barrow only 30 miles away we slowed down and scooped a chunk of ice from the sea. I chopped the ice into pieces and poured a round of gin and tonics to celebrate.

*Silent Sound* arrived in Barrow at midnight. Two other yachts, *Baloum Gwen* and *Ocean Watch*, were already there. These two yachts would become our close friends over the next two months. *Baloum Gwen* was a Belgian-flagged 45-foot vessel skippered by Thierry Fabing. Thierry, a grizzled, chain-smoking Breton, was famous in the French maritime community for his escapades as a lifeboat captain, and over the course of the summer he would regale us with stories of rescuing ships and yachts off the French coast. His crew were mostly French sailors and adventurers, transiting the passage for the pure thrill of it. Thierry had sailed *Baloum Gwen* (White Whale in Breton) through the passage from east to west in 2008, and instead of sailing south and through the Panama Canal he'd decided to make a return trip.

"I have heard that if you sail that way there are many thieves and bad people," he said, curling his lip in disgust. "So I decided to go back the way I came."

*Ocean Watch* was a 64-foot cutter rig sloop on its way around the Americas. She was skippered by Mark Schrader, the first American to circumnavigate the world single-handed via the five Southern Capes. Mark's was a slick scientific expedition sponsored by the likes of Tiffany and the Rockefeller family, and over the course of the summer they'd lend us tools and expertise. They were taking water samples as they sailed with the mission of learning more about the degradation of our oceans.

On our first evening in Barrow we went aboard *Baloum Gwen* for dinner—curried chicken and rice and ice cream for dessert. I sautéed the last of our seal meat and brought it along as an appetizer. Only when we were sitting around a table did I realize how much Hanns, Tobias and I had missed socializing with other people. Thierry's crew consisted of Gill, a retired math teacher who had taken a series of exotic sailing holidays around the world; Patrick, a Belgian marketing executive photographing and documenting the journey for his website; Ariel, who had been a professional sailor in France as a young woman and now worked odd jobs to pay for her sailing adventures; and Aline, who worked in public relations in Paris and found a good philosophical sparring mate in Hanns.

Each time we arrived in port we had the same need for interaction and civilization. We'd accost anyone that walked by, greeting them, pumping their hand and peppering them with questions. "So, what's happening in town? Where can we do our laundry? Where can we find a shower? Is there a place to get a pint of beer? Where do people hang out? Where will YOU be tonight?" All this from three smelly men swaying on their sea legs, their unshaven faces red and chapped from the sun and wind, with huge bags of laundry slung over their shoulders. We wore salt-encrusted boots and were wet from the knees down after rowing ashore. Our tiny, battered dinghy lay on the beach behind us, its oars askew. Once in a restaurant we would all order exactly the same thing—a double hamburger with cheese. The crew of the *Silent Sound* had arrived.

Barrow turned out to be a bit of a disappointment for us after our welcome in Dutch Harbor and Wales. We found it much harder to meet people here than in other towns. Barrow is wind-blown, dusty and ramshackle—a typical Arctic town in other words. Shortly after we arrived in Barrow an easterly storm started blowing at a steady 30 knots. The wind was relentless, cold and dry. It was heavily laden with sand and salt. The wind tore at our hair and clothes, and I always felt a sense of relief when I stepped inside a building, like the calm that comes after a noisy piece of machinery is shut down.

But Barrow had two luxuries that we couldn't get enough of: hot showers and saunas. We made regular trips to the community recreation centre, where we eventually sweet-talked the staff into letting us use the showers and saunas for free. There was also the usual search for an internet connection. We tried the library, but the connection was too slow to upload pictures and video. Then we stumbled upon the Airport Hotel, which had a warm, comfortable lounge complete with a pot of coffee and vending machine full of goodness like chocolate bars and potato chips. We moved in and the hotel reception staff graciously looked the other way. After that, whenever I was looking for a member of the crew I would check the Airport Hotel before searching farther afield.

At street level all Arctic towns share a feeling of desolation and dejection, in contrast to the life inside the homes. Nearly all the buildings need paint because of the constant sea salt, sand and pummelling winds. Houses are plopped down in seemly random locations, most surrounded by a collection of old quad bikes, cars and snowmobiles. Add some children's toys and you have a typical residential area in Dutch Harbor, Wales or Barrow. ATVs tore up and down the roads, approaching with a Doppler whine before howling off into the distance. They were invariably driven by teenagers dressed in NBA-branded hoodies, each of them squinting into the dust-laden wind while two or three friends clutched for handholds as they careened around corners.

The people of Barrow were friendly, even if was initially hard to meet them. Everyone drove around town sealed up in their pickup trucks, trailing a plume of gravel dust. There were no bars—from here on all the Arctic towns we'd visit were dry save for bootleggers—and even the cafes were there more for eating than for meeting, so we had to rely on chance meetings in the grocery store or recreation centre. And most of the people I did finally meet were Filipinos. It seemed that every shop, information office or service centre was staffed by happy, smiling and flirtatious Filipinos, just like the Filipinos I knew in Hong Kong. It made me a little bit homesick for Asia.

They, as everyone else, came to the Arctic for the jobs. It was the same story we'd heard in Dutch Harbor. Everyone moved north for the work, which paid handsomely. In addition, they hoped that being stuck in an isolated town would mean they'd spend less money, letting them save up for that house, education or new life when they returned to the south. In the Lower 48 people were losing their houses to foreclosures and being sent home from their jobs but in the Arctic there was still work for anyone who could brave the cold and isolation.

I met Mariano "Junior" Bascon at the community centre, where he was relaxing on his day off. Junior had moved north from Bakersfield, California several years ago to join a menagerie of family and friends in Barrow. He quickly found a job as a custodian at the local high school that paid $16 per hour, double his California wage. He said he missed the sun and beaches of California, but he had no plans to return. "In California

I was making $8 an hour but I only really got $6 once you count all the driving time to and from work. Here, I can live right by my work and there's no state tax. When I speak to my friends they all say they're having their hours cut or they are losing their jobs. Here, there is plenty of work. But things are expensive—a gallon of milk is $10 here."

Any fresh food not caught or shot in the Arctic must arrive by airplane, raising prices to astronomical levels. But low taxes and generous payouts from Alaska's oil fund help make up for the high cost of living. Oil companies are pouring into the Arctic, creating demand for everything from accountants and scientists to truck drivers and security guards. Roads must be built; tugs and working ships need to be steered through the icy waters. Much of this work is done by the local government, and it remains the largest employer in the Barrow area along with the Arctic Slope Regional Corp, one of 13 regional native corporations in Alaska which operate large businesses such as hotels and transportation.

Alaska pays out an annual dividend to all residents based on its income from the oil fields. In 2008 the payout was $3,269 per person. In 2009 it dropped to $1,305 due to the recession and lower oil prices. Still, for a family with several children, the bonus made a big difference. North American Natives and Iñupiat, the aboriginals of northwest Alaska and the Bering Strait region, get even more, with an additional payout from their regional corporations. Alaska charges no sales tax, which can be more than 8 percent in some US states.

John Dehart, a construction contractor based in Anchorage, said his work began to dry up when the global economic downturn began. John had started travelling north of the Arctic Circle to take on extra jobs as finances got tighter. I met him in a Mexican restaurant as he made his way back to Anchorage after a contract job in a nearby village. "There are certainly more companies from the Lower 48 coming up to bid on jobs in Alaska, jobs that otherwise would only have Alaskan bidders," he said over tacos and chili sauce. But he complained about the quality of workers on his renovation job, and said that even though local governments offered jobs locally first, they had little choice but to bring in outside construction workers. "The pay is better, and even though you have to be away for a few weeks, you know that when you get back home you have a few weeks off to spend with your family."

Pepe's North of the Border, right next to the Top of the World Hotel, was a local institution run by a local celebrity. The restaurant was decorated with paintings of bullfighters and a profusion of chili lights and garish souvenirs. The food was passable, but like everything in the Arctic, it was wildly expensive. A basic burrito cost $20. Fran Tate, the owner, was a fading blonde bombshell in her 70s who still flirted and bantered with her customers. She gave everyone one of her "cheap pens" and promised to send them a calendar at Christmas. Mine never arrived in Hong Kong. Fran arrived from Anchorage in the 1970s as an engineer working on Barrow's runways and drilling sites. In love with the Arctic and unwilling to move back south when her job ended, she started Pepe's in 1978.

One corner of the restaurant was taken over by Fran's office, with heaps of papers, computers and photographs. From here she kept a tally of how many customers came through the door, and, by default, she had her finger on the pulse of the local economy. "Tourism has been terrible this year," she told me in her raspy, smoke-cured voice. "April to October is our best time, when the oil companies are up here trying to sway their customers or whoever it is they buy dinner for. By July 20 of this year we had only 15 out-of-towners. Last year we had 53 by then."

Arctic oil exploration, so demonized in the south, is embraced by many of those who live in these isolated communities. Like Fran, people know that oil is one of their only hopes for economic growth, even as they speak about it with some misgivings and wistful memories of the days before oil. The economy is built on oil now, and Alaskans have come to expect the money that comes with it. Alaska is addicted to its oil, but in a very different way than the rest of the US is addicted to oil.

Barrow is a big town by Arctic standards, with a population of 7,500 including the outlying towns and villages, with another 4,500 living at the Prudhoe oil and gas facility. The largest employer in town is the government, and 90 percent of Alaska's state budget comes from the royalties and taxes paid by oil producers. The Prudhoe Bay oil and gas facilities are about 200 miles to the east of Barrow, and workers regularly leave town for a week of work in the fields, returning home with a fat paycheque.

North Slope Borough is the epicentre of this cash cow. These fields supply about 17 percent of the USA's oil, down from 25 percent in 1988. Although there are large gas reserves here as well, the gas is not being exploited because there is no pipeline linking these Arctic fields to markets in the south.

BP is the biggest player here, and I sent them an email asking for permission to enter their port and tour of their headquarters in Prudhoe Bay. They made it clear we were not welcome. "The oilfields are secure facilities.

The docks are few. They are not public. They are not available for your use," a BP public relations agent wrote back.

Ever since the US bought Alaska from Russia in 1867 there has been a constant fight between federal, state and native interests over resource extraction. Alaskans are battling with the oil majors to regain control over their own land and the wealth that lies beneath it. Alaska has bet its entire future on oil, putting its economy on a never-ending roller coaster ride. Oil pays for the shiny new 4×4 trucks, the ATVs tearing up and down the roads and the snowmobiles sitting on blocks, waiting for winter. The state had just enjoyed a flood of cash following peak oil prices —the industry estimated that the oil price boom doubled their annual state payments to over $10 billion—but Alaska was bracing for a lot less income as the global financial crisis knocked oil prices back down. Before the recent boom the state had struggled financially for many years and there was growing resentment, particularly amongst the Iñupiat, as they saw oil companies hauling away their resources and ruining their hunting grounds in the process.

In 1971 Alaskan Senator Ted Stevens, who later rose to become one of the most powerful men in the Republican Party, designed the Alaska Native Claims Settlement Act to give $1 billion and 44 million acres of land, including subsurface rights, to 12 regional and more than 200 village native corporations. The act was meant to silence natives while the state and oil companies got on with making the really serious money from the state's oil reserves. Those villages that took the cash gave up their right to future land claims, a clause that Stevens thought would solve the state's problem for good.

"The Alaskan Eskimos made a big mistake back then," Frank, one of the hunters I met in Wales, told me. Four decades after that supposed solution, the state and its aboriginal people are still fighting over oil. "They practically gave it away. I hope the Canadian Inuit don't give away their rights like that. I'd like to tell them to hold onto their rights. Go ahead and develop it, but keep the rights for yourselves. Don't lose your land in the process. We lost a lot. Our parents and grandparents were naïve; they trusted Uncle Sam too much."

Two villages did not accept the cash that Stevens offered them. The Gwich'in Athabascan people of Arctic Village and Venetie are at the centre of the current debate over whether or not to drill for oil in the Arctic National Wildlife Refuge (ANWR), a 77,000 square kilometre area on the north Alaska coast. This is the largest protected wilderness in the US and the main calving ground for the Porcupine caribou herd. Environmentalists say that the network of roads, pipelines, drilling pads and gravel pits required for oil exploration would ruin the herd. While the controversy over drilling in Alaska's tundra and forests gains the most international attention, the real bounty in oil lies offshore in the Chukchi and Beaufort seas. Both Canada and the US are gearing up to drill new wells in the Beaufort Sea, a task made easier by the longer ice-free summers caused by climate change.

The people of North Slope Borough worry that the federal government is too focused on national energy security and not concerned enough about preserving wildlife and Iñupiat culture. Bowhead whales and caribou are two of the most important species for local hunters, and exploration activity will affect the migratory habits of both species, the hunters say. Hunting is one of the few remaining links between modern Alaskan life and the ancient Iñupiat culture. Much of the language has been lost and their lifestyle has more in common with life in a Texas suburb than with that of their forefathers. Yet it is still a common sight to see a pickup driving through town with a bloodied caribou in the back, and spring whaling season is a major event on their social calendars.

The North Slope Borough is run from a low, non-descript building in the centre of town, with a row of muddy SUVs and pickup trucks parked in front. I pushed through the front door and asked to see someone who could tell me more about the tension and latent opportunism that defined the relationship between oil exploration and the Iñupiat. Soon I was sitting across a desk from Karla Kolash, special assistant to Mayor Edward Itta. Tall, blonde and exuding an administrative efficiency that is hard to find in the Arctic, Karla had lived in Alaska for much of the past 20 years. It soon became clear she felt this was a David versus Goliath battle, and that she was on David's side.

"We see some communities that are really impacted," Karla said. "You go to Nuiqsut and they are surrounded by development of oil and gas, and they will tell you that caribou patterns have changed. They have to go farther and farther to find them, and when the price of gasoline is so high this becomes more of a problem. Over the years there's been this spiderweb effect across the North Slope, the development is just spreading, and we really don't want to see that. That's our fear, that someday the oil companies will just run right over us."

Karla was no less worried about offshore oil drilling. Shell has spent about $4 billion on Chukchi Sea leases since 2005 and in late 2011 was granted federal permission to drill exploratory wells. ConocoPhillips, the third-largest US oil company, has also spent hundreds of millions of dollars on leases in the area. The Beaufort Sea is also a contested area for exploration, both in the US and Canada. Whale hunters believe drilling will disrupt bowhead whale migration. In the summer of 2009 the borough won a temporary court order to stop offshore drilling. However, in early 2010 US President Barack Obama opened up huge parts of US coastline to oil drilling in the hopes it would win him Republican support for stricter energy laws down the road. In 2011 Shell took a big step forward by winning exploration permits from the Bureau of Ocean Energy Management, Regulation and Enforcement to drill wells in the Beaufort Sea.

"The mayor is opposed to some of this further development, but it is in federal waters, and it is coming," Karla said when I met her in 2009. "What we're trying to do is get more science done. We don't think an oil spill can be cleaned up in the weather and ice conditions we have up here."

Mopping up an offshore oil spill in the Beaufort Sea would make BP's 2010 disaster in the Gulf of Mexico look like a weekly kitchen cleaning. Shell's proposed response plan claims a 95 percent cleanup rate—which is very high even in a less hostile environment. Frigid, stormy and ice-littered seas would make it very difficult to use the skimmers and absorbent booms that were deployed on the BP spill. Canada's National Energy Board says that conditions in the Arctic, including the Beaufort Sea, are too harsh to send out spill-response teams one out of five days. While BP had access to significant maritime infrastructure such a fishing fleet, docks and coastal highways, Alaska's north coast offers little such support. Coast Guard stations are few, and the agency has already said it can't be counted on to help oil companies clean up their spills in the Arctic. A relatively minor oil spill in the Beaufort Sea could very easily turn catastrophic.

Much of the research on the impacts of exploration happens at Ilisagvik College, a blue tin complex surrounded by aging sheds and buildings on a windswept spit of land. The spit protects a shallow lagoon a few miles north of Barrow. The college offers academic, vocational and technical courses. Many of the world's experts on Arctic animals, from bowhead whales to migratory birds, do their research here. Scientists in Barrow are increasingly combining traditional science with knowledge gathered from hunters to get a fuller picture of the wildlife. The community's elders have shared some of their hunting knowledge to help engineers design oil fields with less impact on wildlife. Hunters said raised pipelines had to be seven feet above the ground, not five feet as the oil companies thought, in order to let caribou through. Whale hunters for years said there were more bowheads than the scientists were counting, and eventually were proven right when scientists took local knowledge of migration habits into account. The intensifying research of the impact of oil exploration and climate change has helped Barrow gain at least an intellectual hold on the issues affecting its future. Armed with their new knowledge, the residents are becoming bolder and bolder in standing up against the oil companies, many of which provide funding to the college.

The debate over oil exploration was one I'd hear much more of as I sailed the Arctic coastline into Canadian waters. Communities are struggling to keep abreast of corporations who buy the rights to the oil and ore that lie underneath their hunting grounds. Isolated settlements are vying for attention from corporations looking for places to base their offices and workers—many of whom are moving in from the south. Local workers are eager for oil industry jobs even though their labours are slowly wiping out their hallowed hunting grounds. Alaska is much further down the road of resource exploitation than Canada is, and the more I heard about these conflicts the more I wondered what was in store for Canada.

Several days of easterly wind had whipped up steep waves on the Beaufort Sea. From Barrow we needed to sail almost due east, into the chop. No one wanted to set out into those stormy seas, but by July 20th, three days after arriving in Barrow, the ice charts were showing open water all the way to Tuktoyaktuk, more than 500 miles to the east. I felt pressured to keep moving if the ice allowed. The threat of ice was more than just imagined from now on, even from where *Silent Sound* hung on her anchor. Just offshore, blocking out the horizon, were several massive chunks of multi-year ice. They were much thicker than the sea ice we'd manoeuvred through to get here. The largest ones were grounded and immobile, but slightly smaller ones came and went, turning and shifting with the wind and the tide. It was always a surprise to see that building-sized pieces of ice had silently shifted or arrived during the night. The movement of something that large should be accompanied by the roar of engines, shouts of men, the clatter of steel machinery. But the ice was stealth in its steady drift.

With such a short summer and window of opportunity, we couldn't risk wasting days in Barrow, located at the very start of the passage. Every day Thierry, Mark and I would compare notes and discuss our plans. We spent hours looking at weather forecasts and ice charts, hoping for calmer weather and more open water. *Ocean Watch* was waiting for crew replacements and had no plans to leave until the 26th, but *Baloum Gwen*, like us, was waiting only on the weather. Thierry in particular was getting anxious to make miles. Finally, on the morning of July 21st, the easterly winds had backed slightly to the north. Thierry rounded up his crew and set off, hoping the winds would continue to back and give him a good sailing angle. We decided to wait an extra day for calmer weather. We'd already been in Barrow for four days and had finished all the jobs we needed to do ashore, but Hanns and I agreed that we'd make very few miles beating into that wind, and the few miles we would make would be punishing for the boat and crew.

We waited until the morning of July 23rd and then set off in fog and 12 to 15 knots of northeasterly wind. We rounded Point Barrow and turned east. The sea was clear of ice for the next stage of our journey, but now we came upon an unexpected danger. Even though there is not a standing tree to be seen within hundreds of miles, logs sweep down the Mackenzie River from the interior of Canada and are left bobbing in the murky waters of the Beaufort Sea. The logs are swept onto beaches in long windrows of wood; silent, dead visitors from the south. Afloat in the sea, the logs are just as dangerous as the ice, and hitting one could easily put a hole in our hull. So, instead of watching for ice, we were now watching for half submerged logs. Late in the afternoon we tacked, sailing about seven miles north in order to improve our wind angle and gain more sea room as we sailed past Cape Simpson. By midday on the 24th the wind began to die and we had to use our engine. Our head was also once again causing problems. Hanns announced that the holding tank, which was full, appeared to be backing up into the toilet bowl, which meant the hose leading waste off the boat was plugged. We stopped the boat to make the job easier, and Hanns rolled up his sleeves. An hour later, head fixed, we got back underway.

The wind died entirely as we passed Cross Island on the 25th. It is a low, sandy barrier island about 12 miles offshore, shaped into a fish hook by the swirling currents. The Inuit in the area use it as a staging island for their annual whale hunts. The island appeared in a mirage, floating just above the sea's glassy surface. The mirages were intense in this area and had been playing tricks on our eyes for several days. At one point what looked like a dark form jumped up from behind a small iceberg. I looked through the binoculars and saw it was just another superior mirage, adding a touch of drama to the otherwise flat landscape along this coast. Floating ice appeared as towering carved columns, islands grew hills and features that disappeared as we drew closer, and the sea itself climbed up and over the land.

Mirages, caused by layers of different temperature air, can appear at any latitude but they are common in the Arctic due to simultaneous warm summer sunshine and cold seas. The air just over the sea is much colder than the higher air, which is warmed by the sun. This combination creates a superior mirage, with the different temperature layers causing light rays to travel in varied curved paths. This can make an ice floe or small island in the distance appear to grow vertically into magical shapes resembling towers and turrets. This apparition is known by the Italian name *fata morgana*. Fairy Morgan was King Arthur's sister and the castle she lived in inspired the name. The image changes as you watch it, making it all the more mysterious. The curvature of the light rays also compensate for the curvature of the earth, allowing you to see objects that would otherwise be below the horizon. I spent hours mesmerized by the strange dance and shimmer of mirages on the horizon, and their presence made me question the reality of everything else I saw.

We settled back into the rhythm of life at sea after leaving Barrow. I baked whole wheat bread and served it up with bacon and eggs. There was lentil soup on the stove. The 34 kilograms of dried beans and lentils we bought in Victoria were not a big hit with the crew, and I was the only one to cook them regularly. We'd all begun complaining about cricks in our necks and between our shoulder blades, and we suspected it had something to do with our position at the helm. I wasn't sure if the wheel was too high or too low, and given that Hanns was about six inches taller than me made it even harder to find a pattern we could blame for the discomfort. Either way, there was not much we could do about it but stretch and keep steering. Barrow's saunas and hot showers were far behind us, and we were back to taking sea baths. The water was now 3°C, and while Tobias and Hanns seemed to relish the frigid baths, I hated them and had to grit my teeth so as not to make girlish noises while standing naked on deck, dripping with freezing water.

With heavy fog blanketing the sea we ran the radar as much as our batteries allowed, even though it would not show the small bits of ice and floating logs. The wind was fitful, building to 12 knots from the east, then falling back to three or four knots. It made for frustrating sailing. Even though we were only a few miles offshore the land to starboard was so flat that it was often invisible. We became bored, staring into the murky, featureless sea.

It was raining by the time we crossed the mouth of the Coleville River and its scattering of oil rigs. A few small bits of ice, which had probably floated down the river, bobbed in the grey seas. We picked up XNR79 on the afternoon radio schedule, and he told us the seas should remain clear until Tuktoyaktuk, with the main ice pack located about 40 miles offshore. We stayed well offshore to avoid the many shallows, oil rigs and artificial islands created for drilling platforms. All along the Alaskan coast we could see lights to starboard where exploration companies were making the most of the short summer. Tugs plied the coast, pulling barges loaded with drilling equipment.

Although we no longer had 24-hour sunlight it never got truly dark. One night as I took over the watch at midnight I witnessed the miracle of the never-ending Arctic day. I was sailing at a comfortable angle, standing at the helm and marvelling at the sky. During a clear day the blue sky made the Arctic feel big. Airy. Elegant. When the sun dipped to the horizon things turned truly supernatural. The sea was glassy when I came on deck, and the sun was low on the horizon, yet to set. The light had an intensity and physical presence as if it were bending through crystal clear water. It had heft like a smooth rock in your open palm. Colours ranged from a deep mauve and pink near the sun to a soft blue where the light thinned near the edges of the sky. There was enough wind to keep the sails full while the sea remained smooth, reflecting the backlit clouds. The boat weaved and wobbled as I craned my neck to look at the sky, mouth agape and mind far from the helm.

By about 0100hrs the sun had sunk beneath the horizon and I turned my attention back to sailing. I was engrossed with trimming sails and squeezing out a bit of extra speed when I looked to port and saw a lurid pink cloud where the sun had been. It grew brighter by the minute, and above it hung a bank of black clouds. Between the horizon and me was a low, white fog bank, perhaps two to three miles away but rapidly approaching my position. Within minutes the fog was upon me, hanging about 10 metres above the surface of the sea. It silently whistled around *Silent Sound*'s mast, long tendrils creating a smoky ceiling above the boat.

Slowly the sun, which had only a few hours ago dipped out of sight in a blaze of pink, rose up again from behind of fog. The wind picked up and *Silent Sound* gained speed. The colours I'd witnessed as the sun was setting were now replayed in reverse. From the most startling red and pink the light faded into clear pastels. Within one watch I'd witnessed both a sunset and sunrise, a phenomenon of the Arctic's long summer days. As the sky brightened I passed a few seals bobbing in the waves, curiously following the *Silent Sound*'s progress. I'd watched all this alone as I steered my boat through the Arctic, like a secret of sorts.

# CHAPTER 4
# Adaptation

*Ladies' corsets! For without them there would have been no
demand for whalebone, hence no great whaling fleets of sturdy
wooden vessels, sail and steam, manned by men the like of
whom the world had never known.*
— Charles Brower, *Fifty Years Below Zero.*

It was foggy as *Silent Sound* passed Demarcation Point, marking our
return to Canadian waters. We passed in the dusk of midnight, the outcropping of land barely visible. I made a breakfast of pancakes with maple
syrup to celebrate. By morning the skies had cleared and we began to close
in on Herschel Island. In my mind this had always been a Canadian journey, the thousands of miles we sailed around Alaska almost a diversion.
Not that Yukon waters looked any different. The wind was still weak and
the land was just a low shadow on the horizon, the water a muddy grey.

By noon we had entered the Workboat Passage on the southwest side
of Herschel. The island is part of a peninsula that was dredged up by the
Laurentide ice sheet during the last ice age. As the ice sheet melted, the
sea rose enough to flood the low land in the peninsula's waist, leaving
an island just off the mainland coast. We could have sailed around the
north side of Herschel Island to reach Pauline Cove, the island's only settlement, but decided this channel looked passable and more interesting.
We squeezed through, between the mainland and a long, curling spit of
land with a driftwood hunting shelter at its tip. It was warm day, and the
sky was clear blue and brilliant with light. We squinted at the land and
shielded our eyes to see the sandbars.

The island offered some welcome visual relief from the featureless
coast we'd been sailing along for several days. Its green hills were covered in summer flowers even as patches of snow still clung to the shady
undersides of the cliffs. To the south we could see the outline of the British
Mountains on the mainland. The breeze carried the scent of Arctic flowers,
and a caribou loped along the shore. Not only was the scenery stunning,
it was also the first time we'd seen proper vegetation since leaving Dutch

Harbor. We had covered mile upon mile of open sea, and when we did close in on land all we could see was sand and rock. Herschel Island did not have a single tree, but it was covered by a knee-high carpet of shrubbery and an explosion of tiny flowers that make a brief appearance every summer. It was alive, growing and, as far as we were concerned, green as an English summer meadow.

Herschel was also our first properly sheltered anchorage since Dutch Harbor. The north Alaskan coastline offers very few sheltered anchorages, as the land runs flat and low to the Beaufort Sea. Pauline Cove is the only protected harbour on the 450 miles of coastline between the Mackenzie River Delta and Barrow, where we had spent our first night in a choppy lagoon, then moved to anchor off a beach that was open to the sea. In Wales we had to leave earlier than planned when winds picked up as *Silent Sound* sat at anchor on an exposed shore. Compared to the shores we'd been sailing, Herschel Island and Pauline Cove felt like a protective cocoon.

As protected and lovely as the Workboat Passage was, there was good reason why most boats went around the north end of the island. The muddy water hid shifting sandbars and we had to keep a close watch for rocks and shallows. *Silent Sound* gently bumped the sandy bottom several times as we felt our way through the channel. We peered into the depths in hopes of spotting rocks and sandbars before our keel found them.

As we rounded the last headland before Pauline Cove we could see the hazy outline of an oil rig in the distance, drilling in the shallow waters. Then the still summer air was shattered by a helicopter's thwapping blades overhead. *CCGS Sir Wilfrid Laurier* was at anchor just outside the cove, and its helicopter had gone airborne to check on ice conditions. We had first encountered the giant red icebreaker in Barrow, and our paths would cross several more times as we both sailed eastward through the Arctic.

We lolled in the sun and watched the island slide by. As we entered more sheltered waters the water temperature rose to 9°C and then 15°C. This was too good of an opportunity to pass up. We took turns standing naked on the foredeck with our red shower bucket as we sailed past the *CCGS Sir Wilfrid Laurier*.

Pauline Cove was sheltered from all directions by a long low arm of gravel that branched off the island and wrapped itself protectively around the small harbour. We set our anchor and rowed ashore, eager to explore and stretch our legs. We climbed the bare, open hilltops to get a clear view of the sea and the mainland. A strong wind was blowing, whipping through the knee-high grass and willows. The droppings of bear, musk-ox and caribou were scattered everywhere.

On the north side of the harbour the island's hills rose steeply from the water. To the east the land rose more gently, with a scattering of white crosses in the cemetery standing out against the grass. The old whaling and police settlement stood at the base of the gravel spit, the buildings grey with weather and age.

The small cluster of buildings in Pauline Cove stand in much the same way as they did when this was the hub of Beaufort Sea whaling a century ago. The Pacific Steam Whaling Company house, built in 1893, is still in good condition. Two large warehouses remain in use, as do several of the smaller cabins. The dry, cold Arctic climate is perfect for preserving these historic buildings. Across the cove, dug into the hillside, are several icehouses, one of which is still used to keep meat through the summer.

I'd been eager to reach Herschel Island ever since I began planning the expedition. Many of the most recognizable names in Arctic travel —Franklin, Stefansson, Amundsen, Bartlett—had spent time here, and it served as a major centre for the 19th century whaling industry. Amundsen spent an entire winter here, and his observations of the culture and life of the Inuit in the area contributed greatly to European understanding of the people.

The Inuit name for Hershel was Qikiqtaruk (kee keek ta ruk), meaning "it is island," and the Inuit of the area called themselves the Qikiqtarukmiut or "island people." Until the early 19th century these subsistence hunters and fishermen eked out a living from the frigid environment. But in a story repeated across the Arctic, the Europeans arrived, renamed the place and drove out the locals in less than a century.

Sir John Franklin stopped at the island in 1826, in mid-July just as we were doing, on his expedition down the Mackenzie River. He renamed the island after Sir John Herschel, a British chemist and astronomer. "It is composed of black earth, rises, in its highest point, to about one hundred feet [actually, it's closer to 600 feet], and at the time of our visit [July 17] was covered in verdure," he wrote. Franklin, who took his crew through this same narrow channel between the island and the mainland that we had used, wrote that Herschel Island provided the first sheltered waters he had seen since the mouth of the Mackenzie River, 130 miles away, although the channel "is much interrupted by shoals."

Whaling captains were prominent among the earliest European explorers of the Arctic, and were usually at the helm when scientists and explorers pushed north. So Hanns and I were sticking to the tradition of a first mate or sea master having more experience than the captain, or expedition leader. The whaling captains knew all about Baffin Bay and Lancaster Sound when the British Admiralty still thought the bays were channels.

But the arrival of the whaling industry also sounded the death knell for the Inuit and the resources that made their culture possible. The whalers were hunting the bowhead whale, and its close east-coast relative the right whale. These whales yielded blubber that was rendered into barrels of oil to fuel Europe's lamps. But soon petroleum products replaced animal fat for lighting in Europe. The vanity of the European female populace came to the rescue as ladies began sticking whale bones up under their skirts in the form of hoops and corsets. They had learned that using baleen, the bone around the mouths of the bowhead, was much better for giving shape to the Victorian woman than the bamboo they had been using. Bowhead whales have the longest baleens of any whales, making them the best for the job. So Arctic whalers resumed their hunt and shipped the baleen to the ladies of Europe. Their vanity came at a price. Most of the bowheads were slaughtered only for their baleen, and the wasteful practice nearly wiped out the species.

At first whalers hunted in the warmer southern waters, but soon demand outstripped supply. Whalers followed the bowheads into the Bering Sea, and finally the Beaufort Sea, which still contained a bounty of whales into the late 1800s. Each spring the whalers made the long trip north, around Alaska and into the Beaufort Sea, just as we had done in *Silent Sound*. But it was a long trip for whalers based in southern ports. The Northwest Passage had not yet been discovered, and whalers entered and exited the Arctic by the same route. Instead of making this annual trek, those entering from the west decided to winter in Pauline Cove, putting them in the heart of their hunting grounds as soon as the ice melted in spring. It meant they could spend more time hunting and less time sailing. A police officer patrolling the north reported that 12 whalers with between 1,000 and 1,200 men had stayed on the island or in the Mackenzie River area the winter of 1895–96.

The whaling companies built houses and warehouses ashore, but most of the men lived aboard their ships, at anchor in Pauline Cove. Waiting out an Arctic winter in the late 1800's was a long, tedious and often deadly affair that stretched from September to July. Some ships conducted educational classes, organized hunting parties and published newspapers. Many ships stocked liquor to help pass the time, and this was often traded for Inuit women, carvings, clothes and other goods. At first the Inuvialuit, an Inuit people in the western Canadian Arctic, were happy to see the whaling ships. They hunted for the whalers in exchange for tea, sugar and metal pots.

But soon the growing population overwhelmed the land. While the steady trickle of driftwood that came down the Mackenzie River always provided sufficient fuel for the small Inuit settlements on Herschel Island, the whalers need large quantities to heat their ships, and soon the beaches were bare. The whalers started to bring coal to heat their ships, but the Inuit were left in the cold. Soon the local stocks of caribou and other wildlife were depleted and the Inuit had to travel farther afield for food. The whalers also brought new diseases, which decimated the local population.

In his book *Fifty Years Below Zero* Charles Brower describes an epic party in 1902 that drew Inuit to Utkiavie, the Inuit community next to the Barrow whaling station. They came from communities far and wide and the party, thrown to mark a successful whaling season, went on for many days, with feasting and dancing. The revellers also visited Barrow's ever-present whaling fleet to trade carvings for booze. They got more than they bargained for.

Not long after the party ended and all the guests had left for home a hunter came to Barrow and told Brower that he had found many dead people scattered along the banks of a nearby river. Brower went to investigate, and discovered to his horror that the guests had caught a flu bug from the whalers and died on their way back to their home villages. Men, women and children had died in droves, their bodies left where they fell, scattered across the land.

"All that fall and the next summer we kept getting reports from hunters of bodies discovered along far river banks, sometimes alone, sometimes with a few belongings scattered around," Brower writes. "It is my opinion that of those two hundred or more husky inland Eskimos who so light-heartedly danced with us at Utkiavie, not one was left alive."

Some of those that came north were on a mission to help the Inuit rather than make money off their labour. Isaac Stringer, an Anglican minister, made his first visit to Herschel Island in the spring of 1893. He continued to make regular visits until 1897, when he and his wife Sadie established an Anglican Church mission on the island. Their mission house stands off by itself north of the other buildings and is now home to a flock of guillemots.

Stringer became an Arctic legend for his attempts to bring order to the moral chaos among the whalers and Inuit. He was shocked by the moral degradation that he observed in island life. The whalers were a hard-drinking, cussing lot and the Inuit living on Herschel had developed their own taste for strong drink. To his horror, in a custom well-documented and much enjoyed by early Arctic explorers, Inuit women took numerous lovers amongst the visitors and their husbands seemed happy with the arrangement. Stringer set out to bring the Pauline Cove community in line with his puritanical moral standards.

At one point he struck a deal with the whaling captains to stop giving liquor to the Inuit on Herschel, but the ban was short-lived. "You know that time when they first started to come, they had no priest … they started drinking, they try to kill each other, fought, drank," an Aklavik elder named Peter Thrasher told an anthropologist. "Their wives, they lost them to those white people… When that preacher came, just like that, all the bad people stopped. Bishop Stringer, yeah!"

One year Stringer and another missionary worker were caught in an early winter storm. They walked 60 miles across the tundra to civilization, running out of food along the way. They resorted to boiling their spare moccasins for food. The survival trick made Stringer famous as "The Bishop Who Ate His Boots."

By 1907 fickle Victorian fashion began to move on, and demand for baleen waned. Soon the whaling era was over. But the damage had been done. The whales and the Inuit were decimated by hunting, disease and shifts in the economy too fast for them to keep pace with.

Today, the whalers lie in rows of graves at the bottom of the hill, crosses leaning and weaving across the tundra like a decrepit picket fence. As I walk through the graveyard I sink up to my ankles in the bog. Dark water pools in my footprints. The buzz of mosquitoes is a continuous drone; a white noise that marks the short, explosive Arctic summer. The mosquitoes fly up my nose, into my ears, they stick to my teeth. The motion of waving away the mosquitoes around my head has begun to feel natural, an involuntary twitch I've long ago forgotten about.

Many of the crosses are inscribed with Scottish names—these are the hardy whalers who came here looking for oil and baleen but never left. The dates scratched into the crosses show few long lives and many that ended in their primes. Babies, young men and young women are buried here, showing the whalers made Herschel Island home while they were here.

Life was hard for those that lie buried here. Death was never far away even when the whalers were trying to have fun. On February 19, 1894 a group of men ventured out of their whaling ships, which were frozen into the ice, to play a game of baseball on Pauline Cove. They used ashes from the ships' furnaces to mark baselines and an old sail was set up as a backstop. By the next year the four-team winter baseball league was an institution, breaking the boredom of waiting seven or eight months for the spring thaw and whaling season. On March 7, 1897 a game was in the bottom of the second inning when a blizzard swept in from the Beaufort Sea, blinding the players. Two players and three Inuit spectators lost their way in the blizzard and froze to death.

An Inuit graveyard is situated slightly inland from where the whalers rest. Some of the Inuit skeletons are rising from their graves, expelled by the Arctic's continuous frosts and thaws. Skulls poke from wooden caskets; a bone here, a glimpse of a dark cavern there. Amundsen's description of the graveyard reveals that the bodies were never buried as well as those of the whalers.

"The whale hunters' graves were all well-kept and adorned with painted crosses," Amundsen wrote. "But the Eskimo's presented a most remarkable appearance. It was as if a tradesman had kept his store of goods there, for the Eskimo put their dead into ordinary wooden boxes and deposit them in rows on the bare ground."

I've forgotten myself, walking from one grave to the next, looking for more skulls and bones, when the macabre nature of my survey registers. I'm standing in a field of death. It is sunny and warm on the green hillside, with small flowers blooming in the throes of the island's short summer. My hiking boots are sodden from walking in the ankle deep water and muck. The swamp, heavy with a peaty stench, reluctantly releases my every step with a guttural, slurping sound. The earth may be giving up its corpses, but it is trying to draw me in, I thought. I lingered for a moment more, then hiked to higher ground.

High on the hillside, two graves stand out from the rest. The two Royal North West Mounted Police graves are on dry ground and surrounded by an immaculate white picket fence. In one grave lies Sergeant Stafford Eardley Aubyn Selig, who died in 1911; in the other Constable Alexander Lamont, who died on February 16, 1918, just short of his 30th birthday. Lamont died of typhoid fever, contracted while tending to Vilhjalmur Stefansson, the Icelandic explorer who was born near my own home in Manitoba. Stefansson arrived on Herschel Island after abandoning his expedition ship, the *Polar Bear*, which was stuck in the ice. Stefansson became ill and was eventually rushed by dog sled to Fort Yukon, where he recovered. Lamont was not as lucky.

The police, then known as the North West Mounted Police, arrived on Herschel Island in 1903, a few years before whaling died out. They, like the missionaries, came to protect the Inuvialuit from the hard-drinking whalers. The police were also in charge of reminding the largely American whaling fleet that Herschel Island was Canadian property. Unfortunately, they tried to establish their sovereignty on the cheap, without a vessel of their own, and had to rely on the American whalers for transportation.

The Canadian Arctic's first court case took place at Pauline Cove in 1924 in a building known as the Bonehouse, constructed in the mid-1890s to store baleen and now used by scientists to store their equipment. Judges came from Edmonton to try two Inuvialuit men, Alikomiak and Tatamigana, for murder. It was the third case of locals murdering outsiders. In the first two cases the accused were treated leniently—primarily because the government was afraid of upsetting the Inuit. But this time the Canadian government decided to set an example for the locals and make a display of their sovereignty in the Arctic. The men were found guilty and hanged from the rafters in the same building they were tried in.

The only people to still call Herschel Island home are the MacKenzies, and they outnumber everyone else in the small transient community of hunters, rangers, scientists and adventurers.

Mary Margaret MacKenzie was born in the old family log cabin that stands in the middle of Pauline Cove. She is in her 30s, with tattoos on her arms. She wears a black strappy top and complains about the 20ºC heat, squinting at the sun from under a fringe of hair.

"The Canadian government threatened my mom," Mary says, swatting at the cloud of mosquitoes around her head. "They said she had to move to somewhere with civilization where us kids could go to school or she'd go to jail."

The log house is now a summer camp for her extended family—a brood of children running amok at all hours, waving fishing rods and rifles.

The logs the cabin is built from are a bit unusual, as you won't find a standing tree within hundreds of miles. The last live tree we saw was in Prince Rupert and the next one will be in Labrador. But on Herschel Island, tangled piles of driftwood are swept into the barren Arctic by the nearby Mackenzie River. The tree trunks, worn smooth by the sand and wave, lie thick on the ground. Excavations show that the wood has been used for housing in this area for hundreds of years.

The cabin is covered by a coarse fishing net. "It keeps the bears out," Marjorie Marie, one of Mary's sisters, tells me. "Bears kept breaking in. It didn't matter what we did, they'd just tear the boards away and break windows, doors, anything. Once they're inside they'd really tear it up. Then an elder told us to do this. I guess it scares the bears, they don't like getting tangled up in the net."

The area around the cabin was busy with wheelbarrow traffic as kids hauled each other around camp. Mattresses had been laid out to air alongside fishing nets, knives, coffee mugs, toys and scraps of firewood. The family sits outside the log cabin for long hours drinking coffee and smoking cigarettes, storytelling and reminiscing. Teenagers fiddle with their mobile phones even though there is no signal here, their longing for the conveniences of home hard to disguise.

Mary's husband Sheldon Brower spends hours each day toying with his fishing net, set perpendicular to the beach. He is the great-great-grandson of Charles D. Brower, the Barrow whaler. Sheldon has a wide smile under a bristling black moustache and his body is squat and powerful. When he's not hunting or fishing he does maintenance work for the town of Kaktovic. It's late afternoon and the smooth water creates a body double of him as he crouches on the beach, anchoring his net. A red plastic bucket full of fish sits on the sand beside him.

"Seal have been swimming around in the bay, so the fish are scared off and won't come in," Sheldon says. "Sometimes I get in my boat and scare them off a bit, but they keep coming in." He says that less ice along the land means fewer polar bears in the area, making the seals brazen.

Tobias and I have been staring at the plump Arctic char in Sheldon's bucket. Arctic char are one of the most prized fish in the region, and their habitat extends farther north than any of the other freshwater fish. Like salmon, many Arctic char are anadromous, spending most of their year at sea and returning to freshwater only to spawn. Some varieties spend their entire life in freshwater. Arctic char are different than salmon in that they do not die after spawning, instead spawning repeatedly. But like salmon, they are delicious when they are barbequed.

We have yet to catch a fish with our own hooks and lines. The hunters in Wales laughed at our attempts and told us we'd need a net. We tell Sheldon about our bad luck and then pull long faces, adding that we've been eating a lot of canned tuna. It works, and he offers us one of the fish for our barbeque.

I see Sheldon again the next day, this time with his 10-year-old son. Jonas is wearing a traditional Inuit parka with a furry hood pulled over his head. Underneath he wears basketball shorts, his sandaled feet squishing in the mud and goose shit that surrounds the cabin. Sheldon has been teaching him how to hunt, and they're hopeful that Jonas will get his first caribou this summer. Sheldon would like to pull his son out of school, raise him on the land and educate him at home. But work, government rules and modern life's realities ensure that this will remain a dream. Jonas plays silently with a toy gun and a roughly carved wooden toy boat while his father speaks about him.

"I could teach him better than the school, teach him about the land," Sheldon says with a hint of defiance in his voice. "I never had the chance when I was young. I had to go to a white school and I only learned about our culture later on. I'd like him to learn it when he's young, from me. That's all he needs to know."

Coming here for a few weeks each summer to be "on the land" helps the elders pass on the remnants of their culture. Although the MacKenzie family has now moved to nearby communities of Kaktovic and Barter Island—both of which are in Alaska—they still return to the island each summer. The international border has little meaning to them; these are all their hunting lands. They cross without papers or fuss, moving between their winter home and summer hunting grounds.

The visit to Herschel Island is a retreat that the family looks forward to all year long. Toddlers, teenagers and grey-haired hunters all find a bunk in the old family home. They fish, shoot a few caribou and catch up with the in-laws. The settlements they normally inhabit would seem like the end of the world to the average urban dweller, but the MacKenzies see it as urban living. They enjoy the peace and quiet on Herschel, far from the headaches and hassles of their busy winter homes back in Alaska.

As I walked across Herschel Island I came across the scars where hillsides had simply collapsed in on themselves. Green tundra was interrupted by giant scabs of mud. Herschel Island was slowly sinking—its permafrost melting as the temperatures rose in the Arctic.

Chris Burn, an expert on permafrost from Carlton University, was visiting the island to collect data, as he had done each year for decades. He was one of many scientists pacing around the island in their Gore-Tex clothing, clenching clipboards and making determined strides toward field stations off in the hills.

"We know there has been a 2°C warming of the permafrost in the last century," Chris said. "It's harder to know how much of that has occurred in the last 50 years because of the data we have to work with. This is happening because of higher air temperatures at the surface."

About one quarter of the land of the northern hemisphere is permafrost, ground that remains frozen year after year, through all seasons. In some places the soil has remained frozen to a depth of hundreds of metres for millennia. Changes in air temperature take time to penetrate permafrost. It could take three years for a change in surface temperature to reach 10 metres into the soil. The effect of the heat weakens as it moves deeper but it leaves a trace, called a thermal memory, of the temperature changes on the surface.

Scientists have drilled holes into the permafrost to read this thermal memory, and have determined that surface temperatures have risen some 2°C over the past several decades.

(Farther south, around James Bay, the southern extension of the Hudson Bay, scientists from Laval University have recorded a 2°C rise in permafrost temperatures over the past 20 years and have found that the southern edge of permafrost retreated 80 miles north in the past 50 years.)

Above the permafrost is an active layer of soil that thaws each summer and allows plants to root. The active layer is slowly getting thicker as the permafrost melts, which results in more and larger vegetation throughout the Arctic over time. "In the last twenty years the thickness of the active layer has doubled," Chris said.

The permafrost locks away methane, a greenhouse gas far more damaging than carbon dioxide. As the permafrost thaws it releases the methane, contributing to the warming cycle. The Arctic contributes only a small fraction of methane emissions—most comes from lush tropical forests—but Arctic emissions are rising rapidly due to higher temperatures.

Melting permafrost also creates headaches for municipal infrastructure across the Arctic, from Nunavut to the Northwest Territories, the Yukon and Alaska. Arctic construction costs are already many times what they are in the south due to high transportation costs and the need to bring in engineers and skilled workers. Until now it was common practice to build everything on piles or piers, so the heat from buildings wouldn't warm and soften the earth underneath. But with climate change added to the mix, there is little that builders can do to protect their foundations.

The *Nunatsiaq News*, for example, ran a story about Salluit, a community of 1,200 people on the shores of Hudson Strait in Northern Quebec. Soil temperatures there have risen by 1°C in the past 10 years while average air temperatures have risen by more than 3.3°C in the past 19 years. Landslides caused by the melting soil have become a major concern. In 1998 the town of Salluit had to move 20 houses to safer ground after landslides ruined their foundations. Salluit sits at the bottom of a steep valley, and there is no more flat land to build houses on. Residents are concerned that the clay-rich soil under the town will melt, turn to mud and cause their houses to sink. One of the options under consideration is to move the whole town to another location.

"How do we cope with infrastructure costs that can escalate due to climate change?" asked Chris. "Are we willing to spend double the amount of money to build an arena for a small community? If the government approved a $12 million new arena, will they still go ahead with the plans if it now costs $24 million? And what if in five years the community comes and says it needs to be rebuilt?"

"The budget for the north now is not worth fighting over in Ottawa. The Yukon budget is less than $1 billion out of a $170 billion federal budget. That's not big. But what will Canadian taxpayers start saying if that starts going up? Can we recognize the rising cost of northern life in a transition place of climate change, where climate change is taking place, and cope with that cost?"

Herschel Island is a good place to study permafrost because its hills get very little snow cover in winter. Snow is an excellent insulator—something that I learned while winter camping as a kid, and that the Inuit have known for centuries. Sleeping in a snowbank or igloo is always warmer than a tent. The lack of snow on Herschel allows scientists to study the effects of changing air temperatures on the active layer of soil and the permafrost without interference from an insulating blanket of snow.

"We know that the ground is definitely warming down to 42 metres, but surface temperatures suggest that measurable temperature change is penetrating to as deep as 80 metres," Chris said. "Think of the amount of energy needed to warm that amount of mass, all that soil, to that extent."

Scientists like Chris Burn are still using data collected by early settlers—like Isaac Stringer—more than a century ago. Stringer kept careful temperature records while living on the island. These are some of the earliest recorded metrological records for the Arctic—and are simply unavailable for most other locations in the Arctic. For many parts of the

Arctic detailed temperature records only go back to the mid-1950s, when Canada and the US built the DEW Line. Scientists are also studying the permafrost in the island's old ice-houses—caves dug into the permafrost and used to keep meat during the summer months.

Landslides and sinking infrastructure are only two of the many symptoms of climate change in the Arctic.

As I wandered through the camp at Pauline Cove two scientists came scurrying by, loaded down with a shotgun, clipboards and backpacks full of gear. I'd met Daniel Gallant and Francis Taillefer the day before when they'd returned to the camp after a day in the field. Daniel, an Acadian, was a doctorate student at Université du Québec à Rimouski where he was studying biology, and he was wrapping up three months in the field, studying Arctic foxes on Herschel Island. Francis had extensive wilderness experience and was there as Daniel's assistant.

They had spent three months camping on the tundra, trapping and tagging foxes and trying to learn more about the encroachment of red foxes into what has traditionally been Arctic fox territory. Now they breathlessly told me that they'd caught a red fox in one of their traps and were about to go tag it. They invited me to come along and watch.

The red fox can be about twice as big as the Arctic fox, so when they move into Arctic fox territory they tend to dominate food supplies and the best den locations. This part of the Arctic has a long history of Arctic fox populations. Trapping them for their rich white winter fur played a key role in changing the Inuit from a nomadic culture to one living in communities centered around fur-trading posts. While red foxes have been present in the Arctic for many years, it is thought that warming temperatures may be encouraging their move north. This was one of the theories that Daniel was researching.

"In the early part of 20th century we've seen a great northward expansion of the range of the red fox, past the treeline and into the Arctic tundra," Daniel explained to me as we set off across the island. "This may mean that the red fox displaces the Arctic fox in some areas. This has already happened in northern Europe."

"Once they can establish themselves they will dominate the area. But so far the red foxes are not that established. They're living together now, which is not that common. Normally it is just one or the other. The farther north you go, the bigger the red foxes are. Maybe it is because they go after bigger prey such as ground squirrels. I'm not sure if the Arctic fox can harvest [ground squirrels]. We're trying to see if these two species have the same strategy in the winter. We're not even sure if the red fox stays here in winter."

Francis held a shotgun in the crook of his arm, just in case we encountered a bear, and both he and Daniel walked with the long strides of men who are accustomed to travelling on foot. I ran after them, panting like a sailor who hasn't done much walking for months, my cameras bouncing and banging against my heaving chest.

Daniel pointed to small changes that had occurred on Herschel Island in recent years, all part of the larger shift in the Arctic landscape due to rising temperatures. The grass was growing more thickly than it used to, with new, southern varieties beginning to make an appearance. As the grass grows thicker, lichen, which used to be the dominant vegetation and is a critical element in the diet of the caribou, begins to disappear. These changes in vegetation have the potential to upset the entire Arctic ecosystem.

We crept up to the trap to see the fox, then walked out of sight behind a hill to spread out a groundsheet and prepare the equipment. Tweezers and clippers to take fur and claw samples, a leather collar with a radio transmitter, syringes and vials of anaesthesia to put the fox asleep, as well as an antidote to wake it up.

Once they'd set up their equipment they donned heavy leather gloves and crept up to the trapped fox. Francis held the fox down while Daniel quickly injected it with the anaesthetic. They retreated a few metres and waited for the drug to take effect. When the fox had stopped moving they slipped its leg out of the rubberised trap, inspecting it for damage. The fox had not been hurt. Then they put the fox into a sack and carefully ferried it back to their field laboratory.

This was the fourth fox they'd caught this summer; a pair of red fox and a pair of Arctic fox.

As they worked over the vixen her mate came loping across the hills, stopping to sniff the air and look at us before continuing on his way, a radio collar already around its neck. The next 30 minutes were a flurry of quiet, efficient activity as Daniel and Francis drew blood samples, snipped at the fox's fur and claws and inspected its teeth. Then they weighed and measured the fox, attached the radio collar and prepared to bring it out of its slumber. Once the antidote had been injected they carried the fox to a soft grassy spot, and we sat down on ground nearby to wait for it to wake up. Francis checked on it every few minutes, and soon came back to report the fox had woken up and run off into the tundra.

"We're looking at all kinds of potential hypotheses and pitting them against the climate change hypothesis," Daniel explained. "That's when we'll see if climate change really is the best explanation. It certainly is an appealing one, but we're not yet sure if this change is related to climate change."

The three months of living rough showed. Both of them sported bushy beards and their clothes were ingrained with grime. They had been living in cramped tents, rarely seeing other people, and they freely admitted they'd had enough of each other's company for the time being. In a few days time their chartered bush plane would arrive, taking them on the first leg of their long journey home. "It will be nice to go home, have a shower, a real meal with a glass of wine and of course see my wife," Francis said.

Arctic scientists like Herschel Island for its existing buildings and because it has an airstrip which makes it relatively accessible from Inuvik, the regional administrative centre just up the Mackenzie River. The airstrip isn't much to look at: a stretch of beach has been cleared of driftwood, a small shack holds fuel drums and wind instruments while a windsock flaps in the breeze. Next to the landing strip, and buffeted by each landing plane, a large sign warns, "This beach is not a designated airstrip," followed by a government disclaimer of any responsibility for it. The pilots don't seem to mind, with planes landing almost every day during the peak summer season, kicking up sand as they bump down the beach. They turn and disgorge their load of scientists, instruments, food and gear. Then the pilots, still wearing their flight suits, stop by the camp for a chat and a cup of tea before again rumbling off into the sky, heading back to southern civilization.

I awoke to the sound of gunshots the morning we planned to leave Herschel Island. I scrambled up the companionway and scanned the cove. Atop the hilltop, silhouetted against the sky, were two galloping caribou. Hunters from the camp had spotted the animals and chased them into the hills but had been unable to bring down either one.

Hunting in Pauline Cove tends to be a fairly opportunistic venture, and in this case the disappointed hunters soon went back to their breakfasts. The caribou, in what seemed like a brazen act of taunting, then wandered down into the camp while the hunters were eating. Two park rangers who kept an eye on Pauline Cove quickly laid down the law, telling the hunters they were not allowed to shoot the caribou anywhere near the camp. There were close to 30 people now camped in Pauline Cove and there could have been serious bloodshed if the hunters started shooting their high-powered rifles in the middle of "town." The rangers told the hunters to chase the beasts back into the hills before shooting them.

This sounded easy but turned out to be nearly impossible, as the caribou refused to cooperate. The hunters chased them through the camp, up the spit of sand and tried to guide them back into the hills, but the two caribou instead ran in circles, jumping over driftwood logs and coming tantalizingly close to their pursuers. The hunters watched, their mouths watering and trigger fingers twitching. Children came and joined the chase, whooping and hollering as the animals ran back and forth on the beach. Eventually the hunters lost interest and returned to the cabins and their cups of tea. I crept up to the caribou with my camera to snap a few shots. A few hours later the caribou loped out of Pauline Cove unnoticed and unmolested.

Herschel Island remains a popular hunting ground for Inuvialuit up and down the coast. The island extends far out into the Beaufort Sea, giving hunters access to bowhead and beluga whales and ringed seals. The nearby Mackenzie River also brings warm, nutrient-rich waters to the area. This feeds invertebrates, which are in turn eaten by larger fish, seals and whales. This area is known for its Arctic cod, pacific herring, flounder and char. Traditionally hunters have based themselves in Pauline Cove or on Avadlek Spit near the Workboat Passage. Archaeologists have found evidence that hunters have used both locations for centuries.

While we were on the island a group of hunters from Inuvik had taken over one of the cabins, their aluminum motorboats pulled up on the beach. Inside, the atmosphere was steamy with the smell of woodsmoke, wet boots and earth. Gun cases and camouflage clothing lay scattered across the floor. The hunters rested from their forays into the hills with long hours of lazing around the cabin, drinking tea and telling war stories. They could spend hours comparing gun bores and discussing how they liked to set up their gun sights. Which calibre drops a caribou the fastest? The cleanest?

Some of their stories focused on the changes in the land and wildlife. "In Yellowknife last year they killed a white-tailed deer," one hunter offered. Another talked about the grizzly bear shot on Banks Island, only the third one in history. Several polar-grizzly crossbreeds have now been shot in the Arctic. There was talk of cougar sightings along a nearby river. These are all animals that traditionally have remained farther south but are venturing north with the warmer temperatures. "The only people that don't care about the impact of climate change are those that are living in town and they don't see the changes," one of the hunters said.

Doug Esagok works as a guide for visiting scientists and serves on various wildlife management boards created after the Inuit struck a land deal with the Canadian government in 1984. While the agreement gives communities more control over oil exploration on their land, there's still a difficult trade-off between leaving the land pristine or attracting jobs and economic development. While he often came to Herschel to guide scientists, this time he was here for the hunting.

"When you look at the damage that is done to land, whales and other wildlife, sometimes I think we could just do without it. But it does bring some jobs our way, and we need those," Doug said. "People are still pretty split on the benefits of developing the oil. We don't really know yet what it will mean in the long term. But things are already changing, and you have to wonder what's bringing it on. When I was a kid you could go just outside Inuvik and shoot a caribou. Now you have to travel pretty far. Scientists say the numbers of the Porcupine herd are down, but we say that the seismic [exploration] activity is just scaring them off, and that they have moved to the west and to the east."

Doug tells a story about a snowmobile trip he made to the island in January. It was -50°C but had been much warmer only weeks earlier. The thaw and ensuing freeze covered the tundra in a thick layer of ice, locking away the caribou's food. "We saw a lot of dead caribou laying around. The herd on the island has gone from about 400 animals down to maybe 100 in the past four years. This island has had its own herd for years and years, and now suddenly you're seeing them spread all along the coast looking for food." We would hear the same kinds of stories from hunters in other places along the coast where the thawing and freezing cycles of recent winters had coated the ground in thick ice and caused muskox and caribou to starve.

Doug disputes accusations that snowmobiles, high-powered rifles with magnifying scopes and a wanton approach to hunting have decimated the herd. "More people are living wage-earner lives, with jobs," he says. "So that means there are less hunters and we're actually taking less off the land. It used to be if you'd see a herd of 20 caribou you'd shoot all 20. Now you might only take two or three because you don't need the meat as badly."

Two days after arriving in Pauline Cove we raised our anchor and returned to sea. Our next port of call would be Tuktoyaktuk, about 150 miles east.

It was sunny and warm, our cockpit thermometer showing 20°C, well above the normal highs of 10°C to 12°C for this time of the year. The hunters on the island had been complaining about the heat for days. The sea temperature had been around 15°C since we arrived in Herschel Island, warmed by the Mackenzie River.

There was a light easterly wind blowing as Herschel Island disappeared behind us, and we motored for several hours before the wind turned more southerly and we were able to start sailing. We soon passed Summer Island in Mackenzie Bay. A few small ice floes bobbed in the muddy water, but the sunshine and warm current had already melted most of the ice.

We sailed on a comfortable beam reach for a day and a half before passing Pullen Island to approach Tuktoyaktuk, in the Mackenzie River Delta. I set *Silent Sound*'s sails wing on wing, with genoa to one side and mainsail on the other, and we ran dead downwind for the last few miles before dropping sails altogether and starting the engine. It was near midnight by the time we pulled up to the town dock. *Baloum Gwen* was already there, and we put out fenders and rafted up to her. Her crew took our lines, and we invited them aboard for a drink. They stayed late into the night, swapping stories and notes about the Arctic Coast and the grand adventure we were sharing.

# CHAPTER 5
## Tuk Tea

*We have come not to a northern limit, but to a northern threshold of commercial progress ... on the shores of the Arctic Mediterranean.*
—Vilhjalmur Stefansson, 1944

It was the morning after a party that left most of Tuktoyaktuk groaning in their beds. The town was quiet, with blinds drawn. Old men shook their heads and muttered about the decadence of the youth. Hanns, Tobias and I had been at the party, but we left before things got interesting. Before one of the partiers began tearing up and down the gravel road and snowless tundra on his snowmobile.

I'd met Michael at the party and he'd made quite an impression with his drunken threats to "fuck us up the ass" and beat us up. He muttered the threats through a leering grin. It was the kind of uneasy aggression that could as easily escalate into a fist fight as be laughed off and turned into an awkward joke. Meanwhile his girlfriend swaggered around the party with a bottle of Jack Daniels dangling from her hand, cajoling us to get drunk with her. "Tuk Tea" consisted of a long draught on the whiskey bottle followed by a swig of Lipton ice tea. Her interest in chatting with three visiting sailors was too much for Michael's pride, and we left the party when his boozy threats became tiresome.

Michael was looking much less bold when I saw him on Saturday morning, hanging dog-faced over the porch railing of his subsidized house. He was still wearing the red shorts and T-shirt he'd worn the night before, and there were other indications it hadn't been a restful night. I crossed the street to say hello and he told me he was waiting for one of the Tuktoyaktuk's public maintenance men to come fix his front door, which was hanging crookedly from broken hinges.

"Oh-oh, someone break into your place?" I asked.

"Nope. I kicked the door in myself," Michael mumbled.

"Oh no, lost your keys, eh?"

"Nope. I had the key in my pocket. I just felt like kicking the fucking door down."

Tuktoyaktuk had some of the same big-wage swagger and rough-neck attitude I'd felt in Dutch Harbor and Barrow. Jobs paid very well, but most were seasonal and involved driving heavy equipment in dire conditions, such as down a frozen river in the -50°C winter. This bred a certain type of macho pride. Combine that with strict alcohol control laws and a large dose of boredom and you had the foundations for a rough, hard-partying town.

Hanns, Tobias and I had all arrived at the party dressed in matching black jackets, trousers and hiking boots, and we had VHF radios hanging from our belts. In the Arctic, as in the rest of Canada, hiking boots and Gore-Tex are considered fashionable, but the fact we were all dressed in black made people nervous. It took some effort to convince them that we were not somehow related to the Royal Canadian Mounted Police, whose detachments are staffed by outsiders who come to the Arctic for two-year stints. Then some of the drinkers began asking if we were from Greenpeace. They had learned that I was interested in climate change, and quickly associated that with Greenpeace, a much-maligned group amongst northerners because it objects to Inuit hunting practices. We assured them we were not Greenpeace. Next they learned we were shooting video footage, which made them suspicious we were related to one of the television shows that had recently done features on Arctic life. There were dark threats of what would happen to us if we were affiliated with *Jesse James is a Dead Man*, a show where the host does what he deems to be life-threatening stunts. Jesse had recently been to Tuktoyaktuk, and he had not made many friends.

"Jesse James is a dead man. No, really, he's a dead man," David Lucas said. "I wish he'd come back to town, I'd freeze him. Everyone here hates him. He made the town look bad. He really embarrassed Tuk. I don't know where he got his information from, because it was all wrong. He has no idea what's he's talking about. He talked about his chainsaw freezing out on the ice road. I've never seen a chainsaw freeze. That doesn't happen. He was real cheap bastard as well, he paid the crew only $7 an hour."

The house party took place on our first night in Tuktoyaktuk. Earlier in the day Hanns had set off down the main street with a huge sack of dirty laundry over his shoulder. We'd been told the RCMP detachment might let us use their washing machine. As he was walking down the road he met David and his wife Brenda, and they quickly invited him to their home. Hanns had spent much of the afternoon there, downing a few cold beers and watching TV with David as he did the laundry. By the end of our stay in Tuk the entire crew would be making themselves at home at David's. It was the first time we took over someone's home to do our laundry, take hot showers and use their internet connection, but it was a pattern that was to repeat itself many times over the coming months, giving us a temporary family in every town we visited. David invited us to the house party, and that night he made boozy promises to take us out in his fishing boat to see the beluga whales in a nearby cove as well as give us a driving tour of the area.

David had a round face topped with a prickly brush cut. He drove a white 4×4 pickup truck with a cartoon figure and the name "Animal" painted on the side. He had the same logo tattooed on his body and many people referred to him by this nickname, which his grandfather had given him as a child. But he appeared like more of an overgrown college boy than beast, with a constant smile, loud laugh and easygoing nature. He was of mixed Inuit and white background and was a proud member of the Gruben clan.

The family was led by 91-year-old Eddie Gruben, who founded E. Gruben's Transport, one of the largest Inuit-owned businesses in the Canadian Arctic. In the 1950s Eddie, a hunter and trapper, started hauling supplies and firewood for others on his dogsled. In the 1960s he bought his first dump truck as the Canadian government began to build schools, hospitals and roads across the Arctic. Now the company provides construction, transport and environmental clean-up services across the region and is one of the largest employers in Tuktoyaktuk. Much of their work is cleaning up the polluted and abandoned DEW Line sites strung across the Arctic. Pickup trucks with the Gruben logo on the door rumble up and down the streets and a large portion of the town's men were "working for Gruben."

Like many small town entrepreneurs who make good, Eddie had generated more than his share of tales. Gruben's large industrial complex with offices and hotel, all standing on cement piles to avoid melting the permafrost and undermining their own foundations, had been bought from a departing oil company for one dollar. Now Gruben charged visiting geologists and prospectors $400 a night to stay in one of the spartan dorm rooms. The story of what had driven Eddie to build his company underlined the lingering resentment towards Europeans still felt across much of the Arctic.

"When the whaling ships would come, back in the day, they would need some help from the locals," David told us as he gave us a driving tour of the town. "There was one boat that came in and they needed some help so my grandfather was one of them. I think he was 10 years old at the time. They were paying about 25 cents a day to help off-load a boat. And when it was time to get paid he went to the captain's cabin. There were six in line waiting to get paid, and he heard the captain say to someone 'Just a minute mate, I have to pay off these bloody Eskimos.' He took that to heart and never worked for the white man again. Now he has nothing but white men working for him."

David also fed us. One afternoon when we were camped in David's living room, hiking boots and grubby sailing gear spread across the floor and laptops crowding his table, he laid on our first proper Inuit meal. We had already enjoyed seal meat given to us by hunters in Wales and eaten fresh Arctic char in Herschel Island but David introduced us to muktuk. Made from the skin and blubber of either bowhead or beluga whale, it is rich in vitamin C and a traditional staple across much of the Arctic. He also served dried whale meat and "bipsi," or dried white fish, while Brenda had made fresh bannock, a pan-fried flat bread also eaten by First Nations in the south, as well as a steaming pot of caribou soup. We'd soon learn that nearly every Inuit home had pot of caribou soup bubbling away on the stove, and the only consistent ingredient was the caribou itself. It was always delicious.

Although David and Brenda both had jobs and family connections with the town's biggest private company, when winter came he still often went on unemployment insurance—a perk known as "pogey" to seasonal workers across Canada. Severe winter weather made most of Gruben's work impossible for many months of the year, except for those workers maintaining a 120-kilometre ice road linking Tuktoyaktuk with Inuvik, the government and commercial centre to the south. High living costs, easy access to government assistance and the seasonal nature of most jobs meant it was normal for most workers to rely on pogey for a good part of year. David lived a good life. He had spacious and comfortable home with a massive television to entertain him through the dark winter months. He drove an expensive truck and had an array of ATVs and snowmobiles in his front yard. David made regular trips south to cities such as Edmonton for shopping, rock concerts and short holidays. His daughters from an earlier relationship also studied in southern Canada.

David saw his location and his way of life as proudly Inuit despite its relative normality by contemporary southern standards. Hunting, fishing and a few weeks at a summer camp have become the main identifying traits for many modern Inuit. Eating "traditional food" was another activity that they clung to as a key identifier, and many were adamant that they much preferred wild game to the instant meals and junk food available at the Northern store. Yet very few Inuit in the western Canadian Arctic speak either Inuvialuit or their local dialect. And while hunting still supplies the bulk of their protein and fat, most of them are as at home on the couch watching television with a bag of potato chips as they are out on the land.

Tuktoyaktuk was our first large Canadian port and we needed to check into the country upon arrival. We were told the RCMP detachment could handle the paper work—which we would later learn was a mistake. But I went to the detachment office and the officer on duty looked at my ship's papers and then asked me to send up the rest of the crew with their passports. On Friday morning, the morning after we'd arrived, I asked Hanns and Tobias to clear immigration before the weekend. Hanns cleared in a few hours later, but Tobias first went to make a phone call home and by the time he arrived at the detachment they were closed for the day.

I was highly strung. The pressure of running the expedition, problems with the boat and the growing discord between Tobias and I was already wearing on my humour. His delay in clearing into the country only annoyed me further. It was my duty as captain to make sure my crew had their papers in order, and over the following few days I questioned Tobias several times on the progress of his immigration clearance. The station was closed over the weekend, and Tobias had checked with the police when they would reopen, but his explanation to me fell on deaf ears. It came to a head in the Northern store on Sunday afternoon, when I encountered Tobias in the checkout lane. I reminded him one time too many that he had yet to clear in. "Yes, Daddy," he taunted.

"No, c'mon, I'm just saying..." I reasoned.

"Yes, Daddy," he repeated.

This went on for an embarrassingly long time before I stomped out of the store in a rage. Tobias had come a long way as a sailor, starting as a complete novice, and we still had thousands of miles left to sail. As much as I wanted to send him home on a plane, I needed him aboard. But he had set a precedent for the rest of the summer.

*Silent Sound* and the other yachts tied up at Tuktoyaktuk's town dock were attracting a lot of attention. It was hard not to notice our masts towering above the town, and we were docked directly in front of the gas station and the Northern store. Townspeople drifted by to see the boats. Some of them knocked on the hull to say hello; others simply stood on the dock and took it all in. There seemed always to be a ragtag gang of children near the boat, their bicycles strewn about the dock. They would climb aboard and play with anything they found lying on deck, no matter how sternly I threatened them.

We were puttering about the boat one afternoon when Roy Cockney came skimming over the water in his aluminum fishing boat. He was fisherman and hunter in his late 60s, commuting back and forth from his summer camp just outside Tuktoyaktuk. He stood in his boat, hanging on to our rail, as we told him our story and tried to find out more about his. When he bragged to us about how good the fishing was we invited him to come by for coffee and bring some of his catch along.

The next day Roy arrived with five whitefish. "You'll get to Halifax and turn around to come back to Tuk because you miss the fish," he said, his eyes disappearing into the folds of his face as he laughed. He had a wizened, tanned face. He had lost teeth as he'd added years, leaving him with a gleeful one-tooth smile. He was short and wiry with a woollen cap perched on his head. Many of his statements began or ended with a cackle of laughter.

"Yea, all the people in England, they're all my cousins, all those Cockneys," Roy joked.

"We had a cop here years ago, Sergeant Joe, I call him Miracle Joe. I was drinking, been drinking for 20 years. Sergeant Joe came to my place. I was drunk, but he said he'd take me to AA [Alcoholics Anonymous]. So we started meeting every day and just talking about AA stuff. I got sobered up, and I've been sober for 20 years now. That's why I call him Miracle Joe."

Roy described himself as a full-time hunter and fisherman—an endangered species in other words. He said he had been living on the land for the past 10 years, but also admitted it was only possible because his wife had a seasonal job with one of the Inuit corporations which, with a little help from some of his seven children, supplied enough cash for them to live on. Combining a salary job with the hunting lifestyle was hard. Most salary workers viewed hunting as a serious pastime rather than a way of life. Those with jobs had trouble finding as much free time as was required to feed their families by hunting alone, while those who lived off the land struggled to find the cash to buy those things the wilderness could not provide.

Most of the food they bought came from a Northern store, like the one at the end of our dock. While some towns have competing shops, the Northern store chain remains the commercial hub of each Arctic settlement and sells everything from canoes to fresh tomatoes flown in from the south. Northern stores are owned by The North West Company, the oldest retailer on the continent. It started business more than 340 years ago as a fur-trading post. While it no longer swaps flour and tin pots for fox furs, for most northerners it remains the main commercial link with the outside world. The goods on its shelves are expensive because anything fresh has been flown in. Other goods arrive on the summer barge. You either live on what the Northern store sells or you go out and shoot your own meal.

"That Northern store, it's for the people that earn wages, who work full time," Roy said. "As soon as you get one of them jobs, that's it, you're gonna be buying that expensive food at the store. They don't have time to hunt and fish anymore.

"Many years ago, before we had RCMP and everything, our elders worked so hard some days. They had no time for anything, just work, work. But lately, our time right now, we got TV, computers and everything is changing."

Roy lamented the state of Inuit children as well. While he wanted his children and grandchildren to attend school, their short summer holidays were not long enough for him to pass on all the knowledge he had to share. "The younger ones now, they are always in school, 10 months a year. They don't know what we do in wintertime 'cause they're always in school [while we are] hunting caribou, trapping. But when they're out there, they're always happy and laughing. They really like it."

It's also out on the land that children start speaking their native dialects. Most western Canadian Inuit identify themselves as Inuvialuit, and they have three dialects, which together are officially known Inuvialuktun. In the coastal communities of Tuktoyaktuk, Sachs Harbour and Paulatuk the common dialect is Siglit. Today, it is mostly the elders who still speak the language, and even Roy admitted he had lost much of his own language over the years. "It ties up my tongue; I'm used to speaking so much English. We need to speak with the kids to keep the language alive. But really we don't hardly ever speak it."

He, like most other Inuit of his generation, attended boarding school, where they risked a beating if they spoke their mother tongues. He heard his parents speak it when he came home for the summers, but by then it had become a foreign language to him. "It used to be that the elders would laugh if you spoke and it sounded funny. They don't laugh anymore when you make mistakes. They correct you and want you to keep trying. Anyone would be proud if their kids would speak Inuvialuit but very few do. When we're on the land, hunting and fishing, we speak Inuvialuit, but not in town much."

Roy's stories crossed between the modern realities of Arctic life and the romance of the land. By now it was a few days after the boisterous Friday night party, and he said he had called the police to pick up two of his children who were too drunk for their own safety. The next minute he described how beluga whales communicate with him.

"Belugas will come right up to the boat and you'll hear them speaking to you, making squeaking noises. But they'll only do it if you have no gun or harpoon. If you have a gun, right now they'll take off. It's as if they know."

Despite his wonder at mammals that can detect a weapon, Roy continued to hunt them for food. Most Inuit have a deep respect for the wildlife around them but at the same time have no qualms over killing animals for food—an attitude bred by generations of survival on the land and a view that is hard for urbanites to understand. Whales that may have been communicating with the hunter one minute are shot and harpooned the next, dragged ashore, cut up and distributed among families.

"You gotta survive. That's our main grub, muktuk," Roy explained. "We just get enough for the winter. We don't hunt more than we have to. It's always been like that. I've always known how much my family needs, and if we get too much we know who to share it with. I go with another hunter and for about 11 years, we both have a family, so we'd get one whale, just right for us. We each take half. But now we have big families, so we take two whales."

Just as southerners often misunderstand Arctic hunters, to the common hunter or proud Inuit all those who criticize them are simply labelled as "Greenpeace." Roy was no less defiant than the partygoers we'd met who suspected us of being infiltrators.

"Greenpeace, they have their own way of living. They want to be powerful too, eh? They just want to take this away from us because we've got it. But they can't get it," Roy said, pausing to make sure I understood. "Ninety percent of Inuvialuit, could be more, they don't go slaughter like you see on TV. You go to England and they see that, they think that if we have everything native that we eat, that it's us doing that. I've never seen

Inuvialuit slaughter like that. When Greenpeace see that on TV we get the blame. But us, we don't do that."

Not everyone practised Roy's stewardship. We sailed along the Beaufort Sea coast just days after the annual beluga migration and met southerners who had been in Wainwright and witnessed the hunt. John, the construction worker who had come to northern Alaska for the higher pay, showed me a video he had made of hunters herding the belugas into a lagoon with motorboats. The whales were corralled, the boats circling the pod and jumping over their own wakes as the lagoon turned wild with waves and shouting hunters. Then the shooting began. The hunters tried to harpoon the whales first, with a large inflated balloon attached to the harpoon line to keep the whales from sinking and allow the hunter to keep visual track of the beast. But sometimes the whales were shot without being harpooned, and they escaped the whirlpool of killing. They died later and their corpses washed ashore, wasted. The ones that were harvested were loaded onto a gravel truck and hauled into the centre of town for butchering. John said that when the butchering was done there was still ample meat left on the carcasses. He had shooed away the village dogs and cut off several large chunks for himself. "I felt funny doing it, but it's not really stealing, is it?"

After spending his whole life on the land, Roy had begun to notice changes in the Mackenzie River Delta. He didn't attribute the changes directly to climate change, choosing instead to shrug his shoulders and accept it as nature's mystery. "We've got beaver right here in the harbour, on the ocean-side. You'd never have thought to see beaver here, but we have them, I've seen them," he said. He and others also mentioned an increase in mussels. "We maybe had a few in the bay here before, but not like this. This year there's lots and lots. Maybe the water is warmer, who knows."

The Mackenzie River brings a stream of warm, brown nutrient rich water into the Arctic, creating one of the best hunting areas on the coast. The river starts at Great Slave Lake and then cuts across the Northwest Territories and into the Yukon on a northwesterly path towards the coast, where it spills into the Beaufort Sea in a great meandering delta. It's Canada's longest river and together with its headstreams it runs 4,241 kilometres—the second longest river on the continent after the Mississippi. The Mackenzie has played a huge role in Arctic exploration over the centuries, carrying fur traders and fame seekers to the sea.

In 1789 Alexander Mackenzie, a Scottish explorer working for the North West Company, set off from Great Slave Lake by canoe to explore a river the Dene First Nations people called the *Dehcho*. He hoped that it would lead him to the Pacific Ocean and the Northwest Passage, which remained undiscovered. When it instead deposited him on the shores of the Beaufort Sea, Mackenzie named it Disappointment River. In 1792 Mackenzie returned to Canada to make another attempt at finding the Pacific, and this time he was successful. He travelled overland, over mountains and across rivers, and found the sea in Bella Coola, not far from Prince Rupert where we set off to cross the Gulf of Alaska. Mackenzie was the first man to cross the continent north of Mexico. The river was later renamed in his honour.

Sir John Franklin, the most infamous name in Arctic exploration, also travelled the Mackenzie River. Franklin was lionized by the English for his Arctic travels. However, he was a soft, pudgy man and an unlikely Arctic explorer who relied on his native and French-Canadian voyageur guides to the point of becoming a burden to them. Although he went to sea at the age of 12 and served in some of Britain's major battles, including Trafalgar, he paled in comparison to many of the hardy men that tramped across Canada's great wilderness and paddled its rivers in search of the passage.

Franklin's first expedition in the North American Arctic in 1819, to chart the north coast of Canada in search of the passage, was poorly planned and ended in disaster. After a long overland trek he and his men paddled down the Coppermine River and then charted the coastline east of the river. While their work helped fill in some more of the Arctic map, starvation stalked the expedition, forcing Franklin and his men to eat lichen and even their own leather boots, after which he became known as the "man who ate his boots." (It is a title that was recycled several times for different men, underlining the severity of early life in the Arctic.) Eleven of his 20 men died before they were rescued by natives and the legacy of the expedition was tainted by accusations of cannibalism.

Franklin returned to England in late 1823, where he married the poet Eleanor Anne Porden. She gave birth to their daughter Eleanor Isabella the following year. By early 1825 his wife was gravely ill with tuberculosis, and Franklin was preparing to set off for the Arctic once more. She died six days after he set sail.

But this expedition was better supplied and more successful than his Coppermine River debacle. Franklin was accompanied by Sir John Richardson, a Scottish surgeon and naturalist. Franklin's party wintered at Fort Franklin on Great Bear Lake from September 1825 until June 1826, then sailed down river and reached Canada's northern shoreline in early July before splitting in two to survey the coast to the east and west. Franklin went west to the Alaskan border, charting 610 miles of previously uncharted coastline. Richardson went east, mapping 1,015 miles of previously uncharted coastline. The Mackenzie River had proven itself to be one of the quickest ways to get into the heart of the North American Arctic.

The Hudson's Bay Company financed further Arctic explorations in order to gain control of the northern fur trade, and the Mackenzie River was its highway to the north. Supplies were carried north by York boat and canoe, while furs travelled south to fur trading posts. The river is still an important Arctic highway. It is navigable for about five months a year, and its barge traffic is an important supply route for the entire western Canadian Arctic. The river is frozen from October to May and as soon as the ice is strong enough it serves as an ice road, creating an important transport link between Tuktoyaktuk and Inuvik.

Today it is oil and gas that bring explorers to the Mackenzie Delta and Beaufort Sea. A 2008 United States Geological Survey estimated that the Arctic may hold 27 percent of the world's undiscovered gas and 13 percent of its oil. Some energy consultants have predicted that as much as 30 percent of the world's remaining oil reserves may be in the Arctic. While much of that lies in US and Russian territory, the Mackenzie River Delta is at the heart of Canada's Arctic energy exploration efforts, and a proposed pipeline to southern markets has come to dominate politics in the region. The Mackenzie Valley Pipeline would carry gas and oil to Alberta, where it would connect to the province's oil fields. The pipeline plan was first presented in 1970 by a group of oil companies including Exxon, Gulf, and Shell, spawning a wave of environmental, economic and social studies that continues today. Whether or not the pipeline is ever built, its backers have already made good on the promise of injecting money into the region.

I went to Tuktoyaktuk's Kitty Hall community centre one night looking for someone to tell me more about how the pipeline and oil plans were being received locally. Kitty Hall is named after the traditional Inuvialuit gathering place named Kitigaaryuit at the mouth of the Mackenzie River. For hundreds of years people would gather at Kitigaaryuit every summer to hunt beluga whales, and they would return in winter for games and festivals. A series of epidemics introduced by traders and whalers ravaged the local population, and at the turn of the century much of the community was wiped out. Fear of disease and death kept people away from the gathering place for many years, although now hunters again use Kitigaaryuit on a seasonal basis.

It was a far more benign scene inside the hall. The hall provides alternative entertainment for those who don't drink, or at least not the way we'd seen people drink at the Friday-night party. The hall was cold and cavernous, lit by the sickly glow of fluorescent strip lighting. But the atmosphere was warm despite the uninspiring surroundings. A group of women and children sat in a circle on the floor, squealing and laughing as they played a raucous card game called Snirt. The men sitting nearby snidely referred to it as "the ass crack game" as they watched their amply-padded wives and daughters sit on the floor, their pants slipping down their bottoms. Sun-wizened men with coarse hands and working man's bulk sat on plastic chairs under the glare of fluorescent lights. Roy had come in from his hunting camp for the night and was sporting a white cowboy shirt and his usual impish grin. He teased me about buying my boat, and I offered to swap it with him for one of the many new 4×4 trucks I saw driving around town. He looked around the room and complained about the poor turnout, blaming it on weekend hangovers.

Dennis Raddi, a heavy equipment operator wearing a Harley Davidson headband over his shaved head, talked jobs and the economy as he fidgeted with an empty Styrofoam coffee cup. "Oil and gas development are good for us in the long term," he said. "Lot of people take a short-sighted view of it, and then maybe it doesn't look as good. But it means jobs, money and control for us."

In the past many high-paying jobs had been taken by southerners willing to move north for a season or two in order to pad their bank account, but this was slowly changing. Gruben, the town's big construction company, started a training program for machinery operators in order to increase the local labour pool. But most of the work, oil exploration and otherwise, was seasonal, leaving workers to live off the land and unemployment assistance for at least a part of the year.

"You can't live here without hunting and fishing," Dennis said. "Have you seen the prices of things in the store? It's just too expensive and it doesn't taste good anyway. Thank god for pogey. It's a great big help."

I'd met Eddy Lucas, another machine operator, at the house party where he told me that while Tuktoyaktuk had plenty of workers who could drive a truck or operate a road grader, few had the proper paperwork to take the wheel. Companies needed certified operators for insurance purposes, and Gruben's school was providing exactly that.

"I've been here all my life and don't plan on going anywhere else," Eddy said, leaning back on the railing of the patio and swigging from a beer. "Why would I? Money is good here, family is good, you're free to do what you want. Hunt, fish, whatever. You have freedom here compared to life in the city. The money here is really good so you see more guys coming from down south looking for work. Here there hasn't really been much layoffs. It was really bad about four years ago, but now you sort of get the feeling that it's coming back, and that's because of the oil and gas activity. I know what they say about the environment and stuff, and sure, it's a concern, but for us it means jobs, better money and it would probably mean a road to Inuvik."

The ice road between Tuktoyaktuk and Inuvik has starred in several television shows, putting a swagger in the step of the people who build and maintain it when they find out southerners are impressed by their daring jobs and fat salaries. Each winter they clear the snow off the ice so that it will freeze thicker and faster. Sometimes they drill holes in the ice and pump water over the ice to thicken it. Throughout the winter they clear the ice of snow and monitor it for cracks and weak spots. Ice roads are a fixture across much of the Canadian wilderness, and in every case they offer communities a few months of escape from their usual isolation. Prices in stores plummet when the roads open for the season as it becomes easier to haul in fresh goods and visitors can come and go at will.

"The whole community opens up and we can go places," David told me. "We can go to Inuvik to shop. They have a lot of different restaurants there, and a pharmacy. The stores have all this selection. You can finally get out of town when the road opens."

In Tuktoyaktuk there was a clear sense that better times were ahead. People were already enjoying the benefits of the oil exploration boom in the Beaufort Sea. Tuktoyaktuk is the heart of Canada's Arctic oil business, though it pales in comparison to activity in the US and is only now being revived after two quiet decades. Despite objections to Arctic oil exploration by southern environmentalists, Inuit communities wanted the money they saw their Alaskan cousins enjoying. However, they were also aware that it took decades for Alaskan communities to catch up with the oil companies after being hoodwinked at the start. "Guaranteed, we learned something from Alaska," said Dennis, the equipment operator I met at the community centre. "They took the cash in a lump sum and squandered it. They had no foresight."

In 1984 six Inuvialuit communities concluded 10 years of negotiations to sign a land deal with the Canadian government. The Inuvialuit Final Agreement (IFA) was the first Arctic land deal in Canada, though the government had signed similar deals with aboriginal people in southern Canada. The Inuvialuit agreed to give up exclusive usage rights of their ancestral lands in exchange for land, wildlife management control and money.

The government gave 90,650 square kilometres of land, including 13,000 square kilometres with subsurface rights to oil, gas and minerals, along with about $170 million in aid to the communities of Sachs Harbour, Ulukhaktok, Paulatuk, Tuktoyaktuk, Inuvik and Aklavik. The agreement covers a large area of the mainland coast as well as parts of Banks and Victoria islands. The communities created corporations to receive and manage the land, energy and other resources. Councils were established to oversee everything from hunting grounds to petroleum rights negotiations. As part of the deal, Herschel Island became a territorial park, with the Yukon government and the Inuvialuit sharing responsibility for it.

The IFA was an important step towards giving local communities some collective bargaining power when oil exploration companies came to town. People living in these communities are now receiving the same transfer payments Alaskans enjoy, although at lower rates. "IFA gave us some level of self-government, some level of control," Dennis said. "Without the IFA we had no power. The IFA means we don't have to fight the government on every little issue anymore."

But can oil make the Inuit self-reliant once again and end their dependence on handouts from Ottawa? Given the high cost of living and infrastructure combined with the small tax base, it is hard to picture full independence. "Only if it's the last place on earth with oil," Dennis said. "We can't focus just on oil and gas and expect that to be the only thing we'll live on in the future. We have to have tourism. It would make a big difference for us to have a road down the Mackenzie Valley. That would really help us. The oil will be gone someday, but we'll still have the lure of the Arctic Ocean, the pingos [land formations caused by frost], the whales. They'll always be here. We just have to learn how to market it."

But at the end of the day, if the tourism doesn't work out and the oil runs out, many Inuit share the view that the government still hasn't paid them back for taking their land away in the first place. "The British government said they would take care of the health and education of the native population and that this promise was binding on all governments thereafter,"

Dennis said. "So I don't give a shit what anyone says, they made the law. What we give back is Canadian sovereignty. We're here. It has always been important to us, this land. It's ours and we are proud Canadians."

Drew Fellman arrived in Tuktoyaktuk two days after we did. Drew was a short, wiry man with a dark complexion and a mop of unruly greying hair. He had an easy smile and an absentminded air about him, with an absurd sense of humour that that I found both charming and exhausting at times. Drew, a gifted photographer and film producer, was introduced to me by a friend because Drew had a long-running interest in the Franklin expedition. His first email to me included a photo of his bookshelf of Arctic books, many of which we'd both read. I had met him for the first time several months earlier when he was planning to join me for the entire voyage. However, a long-term IMAX film project came to fruition and he dropped out to pursue his own film. When Anna dropped out in Dutch Harbor I called Drew and he agreed to join us for one month as her replacement. He, like Tobias, was not a sailor, but he had spent long periods on ships and dive boats as an underwater photographer and camera technician.

Hanns, Tobias and I had been handling the boat well on our own. It would be best to have Drew focus on shooting photos, film and take some of the galley duties off our hands rather than train him as a sailor during his short stay with us. He arrived from Los Angeles carrying several large sacks of outdoor equipment, cameras, and a folding two-person kayak. The kayak quickly became a core piece of our equipment because our only dinghy was too small. The kayak gave everyone more mobility while at anchor and it proved to be a lot of fun paddling it around ice floes.

It was refreshing to have a new person aboard, especially someone with new ideas and energy. I had my hands full with running the boat and expedition and we had begun to run low on inspiration. Drew, with his quirky humour, helped revitalize us. His arrival also acted as a salve for the relationships aboard *Silent Sound*, particularly between Tobias and me. He and Tobias shared a similar sense of humour and carefree spirit, and they quickly formed their own little band.

After four days in Tuktoyaktuk we were ready to get underway again. Our fuel and water tanks were full, we'd bought groceries and made minor repairs. The only problem was the ice. The ice charts showed that Amundsen Gulf and the Dolphin and Union Strait to the east both remained heavily blocked with ice.

Canada's ice charts are mind-boggling in their complexity, with a four-tier rating system. The concentration of the ice is expressed as a ratio measured in tenths. A further breakdown of this figure is described as the "partial concentration," or concentration by ice type. A third tier of information ranks the stage of ice development ranging from new ice to grey ice, grey-white, thin first-year, old, second-year, multi-year or ice of land origin, to name just a few. Finally, the system rates the size of the ice floes. All of this information is presented in oval diagrams sprinkled across the charts. Along with these clusters of numbers the government uses a simplified colour-coding system with an array of symbols to describe ice movement, open water and the position of major icebergs.

The first time I looked at an Arctic ice chart I was overwhelmed. Then I began to learn how to block out 95 percent of the information and focus on what I needed to know. Red and orange were bad. Yellow was barely passable while light blue and green were easily manageable. In other words, *Silent Sound* should be able to motor through anything up to 4/10th ice, or 40 percent of the sea area, without too much trouble. Driving through 6/10th ice was difficult to impossible. Entering areas of 6/10th or 7/10th ice meant we most certainly would become stuck. The actual thickness and age of the ice hardly mattered. We wouldn't be busting our way through ice floes, young or old, hard or soft.

*Ocean Watch*, anchored near us in Tuktoyaktuk, downloaded the latest ice charts and invited me aboard to compare plans. The charts showed a stubborn plug of 9/10th ice jammed into the narrow Dolphin and Union Strait between the mainland and Victoria Island. There was open water on both sides of the ice jam, with Paulatuk on the western end of the strait and Cambridge Bay to the east both reporting open harbours. While the ice plug was shrinking in size with every passing day it wasn't losing its density and it remained too thick for a yacht to get through. Winds and currents were also pushing the ice flow into the bottleneck, keeping it tightly jammed as it melted. On some days the ice charts showed a promising sliver of 4-6/10th ice on the southern edge of the strait. This was the route many yachts in years past had taken, as local wisdom was that eventually a southern wind would blow the ice up against the coast of Victoria Island, leaving open water to the south. But now it was a gamble. If the wind turned, the ice could pin a yacht against the mainland coast and drive it ashore.

We were encountering more ice than we would have seen if we had sailed the passage in 2007 or 2008, but ice levels were still far below the

30-year average as a trend towards warmer temperatures slowly melted the Arctic, so we remained hopeful that eventually there would be enough open water for us to sail through.

I'd had enough of Tuktoyaktuk and wanted to be underway. Tuktoyaktuk reminded me too much of Dutch Harbor and Barrow, where modern life had all but wiped out the Inuit culture. I was keen to see some of the smaller communities in the Arctic, where I hoped to find a different view of traditional life. But with the ice blocking our way I was worried we wouldn't have time to visit many smaller communities if we wasted more days waiting in Tuktoyaktuk.

*Ocean Watch* and *Baloum Gwen* decided to leave Tuktoyaktuk and wait in Paulatuk or one of the anchorages near Cape Parry until Dolphin and Union Strait opened. I decided I'd rather sail 230 miles northeast to Sachs Harbour, the only community on Banks Island. People in Tuktoyaktuk described Sachs as a quiet and friendly community that retained more of the traditional Inuit lifestyle than its neighbours. It was a few miles off our track and we might have to sail back to the southern side of Amundsen Gulf to get around the ice, but I was willing to risk spending a few extra days at sea. Little did we know that our northern route would prove to be a lucky break.

# CHAPTER 6
## Sachs Harbour

*For the ice you have been built, and in the ice you shall*
*stay most of your life, and in the ice you shall solve your tasks.*
—Roald Amundsen, 1917

We left Tuktoyaktuk on the afternoon of August 3rd and slowly picked our way out of the harbour. The town sits behind three miles of tidal flats and low-lying islands. Even beyond that much of the water along this coast is only four or five metres deep and littered with sandbanks due to the low profile of the land and the silty flow of the Mackenzie River. *Silent Sound* draws 1.6 metres and on this journey we had sailed many miles in as little as eight metres of water, but these shallows made me particularly nervous. Wisps of fog drifted across the water as we raised our sails and steered *Silent Sound* around the banks marked on the chart. The fog was yet not heavy enough to cause problems, but it would become much thicker and give us a fright before we got to our next port.

The forecast called for fickle winds, fog and ice-strewn seas. Forecasts predicted that we would have to make our way through light 3/10th ice to get to Banks Island, but we were unsure of where that ice had drifted to since the report. Our days of sailing through bright sunlit nights were coming to an end. Summer solstice was now a month and a half gone. Still, the sun remained just high enough that we could see the land and ice at night.

This was Drew's first time at sea with us and I sensed some apprehension in him. He was trying to adjust to life aboard a sailing yacht with three other people who had settled into their own rhythms and habits. Drew was also not impressed with his accommodations. I assigned him the aft starboard bunk, which offered privacy and comfort that the other bunks in the main saloon did not. At the start of the trip I assigned this private bunk to Anna as the only woman aboard. Drew arrived with sacks of camera gear and he was one of the messiest people aboard, so putting him in the corner gave him a safe place to leave his equipment. But it was a long, narrow pilot berth with an entry at one end, and it was hard to get in and out of. The entry into the bunk was squeezed in between the companionway and the refrigerator, with almost no floor space. It was designed to be slept in with one's feet to the stern, but there was no perfect solution. Crawling in feet first was hard to do because the bunk was high and there was little room to manoeuvre, and one had to hang from a handgrip like a monkey and shimmy one's legs up and into the bunk. If one crawled in headfirst it was hard to communicate with anyone standing next to the bunk as one's head was deep in the stern of the boat, and the reading light was then at one's feet. What seemed to work best was to crawl in headfirst and then turn around in the tight space so one's head was at the exit. Then, when one wanted to get out, either turn around again and crawl out feet first or do the reverse of the hanging monkey move. Drew found the bunk claustrophobic and it only made it harder for him to fit into our established patterns aboard *Silent Sound*.

Having Drew aboard acted as a buffer between Tobias and I, but the friction had not disappeared. Once we had left Tuktoyaktuk behind the two of us sat in the cockpit and attempted to discuss the problem and find a solution. Our positions had not changed since the last time we had given things an airing, and I remained angry with him for his antics in the store in Tuktoyaktuk. Tobias objected to how I ran the expedition and life aboard *Silent Sound*, and how I communicated my decisions. He had a fair point, as I was an inexperienced captain and manager of people. Hanns also pointed out my lack of communication of the plans I made. Not everything on the boat and the expedition had been planned as well as it could have been, but I felt vindicated by the fact that we were making progress towards our goal and meeting the challenges as they arose. I felt Tobias's expectations were unrealistic and that he didn't appreciate the opportunity he had by being on this expedition.

We knew each other mainly from his weekend visits to Hong Kong—days and nights filled with parties and pranks on the town. Now he was surprised to find a very different person as his captain. I was more serious, a lot less prone to fun and games and was focused entirely on the expedition. I was not as much fun as he'd hoped. In fact, I had become downright humourless for much of the time. The worst part was that we had lost respect for each other, and our friendship was quickly souring. As we sat in the cockpit we acknowledged that neither of us was satisfied with how things stood. The difference was that as captain I expected Tobias to respect my decisions regardless of his feelings, but I sensed even that was in danger as Tobias glumly went below deck and I carried on with my watch.

Our head once again gave us trouble soon after we left Tuktoyaktuk. Hanns was emptying the holding tank when the hand pump began squirting shit. I had already repaired the head several times in the past month, and this time Hanns offered to tackle the dirtiest parts of the job. The sewage tank was in the forward sail locker next to the anchor chain, buried under a pile of sails, buckets and spare parts. We cleared out the tiny space and Hanns crawled in. We had begun calling these repairs "boat yoga," whether it involved working in the bilge underneath the engine, installing gear in the bowels of the hull, or crawling into the sail locker. Working on a boat often involves contorting your body into the most imaginative and painful positions while gripping a screwdriver in your teeth and torch under your chin, all the while trying to loosen a microscopic screw you can't see and which is corroded with rust. Crucial equipment is mounted in the darkest, tightest corners of the boat where only the shortest screwdrivers and the most nimble fingers have enough room to get the job done. Fixing the head has the additional disadvantage of being dirty, smelly work. Human feces are never a good addition to cramped, pitching and airless spaces. I felt bad for Hanns as he was a head and shoulders taller than me, but I didn't feel bad enough to decline his offer to take on the job.

He began taking the pump apart while I cut up an old milk jug to catch the shit as it ran out of the pump. As he worked I hauled reeking buckets of shit through the cabin to throw overboard. The first time we pulled the pump apart it looked fine, so we double checked the hoses for blockage. Then we put everything back together and tested it. It still didn't work, so we took it all apart a second time, and this time we washed the membrane and held it up to the light, revealing the tiny tear that was at root of all our problems. We decided to bypass the tank and the pump altogether. From now on, everything from the toilet would go directly into the sea. But we didn't have the extra hose or the spare parts to do this, so we began to cannibalize the system for hoses and clamps.

Hanns and I kept up a sarcastic banter throughout the job in order to cope with the stench and frustration of the situation. He was folded double in the sail locker, bracing himself as the boat rolled and pitched in the seas. He tried to draw elaborate parallels between his uncomfortable state and the masochism of French modern dance. It made no sense but he succeeded in getting a laugh. In the end we had no choice but to laugh—we were two guys on a small boat at sea, elbow deep in human shit. Tobias and Drew were taking over our watches and helming the boat, just glad they were not being called to the head to help out. But as the afternoon wore on Tobias became hungry despite the pall of stench that hung over the boat. "Should I barbeque some fish?" he asked, standing back from the head at a respectful distance. We had a refrigerator full of fish from Roy Cockney, the hunter we met in Tuktoyaktuk. Food was the furthest thing from my mind. Our lack of enthusiasm at Tobias's offer turned him back, and he consoled himself with a few biscuits.

An hour later he returned. "How hungry are you guys? Should I start cooking?" Our hunger was rapidly abating with each passing hour as Hanns and I became more frustrated and less timid about plunging our fingers down dark, slimy pipes. We grunted and ignored him. Tobias started cooking despite our lack of interest, and soon the smell of barbequed fish wafted through the cabin, mixed with the putrid smell of our dismantled sewage system.

Late in the afternoon we started putting the sewer system back together and cleaning up the mess we'd created, carefully disinfecting all the tools we used and surfaces we touched while working. The last thing I needed was for the crew to become ill from the bacteria we had spread around the boat. Finally we tested our new plumbing, only to have the new joints squirt water as soon as they were under pressure. We plucked it all apart yet again and left it all open to dry, with plans to silicon the joints the next day. If anyone needed to use the head during the night they would have to squat over a bucket or go over the side of the boat. Frustrated and tired, we sat down to eat the barbequed whitefish. It was delicious.

Meanwhile, we were once again faced with fitful winds. The wind that did show up came from the northeast, forcing us to sail close-hauled, which is slower and less comfortable than sailing on a beam reach. On our second day at sea a light rain began to fall through the building fog, which made it feel colder than the 7°C to 10°C that our thermometer showed. About 40 miles from Sachs Harbour we began to see ice in the water, with a few larger floes glowing white in the distance. Here was the ice as forecast. Some of it was multi-year ice drifting south out of the Arctic Ocean. Multi-year ice tends to be harder and thicker than first-year ice. The ice has spent several years as pack ice and is slowly melting and breaking up as it drifts south. We slowed down, dropped our sails and began motoring for better manoeuvrability. After the initial interest in seeing ice once again, the rest of the crew went below deck and I was left alone at the helm to resume my watch. Soon we were through the first band of ice floes and it appeared we were back in clear water. The wind had picked up from a good angle and I contemplated raising sail again when there was a loud thud that echoed through the hull. *Silent Sound* shuddered with the impact and a huge chunk of ice scraped along the side of the hull with a loud rasping sound. The ice lazily spun away in our wake, split in two by our bow.

"Whoa, whoa, whoa!" Hanns shouted as he came running up the companionway in his underwear. What had sounded like a dull thud from the cockpit was frighteningly loud below deck. The rest of the crew came up behind him, wide-eyed with concern. I was shaken as well. I thought I was watching carefully, but the fog was cutting visibility down to as little as 50 metres at times and I'd allowed myself a short lapse in attention as I'd contemplated raising sails. I felt foolish. This was the second time we'd hit ice, and both times the captain had been at the helm.

The impact wasn't as bad as it sounded. The ice had given way to the bow of the boat, but Hanns was still concerned and began looking at the bow and inside the hull for any cracks. *Silent Sound*, with her reinforced Kevlar hull, had come out of the collision with nothing more than a one-centimetre-long scratch in her paint. I was suddenly very happy for those miserable days spent applying Kevlar to the hull, even though I couldn't be sure if it had really protected us or if *Silent Sound*'s thick hull and sizeable bulk would have knocked the ice aside anyway. Regardless, it was a reminder to pay closer attention. If the ice were to punch a hole in the hull we could be forced into the icy water within minutes. We were carrying full immersion suits in case of emergency, but our chances of survival were very slim if we had to abandon ship. The water temperature often hovered just above 0°C. I tried not to think about the potential outcome of an accident.

Even the largest floes of first-year ice stand only a metre or two above the surface of the water, and the smaller chunks that break off become very hard to spot in the water. Icebergs, which are created when glaciers break apart at their face, can stand 75 metres or more above the sea, while sea ice normally only rises a few metres above the water's surface. These waters were littered with sea ice, not icebergs. *Silent Sound*'s radar was able to spot the largest of the ice floes. But it could not help us avoid smaller pieces, which might not appear on the radar but were still large enough to damage her hull. Now, with the radar on and me closely watching the waves, we navigated through the foggy sea. The radar showed a jumble of ice ahead of us as we picked our way forward. Tobias took over the watch for the final few miles into Sachs Harbour, steering us around ice floes that were hundreds of metres across.

It was from Banks Island, the fifth-largest island in Canada, that Sir Robert McClure spotted one of the final pieces to the Northwest Passage puzzle in 1850. This was McClure's third time in the Arctic and his second expedition in search of Franklin. This time he was back as captain of his own ship, the HMS *Investigator*, although he was not the leader of the expedition.

The two-ship expedition was led by Richard Collinson, who was captaining the HMS *Enterprise*. They sailed from England via the Straits of Magellan and Hawaiian Islands in order to approach the North American Arctic from the western entrance. McClure reached the Arctic before Collinson, and instead of waiting for him as planned he set off into the ice alone. The *Investigator* entered the Arctic by cutting through Alaska's Aleutian Islands and across the Bering Strait, the same route we took 159 years later aboard *Silent Sound*. McClure rounded Point Barrow on August 7, about two weeks later in the season than us. McClure was forced to use five rowboats to tow the *Investigator* through ice in the same place we encountered our first ice. Heavy offshore ice forced him to stay close to the coast as he worked his way east before turning north to Banks Island.

McClure knew that in 1819 William Edward Parry had sailed as far west as Melville Sound after entering the Arctic from the east, but at a higher latitude than McClure was at. Parry had sailed through Lancaster Sound and Barrow Strait along what would become known as Parry Channel. Parry had seen the northern shores of Banks Island from his ship, naming the island for Joseph Banks, an English botanist.

Now McClure, on the southern coast of Banks Island, spotted a channel on the east side of the island that led north, later named Prince of Wales Strait. McClure speculated that this channel might lead him to Melville Sound on the north side of the island. If he was right, he would have discovered a route through the Arctic, the elusive Northwest Passage. It would have been a very different route than was eventually sailed by Amundsen, but today we know that the Northwest Passage is actually a series of different possible routes through the Arctic, not just one.

Winter turned against McClure and his ship became locked in ice in Prince of Wales Strait along the eastern shore of the island. In October, after the ice had closed in on the *Investigator*, McClure took a team of his men and sledged to the north end of Banks Island. From atop a small mountain they could look out across the frozen Melville Sound. He had discovered a continuous sea route through the Arctic, the Northwest Passage. However, it was frozen in ice, and it would never become a viable transit route, even for McClure himself.

The next summer McClure and his men set off to sail farther north as soon as the ice broke up in the hope of sailing their new-found passage, but they were again unable to get through the strait and through to Melville Sound. So McClure turned around and headed south, sailing around the island to attempt reaching the sound from the other side. As long as he could enter Melville Sound from the west he would be able to proclaim himself the first to sail the Northwest Passage. Once again, he was stopped short by ice as winter set in. The *Investigator* was imprisoned in a bay which McClure named Mercy Bay, on the far northern coast of Banks Island.

McClure was unable to free his ship from the ice in the spring of 1852 and his crew faced their third winter in the Arctic. They were suffering from scurvy, frostbite and starvation. Every spring they hoped for open water, but were disappointed when the ice remained firm. By now the British government had sent additional men to the Arctic to find McClure, who had been sent to the Arctic to find Franklin but had been sidetracked by the lure of the Northwest Passage. In the spring of 1853 a crewmember from the rescue ship HMS *Resolute* found McClure and his men.

The *Resolute*, part of a fleet under the command of Sir Edward Belcher, was captained by Henry Kellet and had come to the Arctic looking for both Franklin and McClure. Kellet ordered McClure to abandon ship and hike across the ice to the *Resolute*, which was wintering 180 miles away at Dealy Island, off the south eastern shore of Melville Island. It was late in the season when the ship turned for home, and the *Resolute*, carrying McClure and his men in addition to its own crew, made it only as far as Barrow Strait, forcing the *Investigator* crew to spend a fourth winter in the Arctic. The next spring Belcher and Kellet abandoned their ships and walked across the ice to Beechey Island. There they hitched a ride back to England on summer supply ships, sailing east through Lancaster Sound and exiting the Arctic through Davis Strait. McClure finally arrived home in 1854, four and a half years after setting out.

This journey made McClure and his men the first to transit the Northwest Passage, if we count both their sledging and sailing miles. McClure was awarded £10,000 for solving the riddle of the Northwest Passage. Kellet went on to become a rear-admiral and take commands in

India and China, and today the Royal Hong Kong Yacht Club sits on an island named after him. The M'Clure Strait (using an alternative spelling of the explorer's name) extends west from Melville Sound and forms a gateway into the great Arctic archipelago. It is now the most westerly part of a northern Northwest Passage route that runs on the north side of Banks Island and Victoria Island. Although it was the first Northwest Passage route to be discovered, it was not the first to be sailed. When Amundsen became the first to sail the passage in 1903–06 he took the southern route, the same route *Silent Sound* was now following. The northern route remains less popular because it contains considerably more ice, although it was open in both 2008 and 2007 as climate change melted away its icy defences.

Sachs Harbour, population 120, is the only settlement on an island almost twice as big as Taiwan. Its name comes from the ship *Mary Sachs* of the Canadian Arctic Expedition that visited the harbour in 1913–18, although it would be another decade before a group of Inuit trappers began living there permanently. The windswept town lies at the mouth of the Sachs River, with the town facing south across a small lagoon. Hills rise dry and stony behind the scattering of houses, which are strung out along a narrow gravel road. Boats, large and small, are strewn on the beach in varying states of disrepair and use. The most active part of the waterfront, a sandy beach, is lined with aluminum fishing boats that rest on logs and plastic piping for easy launching into the sea. It was early evening as we approached Sachs Harbour, and all was quiet save for the barking of chained sled dogs.

We stopped the boat just outside the harbour and fished a piece of ice from the sea for our evening drinks, then turned our attention to entering port. The most exciting and challenging aspect of cruising foreign shores is approaching new ports. Each new port involves a search for a good anchorage or place to tie up on dirty wharfs lined with tugs and fishing boats; going ashore to meet new faces, buying a treat that can't be found aboard and getting the lay of the land. The excitement of arrival equals the urge to return to sea once you've been in port a few days.

But with the thrill also comes a dose of danger. Sailors feel safer in deep water miles out to sea than near the shore, and for good reason. While good charts should show the dangerous reefs, shallows and rocks, they are rarely as comprehensive as advertised, and in the Arctic this is particularly true. Many harbours in the Arctic have little or no lateral marks or buoys marking safe water, and sandbars may have shifted considerably since the last chart was printed. Entering at night makes it even trickier.

Our chart showed two low shoals reaching out from the mouth of the Sachs Harbour, with a sandbar connecting the two. The channel into the harbour led over this bar, the depth of which was "liable to change due to ice action" according to the pilot guide. Once inside, the harbour was cut in two by yet another sandbar that, according to the charts, was too shallow for us to cross. We sailed into the harbour in the light of the early evening and made a few turns to survey the depths before finding a comfortable spot in the middle of the outer harbour to drop our anchor. As we did this we watched ATVs drive down to the beach, delivering a row of people to watch their visitors from the sea. Just as we were testing the anchor's hold one of the aluminum boats on the beach was pushed into the water and approached *Silent Sound*. The hunters driving her shouted greetings and asked where we were from. After a few moments of small talk I asked them whether this was the best place to anchor. They beckoned us into the inner harbour, assuring us that the charts were wrong and that there was plenty of water over the bar.

"That's where the barge goes every year, and there's enough water for your boat," one of them said. "Just stay to the left of that red float. That's where the sandbar starts."

I followed his directions, watching my depth sounder as it crept down to two metres over the bar and then climbed back to safer digits. We set the anchor in three metres of water and then gave it an extra tug with the engine in reverse to make sure it would hold. The forecast called for strong winds overnight and there was little room for error in the small harbour. Then we tended to our drinks and the ice we scooped out of the sea before turning in for the night.

When I awoke the next morning the wind was blowing from the north. I turned on the radio and listened to the forecast, which called for strong northerlies and snow. A quick check with the pilot guide confirmed that not only did this sound uncomfortable, it could also turn dangerous if the wind continued to change to a northwesterly. "If sheltering in Sachs Harbour, keep a good watch if the wind hauls to the west or northwest; the ice barrier can move in towards the land quite rapidly in a fresh westerly wind," it read. We couldn't afford to get blocked into Sachs Harbour. I went on deck to check the wind more closely, and suddenly it became easy to imagine that the wind was backing to the northwest. The rest of the crew was still sleeping as I sat at the navigation station listening to the wind whistling in the rigging. *Silent Sound* had started tugging at her anchor, but it was holding well. However, the clank of the anchor chain reminded me of the shallow waters and nearby sandbars. I decided that we would go ashore but keep a close eye on the wind and be ready to leave at a moment's notice if it backed to the northwest.

We rowed ashore to find a young man waiting for us. Jeff, the town's 24-year-old fuel truck driver, stepped into the surf to help pull the dinghy up the beach before excitedly shaking our hands. He wore wraparound sunglasses, a "Poker Stars" woollen hat and diesel-stained work gloves. He had never before seen a sailing boat in Sachs Harbour. Jeff had watched through binoculars from a window in his house as we entered the harbour and dropped anchor. He could see the banners on both rails of the *Silent Sound* displaying our website address. Jeff logged onto his satellite connection and read about us online and by the time he greeted us on the beach he knew each of our names and what we'd done in our last port of call. Others on the beach had done the same. My fantasy of experiencing the social deprivation so lionized in the literature of Arctic exploration evaporated. I had arrived in one of the most remote villages in the world to find out that its isolated residents had Googled me and read my blog. And therefore they knew I was keen to visit them because they were more "traditional."

On the hillside along one side of bay was a haphazard row of houses and outbuildings, separated by large expanses of thin Arctic grass. The residents of Sachs Harbour had plenty of space to spread out. We hiked up the hill towards the village store, stomped the sand off our boots and went inside. We had begun monitoring milk prices from port to port, and Sachs Harbour took our milk index to a new high of $22 for a four-litre jug, about four times the price in southern Canada. But wages, if you could find a job, didn't match the milk prices. On the store's bulletin board the RCMP was advertising for jailhouse guards at $27.54 per hour, while a local company offered $23.00 an hour for truck drivers. An hour of work for a jug of milk.

We were browsing the store shelves when Joey Carpenter burst through the door with an enthusiastic greeting. Joey was wearing a heavy parka and a toque over his grey hair; iridescent sunglasses hid much of his ruddy, wrinkled face. He was dressed like, and had the energy of, a teenager, yet the lines on his face suggested he was getting on in years.

"I've been looking everywhere for you!" he said. "You have to come over for coffee. I live next door."

Everyone in the tiny town could claim to live next door to the store and post office, but Joey was particularly close because he was the postmaster. We waited a few minutes as he sorted the day's mail and then walked the few metres to his house with him. Joey's wife Margaret greeted us with a kitchen full of food. Caribou soup bubbled on the stove, and next to it was a cured leg of caribou. As a special treat, Margaret offered us braided seal innards. Woven into a thick plait and then boiled and salted, it was rubbery and mildly fishy tasting. Things hadn't changed much. Caucasians arriving from the south by sailing boat, curious to learn about the Arctic, and gratefully accepting food from the Inuit, regardless of how peculiar it was according to their tastes.

Seal offal was great, but when it came to paws Margaret said she preferred those of bears to those of seals. "The other day I had bearded seal paws. I had too much and my stomach was so full it really hurt in the evening. I prefer polar bear paws to bearded seal flippers. I call polar bear paw polar bear jujubes because it's so chewy and soft and breaks off really easily in your mouth."

Margaret appeared tickled to feed us, admitting she missed having her own children at home. Her own son had drowned in 1986. Margaret had a gleeful open-mouthed laugh that engulfed her whole body and ricocheted off the walls. Otherwise her voice was soft and wavering with a mild stutter. She had a warm, motherly beauty about her, with high cheekbones and dark earnest eyes, her long greying hair tied back from her face.

Joey sat at the dining room table working on a caribou brisket. The hunters had chased the caribou before shooting it, pumping its meat full of adrenaline. Joey described it as "sweat," and he was carefully scrapping a stringy slime off the meat as we chatted, readying the brisket for dinner.

Joey told us an old story about two Inuit hunters who were attacked by Quechan Indians. North American Indians were bitter enemies of the Inuit. One of the Inuit was a shaman. The Indians shot an arrow at the Inuit and the arrow went right through the shaman without killing or marking him. Then the arrow turned and struck the other Indian attacker and killed him. The Inuit escaped unharmed.

"I still believe it. You have to believe it for it to work. It's also a bit up here," he said, tapping the side of his head. Then he conceded that, "you can't really apply that kind of belief today. I think you have to be in that kind of culture for it to work."

Joey and Margaret lived in one of the most remote corners of the earth and their fridge contained very different foods than you'd find in a suburban

Canadian home. But on the surface, looking at their TV and computers and connectedness with the rest of the world, they could have been on the outskirts of any southern city. The television was showing a live baseball game, Boston Red Sox at New York Yankees (the Yankees won 13–6).

Joey told us he had paid for high-definition satellite service but had yet to figure out how to set it up. Earlier in our visit Drew had told him that he worked in television, and now Joey asked if Drew could use his expertise to help him set up the new satellite service. Drew, despite being a film and television producer rather than television repairman, gamely agreed to help. Out came the various bits of equipment, cables and manuals. Joey went outside and climbed a ladder to the roof, wiggling the dish and waiting for Drew's shouted instructions, which were relayed through the open front door by Tobias, who was standing in the hallway. The dish wasn't working. Finally Drew rang the satellite service help line for advice, and his call was answered by a woman in a call centre in the Philippines. After a long chat about various technical details while adjusting cables and knobs, it was clear Drew and Joey were no closer to watching high-definition satellite TV than they had been a few hours earlier. The Filipino service agent asked for an address, and Drew answered her as best he could.

"Well, we're in the house next to the Co-op store," Drew said. "In Sachs Harbour, Northwest Territories. It's on Banks Island, in Canada."

There was a long silence as the woman tried to enter this address into her system without much luck. "There isn't really a street address. We're beside the Co-op," Drew told her. The agent then offered to send a technician to Joey's house to fix the problem "Oh, that might take a while and I'm not sure we're willing to pay for that," Drew replied.

No need to worry, she reassured him, the satellite company would give Joey a $99 credit to help pay for the service call. At this point the joke was running thin and Drew had given up on trying to explain where we were and that $99 wouldn't pay for many miles of Arctic travel. He hung up and advised Joey to order a new satellite dish.

Margaret, meanwhile, was on her computer, giggling her way through a live video chat with her daughter in Montreal. Her daughter held her fat baby boy in front of the computer camera so his grandmother could marvel at him.

"Hellooo! Hello!" she crooned at the baby on her screen. "Look at his eyes, they're so big!"

Margaret had become an online card shark and pressed Tobias into downloading some new gaming software she was having trouble with.

She was demurely confident in her poker skills. In truth, this timid grand-mother had become deadly serious about the game.

"When I got my first computer I downloaded Poker Stars and I stayed up for three days playing poker for play money. After that I had to slow down because three days is too long," she said before breaking into embar-rassed laughter. "I play for play money. Poker Stars I play for real mon-ey on free roles. And sometimes when I'm lucky I come out on top. The most money I ever made was two dollars and some cents.

"I like the skill of poker and one of these days hopefully I become real-ly pro at playing Texas Hold'em. I might end up in the United States and playing with David Granados and those pros. When I play with the guys here at home, I just really like the challenge. It makes me feel good when I win. It's only been a few times when I've cleaned everybody out. Once when I was playing with them I went broke, and then I found a toonie [$2 coin] and I cleaned everybody out with a toonie. I made about $1200! The next time they were gonna play they said, 'no women allowed'. I said I'd still play, 'cause they were playing in my house and they had no say."

It was near midnight when we returned to *Silent Sound* for the night. A light snow was falling. We rowed through the cerulean waves, marvel-ling at the beauty around us. I could smell the tangy life of the sea in the wind blowing in from far beyond the horizon. Fish and foam and Force 10 storms lingered in the air. *Silent Sound* was covered in a thin white coat of snow. We clambered aboard, lit the heater, and snuggled deep into our sleeping bags for the night.

David, whom we met in Tuktoyaktuk, had encouraged us to visit his uncle John Lucas Sr, a hunter in Sachs Harbour. It is still snowing the next day when we walk to John's house, built near the shore. His yard is a jumble of bones, scraps of hide and the equipment of his trade. Snowmobiles, ATVs and sleds stand ready for the next trip into the wil-derness. John Sr, like many of his neighbours, has saved his caribou antlers through the years, and has stacked them into a decorative tow-er. The prickly stacks of greying bone marked which homes had hunt-ers living in them. John Sr's tower, which rose well above my head, was taller than anyone else's.

The porch of John's home is filled with outdoor clothing, fur hats, boots and rifles. We wade through the clutter and go inside, where his wife Samantha has decorated the home with a collection of wind chimes and photos of John Sr posing beside dead polar bears. Rows of photos show him, and often a paying client he has guided on the hunt, standing over fallen bears and other game. The bookshelves contain mostly hunting magazines and rifle catalogues. A pot of Arctic char chowder bubbles on the stove, filling the house with the warm and comforting smell of food.

John Sr wears heavy plastic eyeglasses with thick lenses. His face is flat and dark. He has a soft, quiet voice and he hardly moves his lips when he speaks. When John Sr does speak he strikes me as someone who would rather not be speaking at all.

He moved here from Reindeer Station, near Tuktoyaktuk, to take advantage of the good hunting on Banks Island. John Sr has spent more than 40 years trapping and hunting, and in that time has seen snowmobiles replace dog teams and traditional navigation techniques give way to the global positioning system. "Up here you don't have to worry about anything. You don't have to buy meat, there's so much of it out on the land. I was very fortunate to experience the last part of the dog team years. If I didn't I don't know where I'd be now. I learned a lot from some of those old guys," he says. "I don't use GPS but my sons do. It's good for the younger generation. Then we don't have to worry about them. They don't know the traditional methods of navigating out there, like watching the wind direction, the snowdrifts."

John Sr hunts and traps with his four sons. John Jr, home when we arrive, supplements his hunting income by working for the Aulavik Park, created in 1992 to protect a large tract of wilderness at the northern end of Banks Island. The park, which has a visitor centre in Sachs Harbour, only attracts a handful of visitors per year, including a few whitewater rafting expeditions.

John Sr and his sons travel into the interior of Banks Island and along Prince of Wales Strait to where the wolves are. A pristine fox fur will bring $60, a wolf $600 to $700, and a polar bear $3000, he said.

"Going on the land is not cheap nowadays. A snowmobile will cost you $10,000, and then you have to pay the fuel on top of that," John Sr says. "From here to the end of the island we use about 160 gallons of gas. At $40 for a five-gallon jug you need a lot of wolves to pay for a trip. We got 40 wolves once. The wolves up there don't know about people, they're not afraid. They'll run right at a guy 'cause they don't know humans."

John Sr scoffs at the non-hunters in his community who come to him asking for fresh meat because they know he hunts. "We're slowly losing our hunting traditions," he laments. "Once we quit, it's all gonna be gone. A lot of the people no longer want to get their hands dirty. Kids don't even want to eat the native food. I'm a subsistence hunter in the Arctic. I'm not trained for other jobs. I have no education."

John Sr also runs a guiding business charging big game hunters $30,000 for a shot at a polar bear. At that price a client gets two weeks of tundra travel by dogsled and constant attention and guidance from and experienced Inuit hunter. If they're only after muskox, which are more plentiful on Banks Island than anywhere else on earth, they pay $5,000.

"It's a lot of work to take out a white guy. You have to babysit him 24 hours a day. To me it's like taking a fully grown kid. He's gotta learn everything in two weeks."

John Sr tells a story about taking a client out on a hunt during the Arctic winter. After numerous cups of coffee and hours of shivering in the cold waiting on their game the southerner needed to relieve himself. But the prospect of unzipping and letting his valuables dangle in the -50°C cold didn't appeal, so he turned to John Sr and asked what he should do. "I told him, 'I ain't gonna hold it for you!'" It's the only time I hear John Sr laugh.

The declining fashion of fur coats and a US ban on polar bear skins has wiped out a big part of John Sr's guiding market. In 2007 the US Geological Survey predicted that two-thirds of the world's 25,000 polar bears could disappear within 50 years because of sea ice loss. A year later the US listed polar bears as "threatened" under the Endangered Species Act, automatically triggering an import ban and making the polar bear the poster child of Arctic climate change. Inuit hunters dispute this, and say the bear population is rising, not falling. They say scientists are basing their calculations on surveys made by helicopter over a short time period, while their information is gathered through wide-ranging travel throughout the year.

The US accounted for about half of the polar bears exported by Canada through the 1990s, and hunting the animals generates about $3 million in annual revenue for Canada's north. The ban has seriously dented John Sr's business, and he says if it remains in place he'll have to look to Japan and Europe for new clients.

While John Sr doesn't agree with nearly anything scientists have to say about changes in the Arctic, he has noticed subtle shifts in everything from birdlife to the prevailing wind, all of which may be caused by a warming climate.

"Life is changing a bit. It's getting a bit warmer and we're seeing new animals like wolverines and grizzlies. In summer we see some different birds and in winter we run into grizzly bears. It's happened before, but it's becoming more common now. It's odd. We see more thunder and lightning now than we had in the 1960s. There's also a lot of westerly winds. We never had that before. Here the normal wind is easterly."

The northern hemisphere is roughly divided into three latitudinal bands of wind: the northeast trades just above the equator, westerlies farther north, and polar easterlies in the high Arctic. The wind bands are slowly shifting north, bringing more westerlies to the Arctic.

John Sr also repeats the same concerns we heard in Wales about the dangers of thinner ice. Thick, multi-year ice, once common in Sachs Harbour, is now becoming rare.

"All the ice you see now is from this year," John Sr says. "This makes it a lot more dangerous because it's so hard to predict where it will open, when it will open. We used to go way out there and camp out on the ice. Now we're sometimes not sure if we should do that. You'll find open water four or five miles out. But we have to go out there 'cause most of the bears are way out on the pack ice, 80 or 90 miles out, near where the young ice opens up, 'cause that's where the seals are."

Travelling through the Arctic on a small sailing yacht earns you a very different reception than if you arrive by airplane and stay in the local hotel. People in the Arctic take great pride in their ability to survive and remain active in the worst conditions Mother Nature can throw at them. Braving those conditions aboard a yacht gave us some credibility with them. Sailing yachts are also a rare sight in the Arctic, attracting further attention. Towns such as Tuktoyaktuk, Cambridge Bay and Gjoa Haven are key ports for any yachts transiting the Northwest Passage, but communities such as Sachs Harbour that lie just off that route rarely get casual visitors by sea.

However, we see constant reminders that these waters were once sailed extensively. Wooden schooners lay beached in many of the towns we visit. Sometimes a broken keel and a few weathered ribs are all that remain. Other wooden boats are more complete, dragged up on a beach for the winter but never to return to the sea.

Joey showed us a film made by his father in the 1920s, with scenes of trappers sorting hundreds of snowy Arctic fox furs while rows of shy Inuit stand staring into the lens. The shaky monochrome images show everything from foot races to scenes of everyday life on the land. And in the background of every scene stand the masts of the trading schooners.

Joey counted the introduction of schooners as one of the most important factors that changed the Inuvialuit way of life in the early 1900s,
along with the missionaries and whalers who came to the Arctic and introduced changes to the native way of life. "It allowed them to travel, open
new areas for hunting and economic reasons," Joey said. "If it wasn't for
these schooners, they wouldn't have been able to come here to trap. They
would have had to stay on the mainland. White [Arctic] fox fur became
fashionable in the '30s and '40s, especially for the ladies down south, and
that's what attracted people to come here. I'm guessing it was word from
people like Natkusiak, Stefansson's guide, that people on the mainland
learned there was a lot of white fox on island. They came here in the late
'20s and stayed."

Vilhjalmur Stefansson, the Arctic explorer who brought typhoid fever
to Herschel Island, spent much of his time in this part of the Arctic. He
and his Inuit guide Natkusiak explored Banks Island and brought back
word of the wildlife bounty that existed in the remote interior of the island.
His stories attracted the first hunters and trappers to settle here in 1929.

Just outside Joey's house sat the *Fox*, a 35-foot schooner owned by
Angus and Mary Elias, who were amongst the first people to live in Sachs
Harbour. Joey had dreams of restoring the *Fox* and turning it into a museum piece, but with every year he waited, it became harder to do so. She
was a working boat, without many extra flourishes, but she had strong,
pretty lines. Now the hatches yawned at the sky, allowing season after
season of rain and snow to rot the *Fox* from the inside out. Joey and I
crawled inside the hold and he told me the story of the *Fox* and the other
schooners that used to ply these Arctic waters.

"Angus and his family either wintered here in Sachs Harbour or on
the west coast of Banks Island every winter, trapping white foxes," he said.
"In the summer, about July, when the ice left and melted, they brought
the yearly catch of fox, their family and extended family. Sometimes they
brought all the dogs, 25 dogs and 20 people. It would take them about
40 or 50 hours to sail to Tuktoyaktuk."

Once on the mainland they would sell their furs, buy supplies for the
next winter and spend time with their extended families. Many of the
Sachs Harbour settlers originally came from Tuktoyaktuk, and the voyage across the Amundsen Gulf was an annual pilgrimage home for them.

"They'd always delay coming back [to Sachs] as long as possible,
because everyone here had family in Tuk, so it was hard to leave them.
They were pretty well isolated in winter," Joey said. "In late fall the storms

get bigger, you get big west winds, and the ocean gets really rough. The trips could be pretty dramatic."

A few weeks later, when I arrived in Gjoa Haven, I met George Porter, whose father was the original owner of the *Fox*. George, at 78 years old, was a respected community elder with a lifetime of stories to share. As soon as I told George that we visited Sachs Harbour he asked if I saw the *Fox*, then proudly told me that he used to sail on her.

"From here we used to go to Herschel and back," George told me. "I remember the boat well. My dad bought it in 1936 for $14,000. My dad had it for five or six years, and then I went to school and he had no more help, so he sold it."

"It was a good schooner, a good boat. Those old engines, 60 horse-power, there wasn't much grease to put in them. We'd start it with a big flywheel and a long bar. It came with sails and everything when he bought it. My grandfather was a whaling captain, so my father grew up know-ing how to sail."

Now the boat's engine had become a rusty iron hulk sitting in a hull littered with trash and scarred with vulgar spray-can graffiti. The engine, along with the anchor and heavy chain, would be the only pieces remain-ing in a few decades as the wooden hull of the *Fox* rots away on the beach. George remembered the *Fox*, and many of the other schooners beached throughout the Arctic, as living things, crossing straits and bays during the short summers and playing an important role in the survival of the Inuit. The wrecks scattered across the Arctic were some of the few remain-ing friends that shared those years with him.

"The old Inuit owned them," George said. "There were a lot of boats at one time. As soon as the old people were gone, no one wanted the boats. They travelled a long way. People living in Banks Island, Paulatuk; they all had to go to Tuk to get freight and food. A guy could make $60,000 in trapping. Paying $14,000 for a boat was easy."

Christian Theodore Pedersen brought many of the schooners to the Arctic. An ex-whaling captain, Pedersen created the CanAlaska Company to compete with the Hudson's Bay Company for Arctic furs. Hudson's Bay, the most powerful company in Canada's fur trade, relied on a network of trading posts located near the source of the fur; its new American com-petitor chose to make his fur trappers more mobile. Every year Pedersen would sail north in the 600-tonne *Patterson* from San Francisco to the Beaufort Sea and Herschel Island to meet his trappers spread around the Arctic. And every year he would bring with him one or two new schooners that had been built to order in San Francisco's George W. Kneass Shipyard. The schooners were sold to trappers and merchants, helping to slowly expand the web of civilization across the Arctic.

The *North Star* was the biggest of these schooners, and she was originally co-owned by Joey's father Fred Carpenter, one of the founders of Sachs Harbour. The *North Star* cost $23,000 when she first came north in 1936, which was a fortune to spend on a boat during the Great Depression.

"My father's schooner had a 35 horsepower engine similar to the *Fox*. She was 55 foot—a beautiful boat," Joey said.

I know the *North Star* because she was docked near *Silent Sound* in Victoria's Inner Harbour, perhaps the only schooner of her type and generation to remain afloat. She was originally rigged as a schooner. Her second owner, Sven Johansson, re-rigged her as a three-masted square-rigger in the 1970s. Sheila and Bruce Macdonald bought her in 1996 to live aboard year-round. They sailed the Pacific Northwest on her, exploring the coastline and participating in boat shows.

Back on the *Fox*, it was clear most schooners did not fare as well as the *North Star*. When hauling freight was no longer profitable, schooners were left on beaches to rot. "When the government created NTCL [Northern Transportation Company Ltd], they started hauling freight from Hay River to Tuk and all along the coast," Joey said. "They could haul freight for cheaper than it cost to operate these boats, so there was no need for these boats. So they put them up on beach and that's where they have stayed since the early '60s."

As we travelled east we came across more wrecks from the Arctic's rich sailing history. Amundsen's *Maud* is submerged in Cambridge Bay, with little remaining of her but a few skeletal ribs braving the harbour waves. Having failed at her mission, she was left to rot in the Arctic, while Amundsen's ship the *Gjøa*, which brought him success, sits venerated in an Oslo museum.

Amundsen had the 36.5 metre *Maud* built in Norway in 1917 and named her for Norway's queen with all the dry wit and practicality one would expect of a polar explorer of his stature. He christened her by smashing a chunk of ice on her bow instead of the customary bottle of champagne. "It is not my intention to dishonour the glorious grape, but already now you shall get the taste of your real environment," he said. "For the ice you have been built, and in the ice you shall stay most of your life, and in the ice you shall solve your tasks. With the permission of our queen, I christen you: *Maud*."

In 1918 *Maud* set sail through the Northeast Passage over Russia. Amundsen hoped to become frozen into the polar ice cap and drift over the North Pole, following Fridtjof Nansen's theory of polar drift. He was unsuccessful and *Maud* eventually made her way to Seattle, where the Hudson's Bay Company bought her and renamed her *Baymaud* in 1926. She resupplied the company's far-flung trading posts across the western Arctic and was based in Cambridge Bay. *Baymaud* didn't serve the company long. In the winter of 1926 she was damaged by ice and moored in Cambridge Bay for use as a warehouse, machine shop and wireless station. She sank a few years later, and has remained there ever since.

A Norwegian group is fighting to bring her back to Norway, with plans to put her in a museum along with the *Gjøa*. Keep the Baymaud in Canada, a committee of 20 Cambridge Bay residents, are chagrined that Norway might grab a piece of Arctic history from under their noses and are fighting to keep the ship. However, the *Baymaud*'s many years of neglect undermine their arguments for preserving their heritage themselves.

But the *Baymaud* was not completely forgotten. Tom Hallidie, the man who refitted her in Vancouver before the Hudson's Bay Company brought her north, looked to her for inspiration when he designed the *St. Roch*. The *St. Roch*, a Royal Canadian Mounted Police schooner built to cruise the Arctic, had an ice-strengthened hull designed to ride up and over the ice floes and room for large sled dog teams. Thirty-eight years after Amundsen made the maiden transit of the Northwest Passage the *St. Roch* become the second sailing ship to travel it and the first to do so west to east. She was also the first ship to completely circumnavigate North America via the Panama Canal. The *St. Roch* is now the centrepiece of the Vancouver Maritime Museum.

Just down the beach from the *Baymaud* lies the *Eagle*, a longliner fishing boat. She was purchased in Tuktoyaktuk in 1954 by Father Steinman, a German Catholic priest. He towed the boat to Cambridge Bay and it leaked badly the entire way. Later that year, before he had a chance to refurbish the *Eagle*, he was transferred by the Church. He was forced to leave his boat behind. The *Eagle* sits on the shore just south of the stone church the priest built.

We need to get moving if we don't want *Silent Sound* to end up locked in ice in Sachs Harbour and die on its shores like the *Fox*. On Friday afternoon all the people we've met in Sachs come aboard for coffee and to say farewell. John Sr, John Jr, Joey and their friends crowd into the saloon or stand in the cockpit, smoking cigarettes, drinking coffee and talking about Arctic hunting and sailing. The hunters immediately assess *Silent Sound*'s usefulness as a hunting boat; John Sr speculates on how she would perform as a whaling boat, or as a base for hunting wolves on the northern shores of Banks Island. I find it amusing to think of *Silent Sound* used for hunting, but to them a boat is useless unless it somehow assists in capturing whales, bears and seals.

John Sr and John Jr give us a sack of frozen fish, muskox and geese as a parting gift. Once again hunting *Silent Sound* style has worked. We will have plenty to eat until our next port of call.

I tune the radio to the weather forecast and chat with XNR79 as our guests clamber into their aluminum skiff to ride back to shore. The plug of ice in Dolphin and Union Strait is slowly diminishing, but the ice concentration remains at 7/10th to 9/10th, which is much too heavy for us to sail through. The pilot guide says this ice is normally gone by the end of July, but this year, despite climate change, it remains stubbornly in place due to a mix of unusual weather conditions. The ice has nowhere to go as it packs into the narrow strait, and it will likely remain there until it melts. Cambridge Bay, one of the biggest towns in the Arctic with a population of 1,100 people, is our next refuelling stop. It is free of ice if we can just get through the ice-choked strait. *Ocean Watch* is waiting in Pearce Harbour and *Baloum Gwen* in Paulatuk, both on the mainland coast and on the same side of the blockage as we are. Although we're not racing each other through the passage, I'd hate to see them move ahead and leave us behind, trapped in the ice. We have trouble reaching them by radio but XNR79 relays a message from them that they have no plans to tackle the ice for several more days.

It appears we have made a good decision by turning north to Banks Island instead of joining them to go straight east from Tuktoyaktuk. The charts show some ice to the south in Amundsen Gulf, but if we stay north we should have mostly clear water for our 200-mile voyage to Holman. The town has been renamed Ulukhaktok but it remains better known by its colonial name. Ulukhaktok is a small village on the west coast of Victoria Island. To get there we need to sail around Nelson Head on Banks Island and across the mouth of Prince of Wales Strait. Ice charts show Ulukhaktok's harbour to be open except for some small bergy bits along the shore, but our friends in Sachs Harbour pass on word from their relatives in Ulukhaktok that the harbour is still blocked with ice. We have little choice but to gamble and hope the ice charts are correct by the time we arrive.

We sail away from Sachs Harbour under clear, sunny skies. The sun continues to shine late into the evening, picking out white icebergs on the horizon. The wind is well aft at a gentle 10 to 15 knots as we gybe our way down the coast of Banks Island. I have been craving Chinese food for several weeks, so I use some of the meat from John Sr and make muskox fried rice.

By the afternoon of the next day we're passing Nelson Head, which rears 365 metres from the sea. McClure named it for Lord Nelson because he imagined that the rocky cape resembled the famous sailor. The whole southern coastline of Banks Island is made up of beautiful but unwelcoming cliffs of pink, white and buff quartzites with streaks of dark basalt. This coast is unprotected and offers no shelter, leaving sailors little room for error. If the wind were to turn, an onshore storm to blow, we would be dreadfully exposed.

Instead, on our second day at sea, the wind died and a light fog rolled in. The temperature wavered between 2°C and 5°C near Banks Island, but as we approach Ulukhaktok it warms to 11°C. Victoria Island, bigger than Great Britain, comes into view with its miles of rolling brown hills. We spend the day sailing along the coast and then prepare for arrival in Ulukhaktok. We have two bays to choose from. To the east is Queens Bay, with a string of houses wrapping around the shore. Large chunks of ice bob in the middle of the bay and our charts show some shallow bits. On the west side of town is Kings Bay, recommended by the pilot guide. We choose Kings, coasting into the sheltered anchorage in the warm afternoon sunshine.

Our arrival has drawn a crowd of people to the water's edge. We shout across the water, trying to find out how deep the water is next to the rough landing dock. Not deep enough, they inform us, so we drop our anchor a hundred metres off the beach. On one side of the bay we have the spread backside of the town, complete with heaps of rubbish and long abandoned snowmobiles. On the other side a row of low mountains glow brownish red in the afternoon sunlight. An abandoned settlement lies at the foot of the mountains; a wooden shack leans crazily next to a small stream.

The crowd shouts greetings and beckons us ashore, but for the moment we're happy where we are. We pour a round of drinks and toast our successful, if short, two-day passage and lean back to enjoy what remains of the afternoon.

# CHAPTER 7
# Skinning Seals

*In those days people listened to the rules but of course some people never listened to the older people even when they were told. Some never did anything all their lives, and of course they had a shorter life than the others.*
—Nicolas Irkotee, *Inuit Land Use and Occupancy Report*, 1974

A dozen ring seals lie on the beach. Half of them are pink and naked, their exposed blubber shimmering in the sunlight, while the others still wear their coats. A child in pink sweater and rubber boots sits on the beach, stirring the sand with her fat fingers and babbling to herself. A runnel of snot slides down her lip, disappearing back into her nose with the occasional sniff. Her mother and grandmother work nearby, bent over the carcasses of seals, slashing at them with long strokes of their ulu knives. The women stand up, putting their hands in the small of their back and stretching with a sigh as they gaze across the bay. Ice floes bob in the water, slowly melting in the warm sunshine. The beach wraps around the bay in a perfect arc. Behind the beach is a narrow gravel road, with a row of houses beyond that. Ulukhaktok is quiet except for the drone of ATVs criss-crossing the town. The steep hills of Victoria Island rise up in the distance, barren and void of any vegetation.

Jean Ekpakohak is in charge. I recognize her from our visit to the local school, where she was overseeing a class of giggling first-graders and teaching them Inuktituk through games and songs. Today she's again a teacher. Jean has thick, weathered hands that glisten with seal fat. When not clutching an ulu knife, her fingers pinch a smouldering cigarette. Her dark eyes squint as the smoke wafts past her face. She's a large woman dressed in black track pants and black windbreaker, her greying hair tied back in a messy knot. Her brow wrinkles when she speaks in slow, measured tones. But all the seriousness disappears when she laughs with her head thrown back, round face scrunching up into a gleeful smile.

"Cassandra here is my granddaughter, same to Mystina," she says, pointing to a sullen teenage girl who has come to the beach to bum a light off her grandmother, and then to the toddler sitting on the ground. Cassandra, with earphones plugging her ears, smokes her cigarette and wrinkles her nose at the seals. Soon a boy arrives in a cloud of dust astride his ATV and rescues Cassandra with an offer to go fishing. Mystina remains behind with her grandmother and mother, Julia.

Jean gives instructions in Inuktituk and Julia responds with a mixture of English and Inuktituk. They murmur back and forth about which seals to skin next and how much fat is being left on the hides. Julia is as thin as her mother is stocky, her straight dark hair falling into her face as she bends over to cut at the carcasses. She is wearing a pink sweater and rubber boots, the same as her daughter. Together, they match the colour of the skinned seals. Julia says little, remaining bent over her work while her mother chats.

Jean also is not eager to chat at first, but eventually begins to offer up details of her life. "I still live the Inuit way. I've been living off the land in the Arctic, hunting and fishing, all my life. We hunt everything, seals, caribou, polar bear, muskox, char."

"I went to a Canadian government residential school, which means I had to educate myself. The schools didn't teach us anything. They were really bad and we all hated it. With all that abuse and stuff that went on, because of that when they built a school here in 1964 I quit going to school thinking the school would be the same way as residential school. So through the years as I grew up I educated myself by reading, writing and being a politician."

Canada's residential schools were a horrific chapter of our national history. The government forcibly took Inuit and Native American children away from their parents and stuck them into church-run boarding schools that were sometimes thousands of miles from home. They were beaten if they spoke their native languages. The teachers and priests often abused them physically, sexually, mentally and spiritually. Many children died in the homes. The Canadian government has since offered its sincere apologies, but the scars are still visible across the country.

The residential schools were meant to help the aboriginals assimilate with their European conquerors. Another equally demeaning assimilation tactic was the leather dog tags the Inuit were forced to wear. The Europeans had trouble pronouncing and remembering everyone's Inuit names, so they baptized them and gave them Christian names, as well as a handy registration number. This name and number was stamped on a leather disc embossed with an image of the British crown and hung around their necks. The practice was only stopped in 1978.

Jean serves on school boards and community committees, keeping alive her traditional knowledge while also educating her neighbours on the way government works so that they can regain control over their communities. Teaching Inuit children about their own culture is an important part of creating that sense of empowerment, she says. These are the Copper Inuit, named after the metal they once mined in the surrounding hills to make tools and weapons. Both Banks and Victoria islands, as well as the nearby mainland coast, are traditional homes of the Copper Inuit.

"Our kids don't need to only learn about pigs and cows and hens, 'cause we don't have that," Jean says. "We have muskox, caribou, seal and fish. How do you teach a kid the sound a cow makes? Moo moo. How can a kid know that if they've never seen a cow?"

Jean returns to her work as she talks, drawing a seal skin taut over a board set at an angle in the sand. Then with strong efficient strokes of her ulu she carves the fat off the skins. The knife makes a hollow rasping sound against the skin-covered board. The name Ulukhaktok comes from the large bluff that towers over the town and it means "the place where ulu parts are found." The mountain's thinly layered slate was ideal for making the stone knives. The ulu that Jean holds is made of steel, but its shape and use have not changed much over the years. Once the skin has been flensed she takes it to the water's edge where several more skins lie fur-down, soaking in the frigid seawater. They look like giant pink sores on the beach.

Just before we set off for the Arctic the European Union banned the import of all seal products. This angered Inuit hunters and artisans and prompted Canada's governor general Michaëlle Jean to skin one of the creatures and eat a piece of its heart, raw, to demonstrate solidarity. The political storm around the issue of seal hunting was hugely unpopular with Inuit, who generally took the view that southerners didn't know what they were talking about and should mind their own business.

Much of the controversy surrounds the clubbing of baby hooded seals—which have downy white fur—in northeast Canada. There it had long been common practice to club the baby seals for their fur. The practice is now outlawed and was never adopted by the Inuit in the central Arctic. Still, the European ban covers all seal products from Canada. Jean and Julia's work, gory as it might appear at first glance, reflects an underlying respect for the animals and also the daily central role these animals play in their lives.

In Gjoa Haven, George Porter, a respected community elder, would invite me into his kitchen for tea and discuss the issue. "The price of furs is really low because of Greenpeace. I wish that guy [Mr. Greenpeace, I suppose] was here, I'd shoot him right now," George said, nearly spilling his tea as he warmed up to the issue. "In Newfoundland they club them. They blame us of doing that too, but we shoot them to kill them, we don't make them suffer. I wish they could come here one winter. I'd bring them on the land and let them hunt. They'd starve, and then I'd give them a gun, tell them to go hunting. Cut through six feet of ice to look for seals. Then they might think differently."

The skins Jean is working with will be dried and then scraped again. Some will be sold to make crafts and clothes to sell to the occasional tourist or non-hunting families. The seal meat will be packed into freezers to be eaten later. Usually the meat is boiled, which Julia says is the best cooking method because it brings out the rich flavour of the seal. Barbequing seal, as we did aboard *Silent Sound*, ruins its flavor, she says. Most of the blubber, no longer needed to fuel ancient seal oil lamps, will be thrown away.

"I prefer traditional food over white man food," Julia says. "That's the way I was brought up—and my kids. Not everybody is the same way. Some don't have the means or the transportation to go and get it. It's really hard for some families. That's why you see them live on store-bought food."

Julia is skinning the seals faster than her mother can flense them. She sharpens her ulu between seals, drawing the curved blade over the stone with long rasping strokes. "It's scary and sharp," Julia says as she tests the new edge with her thumb. "I've had my mom and dad sew up my fingers a lot. My mom started teaching me how to do this when I was five or six years old."

The wave-worn pebbles chime like broken glass as she drags the next seal across the beach and flips it over for skinning. Once Julia has the seal in position she carefully makes a cut around the flippers and head, which are left on the carcass. Then she makes a long cut along the belly to free the raw torpedo of meat and blubber from its hide. One hands pulls at the skin while the other holds the ulu to slash away at the blubber. Julia squats as she works, straddling the carcass and expertly flipping it from side to side as she skins it.

"I hope that my granddaughter becomes better than what I became," Jean continues. "A mother, grandmother and a teacher is what I became,

Cameron and his father clean the hull of *Silent Sound* before reinforcing it with Kevlar.    *photo/Tobias Neuberger*

Ian Hansen, a generous supporter and inspiration to the crew, visits *Silent Sound* before she sets sail for the Arctic.    *photo/Tobias Neuberger*

*Silent Sound* sails out of Victoria Harbour on June 6, 2009    *photo/Drew Fellman*

Chris Pielou, scientific advisor to the expedition, aboard *Silent Sound*.
*photo/Tobias Neuberger*

*Silent Sound* in Dutch Harbor    *photo/Tobias Neuberger*

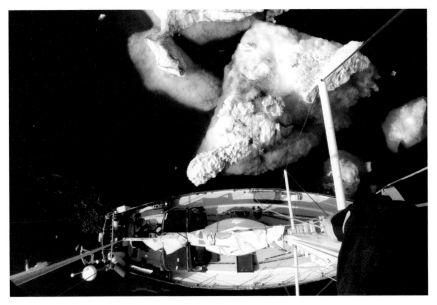

*Silent Sound* winding her way through the ice near Barrow, Alaska    *photo/Tobias Neuberger*

Drew Fellman    *photo/Cameron Dueck*

Hanns, Cameron and Tobias telephone home from Dutch Harbor    *photo/Tobias Neuberger*

Tobias and Cameron with hunters in Wales, Alaska (*L to R Dan Richard, Frank Oxereok Jr., Ruben Ozenna*)    photo/Tobias Neuberger

Child in Barrow, Alaska    photo/Tobias Neuberger

Walruses stand guard near Point Barrow, Alaska. This was the crew's first encounter with ice.    *photo/Cameron Dueck*

Tobias and Hanns do a delicate balancing act in the tiny rowing dinghy.
*photo/Cameron Dueck*

Daniel Gallant and Francis Taillefer tagging a fox on Herschel Island, where they were studying the northward migration of red foxes, which may be due to climate change.    *photo/Cameron Dueck*

Joe Cockney, a hunter in Tuktoyaktuk, aboard *Silent Sound*    *photo/Tobias Neuberger*

Joey Carpenter in the hold of the *Fox*, a wrecked wooden schooner that once sailed the Arctic seas laden with furs.    *photo/Cameron Dueck*

The village of Ulukhaktok on Victoria Island    *photo/Cameron Dueck*

Ulukhaktok    *photo/Cameron Dueck*

Cameron with children in Ulukhaktok    *photo/Cameron Dueck*

Jean Ekpakohak, an Ulukhaktok elder, skinning seals on the beach    *photo/Cameron Dueck*

*Silent Sound* negotiating the ice off Victoria Island    *photo/Drew Fellman*

*Silent Sound* aground on a reef just outside Cambridge Bay    *photo/Tobias Neuberger*

Cameron and Hanns take a break from engine repairs in Cambridge Bay

*photo/Drew Fellman*

Hanns Bergmann    *photo/Drew Fellman*

Tobias Neuberger    *photo/Drew Fellman*

One of many dinners with our friends aboard *Baloum Gwen*, captained by
Thierry Fabing *(far left)*    *photo/Tobias Neuberger*

Jacob Atkichok hunting for seals near Gjoa Haven    *photo/Tobias Neuberger*

Jacob washes his hands in the sea following the caribou hunt (Gjoa Haven)

*photo/Cameron Dueck*

Cameron and Tobias guide *Silent Sound* through the ice    *photo/Drew Fellman*

Using Drew's collapsible kayak to get a closer look at the ice    *photo/Tobias Neuberger*

Paddling through snowflurries in Pond Inlet    *photo/Tobias Neuberger*

but I want her to maybe become a better person; like a doctor, lawyer or something. She's got to make the best of both worlds. Learn our culture in order to survive, and in order for her to have a good life she has to educate herself and learn the white man's way as well. They have a choice. They can go the white man's way or live the traditional way. They can choose. I didn't have a choice. I have seven granddaughters and five grandsons and I don't know what they'll do. Some will stay here and live off the land but some will go south and live in the city. It's their choice."

Mystina watches in silence, tossing pebbles across the beach and occasionally following the women to the water's edge. It is quiet. The sun is warm and bright. We can hear the distant howl of boat engines, and occasionally the crack of a rifle from hunters shooting seals in the next bay down the coast. The water in the bay is still and smooth and throws up intricate reflections of the drifting ice floes.

"Our culture, learning how to do things the Inuit way, it is always there," Jean says. "Some of the kids will turn away because they don't want to learn, others will be interested. You can't force them. It's just there if they want it. They can learn by watching us."

"The name that was given to us, the Eskimo, it's not really what it really means. Eskimo was given to us by the Indians, and it means eaters of raw meat. But we don't only eat raw meat. We're called Inuit, which means people of the land. Real people, that's what it means. Inuit means a whole person, not half a person, half an animal, but a real whole person. That's what we call ourselves."

And with that the day's skinning is done. Jean throws the scraps of fat into the sea where the gulls squabble over the pinkish blobs. She draws a blue plastic tarp over the carcasses on the beach, weighing it down with rocks. Then she collects her knives and skins, takes one last look across the bay, and turns to follow her daughter and granddaughters up the beach.

Ulukhaktok depressed me even after meeting the likes of Jean. The school we visited was filled with listless children and teachers weary from their losing battle. The rate of fetal alcohol syndrome is higher in some Inuit communities than the Canadian average, and it showed in the children. ATVs were as common as mosquitoes, with bored teens mindlessly cruising up and down the gravel roads on them, kicking up plumes of gritty dust. Nearly every building and vehicle in town showed signs of wanton vandalism. At one end of town sat an abandoned orange and silver Co-op company truck emblazoned with the slogan "Locally Owned." All its windows were smashed and tires slashed. The doors to the nursing station were kept locked for fear of vandals and guard dogs were chained to the front door of the police officer's home.

On our first afternoon in Ulukhaktok I wandered through the town and met Adam. He was draining a heating oil tank in order to repair a leak. Next to him stood a friend, watching the work while his truck sat with its engine idling. Our conversation went on for 20 minutes and still the truck sat idling. I asked him if he left the truck running because he was worried it wouldn't start again.

"What do I care? I don't pay for the gas," he responded.

That seemed to sum up the pervading attitude of the rubbish-strewn town. The isolated town was stubbornly refusing development. De Beers was looking for diamonds on Prince Albert Peninsula, about 200km north of the community, but the company was running into local opposition despite their promises of jobs and economic development. "We don't want no development there. That's where our caribou calve. Diamonds are useless unless they're on the end of a tool anyway," Adam concluded.

The people, as always, were friendly. Especially the packs of young children, who roved the town and played on the beach and bits of grounded ice. Some rode bicycles, others ran behind. But they were all curious about who we were, why we were there and what life at sea was like.

We made an unexpected friend in Patrick, a young mentally disabled man. He was full of information, questions, and pride in his part-time job, and was eager to show us around his town. Every time we returned to the boat for meals or at night he would remain on the shore, shouting questions to us.

"What are you having for supper?" he would holler across the water, his voice echoing off the hills. We would shout back and forth, carrying on a stilted prandial conversation until we became bored of the game. He spent hours on the beach during our visit, and continued to shout questions long after we disappeared below decks in the evening.

There was one question repeated by nearly everyone we met, young and old alike. "Have you seen our barge?" Ulukhaktok, like most Arctic communities, relies heavily on an annual supply barge that brings everything from fuel to food and new furniture. Anything that cannot be delivered by barge must arrive by airplane, greatly raising its cost. This year a second barge company was competing for business, which meant that Ulukhaktok would enjoy the luxury of two barges in one summer. Shelves at the few stores in town were nearly bare and what was left on them was exorbitantly priced. Milk, delivered by airplane, was $5.50 a litre, matching prices in Sachs Harbour. If you were after something sweeter, there was canned "Crush" soft drink, available in a variety of revolting fruit flavours, at $45 per 12-pack. If you wanted something a little more mainstream, say a Coke, and bought it chilled, you would pay $5 a can. Suddenly the slightly foul water in *Silent Sound*'s tanks seemed quite appealing by comparison.

Ulukhaktok is a larger, rougher town than Sachs Harbour. Neither settlement is on the normal route taken by the few yachts that sail through the Northwest Passage. Our arrival was an event. On our last day in town we met an old man who had come down to the water's edge to admire *Silent Sound*. Stooped and watery-eyed, he said it was the first sailing boat he remembered seeing anchored in King's Bay since the days of the fur schooners.

But on the beach, at the very back of the bay near where Jean and her family had skinned their seals, sat a strange sailing contraption. The *Ulu* was one of the ugliest boats I'd ever seen, and no prettier for being high and dry on her hard stand. Painted a dull black, she was all protruding edges and sharp angles, with a runty rig and weather-beaten cabin. Her lifelines were made of twisted barbed wire, giving her a sinister touch. The *Ulu* was owned by Harold Wright, who lived in a ramshackle home just up the beach from the boat. I went to his home and banged on the door repeatedly without getting an answer. I was hoping to confirm the story that I'd heard in bits and pieces around town. People told me that Harold had built the boat out of old fuel drums and scraps of metal he scrounged from the rubbish piles, and that he occasionally refloated her to haul small amounts of freight around the Arctic. On cursory inspection, I'd say that story could be true. I admired his pluck and creativity, and was sorry not to meet a fellow sailor such as he.

Ulukhaktok is built along two bays, King's and Queen's. Queen's Bay has all the action. Hunters pile into the boats pulled up on shore, loaded with rifles and fishing nets, and zoom off for a day of hunting. The sound of their engines drones on long after they are out of sight, echoing off the naked hillsides. When the crews return they unload rifles, fish and seals onto the beach. *Silent Sound* was anchored in King's Bay, which remained quiet. Our beach was littered with rubbish—piles of broken toys, old snowmobiles and other detritus of modern life. When I told a woman where our boat was anchored she laughed. "Oh, near skid row!"

Perhaps it was our surroundings that spawned our halfwitted idea for entertainment. Hanns and I were on the beach, waiting for Drew and

Tobias to come ashore. Hanns had found a wooden child-sized baseball bat in the rubbish pile on the beach, and he was inspired by the baseball game we'd watched on television at Joey's home in Sachs Harbour. New to the game, he gave the bat a few experimental swings, deciding he was a lefty. I picked up a suitably round rock, paced off what I thought was a reasonable distance, and fired him a pitch. Hanns connected. It was a clean drive at the pitcher, and I probably hadn't paced off the full regulation distance between the plate and mound. I didn't have time to move, and a split second after hearing the sharp crack of rock on wood I felt the even sharper collision of rock on bone. I doubled over with pain and laughter. My arm swelled and turned purple and hurt for weeks. Hanns brought the little green bat aboard *Silent Sound* with him, but we never played baseball again.

We sailed out of King's Bay with the forecast calling for 20 knots from the east but dying by the time we'd reach Dolphin and Union Strait, where we would need to tack upwind. There was scattered ice outside the bay, and we had to slow down for the first few miles as we weaved through the floes. The edge of the heavier ice that was plugging this part of the passage was clearly visible off to starboard, and it remained in sight for the next several days. A constant warning and threat; a growling dog straining at his chain.

That ice would dictate our next move. The latest ice charts showed that if we hugged the western and southern coast of Victoria Island we would sail through 4/10th to 6/10th ice with patches of clear water. This corridor of navigable water could lead us right through Dolphin and Union Strait. Charts showed open water around Cambridge Bay. Beyond this the ice remained impregnable, blocking Victoria Strait and Larsen Sound to the east. The ice was not melting as fast as it did in 2007 and 2008 but ice levels were still well below the 30-year average.

By midnight the wind had died, which was just as well, as we were weaving our way through ice that began as 2/10th ice but quickly became more concentrated. The coastline and horizon were distorted by dancing mirages, made all the more interesting by the floating ice and the bright pinks and oranges of the Arctic's long sunsets and sunrises. Shimmering pools of coloured light were bent and warped until blue towers of ice rose up, supporting impossibly big pancakes of ice upon their heads. Small inlets along the shore were stretched into rivers that zigzagged and started and stopped, leaving islands of blue on the otherwise dun-coloured hills. The floes tilted and sank in the water as they melted, creating a fantasyland of grotesque and animalistic shapes brought to life by the wavering mirages and soft midnight sunlight. At one point, as I looked through the binoculars, I could see a white four-legged creature that stood out against the sunset sheen behind it. But the longer I looked, the more the creature began to look like a small hummock of ice. We had not yet seen a bear on this journey, and we badly wanted to see one.

The 24-hour sunlight and watch cycle were distorting our sense of morning, night and mealtimes. As we skirted the Victoria Island coastline around 2300hrs one "night," Drew was inspired to cook the geese given to us by the Lucases in Sachs Harbour. Drew had slipped into an odd watch cycle. Awake when anyone else was stirring, he spent much of his time at sea cooking or working on his laptop. Or entertaining the crew with his sophomoric humour. I had not put him into the regular sailing watch, but he was contributing all the same. Now he cleaned the geese and tucked them into bread pans for baking. At the same time, Mother Nature staged a light show. The heavy ice to starboard had flattened the ocean swell and the air was perfectly still. The surface of the sea was smooth as glass, reflecting dark blue clouds and the pink glow of the sun that hung just above the horizon. *Silent Sound* glided between the two parallel planes of sky and sea. Jupiter appeared as a bright orange dot, perfectly reflected in the water. Behind us the sun's rays bounced off our wake, symmetrical and clean in the smooth water, to create a disco ball of light. Occasionally bits of ice, carved into fantastical shapes by the lapping sea, rose out of the water and caught the coloured light. We could hear the ice cracking and sighing as it slowly succumbed to summer. At this latitude the sunset lasted for hours—long enough to cook two geese, their scent wafting up to the deck to call the crew together for a midnight meal. The warmth of the boat's saloon, together with geese given to us by friends and the camaraderie of being aboard a ship at sea created one of the most memorable nights of the journey.

It was relatively warm as we sailed along Victoria Island, with our cockpit thermometer showing highs of 10°C. During the day we sat in the cockpit without our oilskin jackets, basking in the warmth. The ice was brilliant white in the sunlight. The floes were riddled with holes and crevices, like pieces of wood ravaged by termites. Slowly the ice sank lower and lower into the water, and each wave tore off another piece. On the ice sat seals, sometimes in pairs or small groups, but often alone. They lazed in the sunshine watching *Silent Sound*'s approach, then at the last minute they plopped into the water. The water was crystal clear and a deep blue. As we approached the ice floes we could see how they flared out under the water, glowing with a bright aqua light.

The reflection off the ice is what protects Arctic seas from warming up. But with more ice melting every year, the heat of the sun is no longer reflected and is instead absorbed by the sea and land. Each year there is less ice and more heat absorbed, slowly ratcheting up the temperature of the entire Arctic. The ice is slowly losing its battle with summer.

We spent much of the next day sailing within sight of the low rolling hills of Wollaston Peninsula. The farther south we sailed the flatter and more featureless the land became. Then we reached the ice that we'd been watching for the past two weeks. Even though it was melting and slowly shrinking, it continued to block most of Dolphin and Union Strait. But we had found its weak point, along the shores of Victoria Island. Between the ice and the land was a narrow strip of open water leading southwest, towards our target. We slowly motored forward in 7/10th ice, sometimes backing up to try a different route when one lead ended in a dead end. The ice kept pushing us to port, towards the island, with heavier and thicker ice threatening us from the seaward side.

On the morning of August 12th we had the wide, shallow Simpson Bay to port. Our ice-free lane led into the bay, while the main strait was blocked. We had little choice, but even so going into Simpson Bay was not an attractive route. The pilot guide warned of "a number of large shoal patches (position approximate or existence doubtful)" within the bay. The north shore in particular is tricky, and this was the shore that we were forced to approach.

Hanns climbed the mast with the binoculars to get a better look and shouted instructions to the helm. We turned into the bay, sailing almost due east, deep into the indentation, in the hope that our open water lead would continue and allow us to squeeze between the ice and land. If the wind were to change direction now, *Silent Sound*'s hull would be crushed like an eggshell. The ice would rapidly sweep into the bay and squash us against the rocky shore. I kept one eye on the depth gauge as we slowly advanced. Hanns remained dangling from the masthead while we sailed deeper and deeper into the dangerous bay. Finally the ice allowed us to turn back towards the deeper waters of Dolphin and Union Strait. We had made it through the worst ice chokepoint of the season.

The decision I had made in Tuktoyaktuk to go north instead of waiting along the mainland coast had paid off. On that evening's radio call with XNR79 we heard that *Ocean Watch* remained at Pearce Point, on the south side of Dolphin and Union Strait, waiting for clear water. I advised Mark and his crew to sail north and follow the route that we just taken. However, by the time they reached our track the ice had closed the narrow gap we were able to sail through. We had escaped disaster by mere hours. *Ocean Watch* dropped anchor to wait for the ice to clear, but instead the ice continued to close in on them. They were forced to beat a hasty retreat, leaving their anchor behind to be retrieved later. *Baloum Gwen* was also on the other side of the ice, but waited until a southern lane of open water opened. All of us felt fortunate compared to the 17-foot open Norseboat *Arctic Mariner* that was stuck in the ice in the middle of the strait. The two Royal Marines who were attempting to sail and row the passage pulled their boat up on the ice and waited for clear water.

In the midst of our worries over the ice we had crossed from the Northwest Territories into Nunavut, Canada's first aboriginal governed territory. Created in 1999, its name means "Our Land" in Inuktituk. The territory has its own legislative assembly and Supreme Court, but there are no political parties. Instead, leaders run as individuals. Nunavut, like the Northwest Territories, out of which it was carved, has a consensus government, which blends a parliamentary democracy with the Aboriginal values of maximum co-operation, leadership resources and common accountability. Canada's newest territory is bigger than Mexico, but only about 33,000 people live in all that space. Nunavut covers most of the Canadian Arctic Archipelago and a large portion of the Canadian mainland above the Arctic Circle. The vast majority of those living in Nunavut identify themselves as Inuit

These waters were the missing key to the Northwest Passage for half a century. Explorers blindly groped their way through the islands sprinkled across the strait but failed to find a way through. Ships entering from the east were able to make it down Peel Sound but ice and ignorance prevented them from slipping through Dolphin and Union Strait and into the Beaufort Sea. Ships approaching from the west made it through to Cambridge Bay, but then failed to find a route north to Peel Sound.

Sir John Franklin sailed these waters during his 1819 expedition, when 11 of his 20 men died despite having resorted to eating their own leather boots in search of nourishment. He followed the Coppermine River into Coronation Gulf, making it as far as Turnagain Point on what is now Kent Peninsula. He returned a few years later to lead a river expedition with John Richardson, George Back and Edward Kendall. They sailed north down the Mackenzie River to explore the Arctic coastline. Once they entered the Beaufort Sea Franklin and Back went west while Richardson and Kendall sailed east, naming this strait after their boats, *Dolphin* and *Union,* in 1826. But they did not solve the Northwest Passage riddle.

From 1837 to 1839 Thomas Simpson and Peter Warren Dease, both working for the Hudson's Bay Company's fur traders, travelled extensively along the mainland coastline of Coronation Gulf in search of new business. They sailed eastward, past Turnagain Point and on through Queen Maud's Gulf and Simpson Strait into what is now called Rasmussen Basin near Gjoa Haven. Simpson and Dease journeyed through areas surveyed by several earlier explorers and named Victoria Island, yet they were unable to piece it all together and discover the entire Northwest Passage route. The passage explorers had spent years looking for was tantalizingly close, but yet more than half a century away. A string of unsuccessful attempts would follow, and while each expedition failed to capture the grand prize, each one would colour in a little bit more of the vast blank areas on the maps of the Arctic.

In 1845 Franklin set off from England on his third Arctic expedition, determined to find the Northwest Passage. It was the grandest attempt yet, backed with all the resources of the British Admiralty. Franklin, his 128 men and two ships, the HMS *Erebus* and HMS *Terror*, were last seen by whalers in Baffin Bay as they waited for clear water to proceed into Lancaster Sound. Records stashed ashore by his men showed that Franklin's ships made it south through Peel Sound before being frozen into the ice, while his men died trying to walk to the mainland.

The next decade would be spent trying to find Franklin, although many of the search parties were thinly disguised explorations in their own right. In 1848 Sir John Richardson, a Scottish naval surgeon and naturalist, and John Rae, a Scottish doctor who would spend years crisscrossing the Arctic on foot, led an expedition to explore the mainland coastline between the Mackenzie and Coppermine rivers and search for Franklin. The expedition, which trekked overland and used small coastal boats, contributed significantly to the maps of the area but failed to find Franklin or the Northwest Passage.

In 1852, Sir Richard Collinson, an English naval officer, sailed the HMS *Enterprise* through these waters, the first large ship to do so. In charge of both the *Enterprise* and the HMS *Investigator,* Collinson had left England tasked with finding what had become of Franklin. The *Investigator* was captained by Sir Robert McClure, the Irish officer who would sail off into the Arctic ahead of his boss, only to get frozen into the ice of Mercy Bay on the north coast of Banks Island. Collinson, after spending one winter at Banks Island waiting for McClure, eventually turned east, sailing through the very waters we were about to enter. His voyage added little to the knowledge of this area and he knew he was following routes already sailed by Franklin, Simpson and Dease. However, a half-century later the notes he made while in these waters helped Amundsen make the first transit of the Northwest Passage.

"He had throughout done excellent and reliable work," Amundsen wrote of Collinson. "His soundings and survey of this narrow and foul channel were very helpful to the Gjøa Expedition... He guided his great, heavy vessel into waters that hardly afforded sufficient room for the tiny *Gjøa*."

Amundsen viewed Dolphin and Union Strait, as well as Coronation Gulf and Queen Maud Gulf to the east, as the hardest portion of the entire passage, and he slowed the *Gjøa* down to a crawl to avoid running aground on the many reefs and small rocky islands. "We would rather sacrifice a few hours than jeopardize our vessel in these very hazardous waters, with a ragged stone bottom and shallow water under the keel, an unsafe compass, and a small crew," he wrote.

A century after Amundsen guided the *Gjøa* through this strait it remains a treacherous bottleneck, and aboard *Silent Sound* we were on the alert. Currents reaching several knots regularly sweep through the strait. These currents had played a big role in plugging the strait with ice for the past several weeks. The pilot guide recommended that the strait be transited only during the day as the low headlands offer poor radar fixes and there are numerous shoals that could rip the bottom out of a boat. Northerly winds are most common here, but easterlies and westerlies also blow up, making for unpredictable sailing conditions.

As we motored through the strait Tobias drew our attention to a vibration in the boat he had begun to feel. I had also noticed an odd vibration while standing at certain points above the engine, but dismissed it as a loose floorboard. Now we opened the engine compartment for an inspection. It was possible that we had hit a piece of ice with the propeller, bending it, or even worse, bending the shaft. Ian Hansen, our friend in Victoria, had given me an expensive spare propeller as a going away present. But changing the propeller would be a big job, requiring us to beach the boat or dive into the frigid water to access the propeller. The drive shaft appeared to be spinning smoothly, but the engine continued to vibrate more than usual. I checked the alternator belt and every other moving part I could think of, but everything appeared snug and in good condition. Tobias and I blindly groped at the metal brackets supporting the engine. The engine mounts were deep inside the dark, dirty bilge, and almost impossible to see, but we checked them as well as we could by feel. They felt fine. We were only a day or two away from Cambridge Bay, so we throttled the engine down to lessen the vibration and decided to take a closer look at the problem once we were in port. Once there we would discover what great risk we had put *Silent Sound* and ourselves in.

That evening we passed Lady Franklin Point and entered Coronation Gulf, named by Franklin in honour of the coronation of King George IV. As we rounded the point I spotted activity on the shore. It was rare to see people when we were hundreds of miles from the nearest town, so the sight of an ATV driving along the beach immediately attracted my attention. An old DEW Line site occupies the point, and I watched through my binoculars as people shuttered their camp and set off on an aluminum boat. Soon they came zooming up to *Silent Sound* to say hello, as curious to see other humans as we were. They were conservation officers from Coppermine, renamed Kugluktuk, a town on the mainland side of Coronation Gulf. Hanging across their bow was a caribou they had just shot. They were driving a Zag Fab boat built in my hometown of Riverton, Manitoba, and seeing it gave me a twinge of homesickness. We stopped to chat, and they told us that we were the first transiting boat they had seen that year. They expressed surprise at the amount of ice that remained in these waters, adding that in recent years the strait was open by this time. Even the pilot guide advised that these waters were normally clear of ice by the end of July. After a few minutes of chatting they sped off, once again leaving us alone in the empty expanse.

It was the middle of the night when we sailed between the towering cliffs of the Richardson Islands—offering some geological relief after many miles of low and featureless coast. We followed the charted course, surveyed for depth and assured to be free of reefs and sandbars. By early afternoon the next day we were sailing past Turnagain Point and entering Dease Strait. We were passing Kugluktuk, as well as numerous other islands, inlets and settlements that loomed large in the history of Arctic sailing and exploration. I wanted to stop and visit each place, but we had to push on if we wanted to spend a few days in Cambridge Bay and still have time to make it through the passage before winter set in.

Cambridge Bay marked the halfway point of our journey. We had sailed more than 4,600 miles in just over two months. We had begun to calculate our time at sea, miles sailed and the length of our shore visits carefully. I wanted to arrive in Halifax in early October, which left some 3,500 more miles to sail in 55 days. At our current pace of about 100 miles per day we were left with just 15 days of shore time between Cambridge Bay and Halifax.

August 14, 0830hrs

We have made better time than expected through Dease Strait and soon we see Cape Colborne, marking the entrance into Cambridge Bay. The land around Cambridge Bay is featureless except for Mount Pelly, which rises to 220 metres just north of the town. We're still some 30 miles away from Cambridge Bay but it's a straight shot as I hand the watch to Tobias. I have plotted a course on the electronic chart plotter in the cockpit, all he has to do is follow the red line and we'll be in town for lunch.

I go below deck and prepare for a hot shower. We are freely using the remaining water in our tanks because we can take on fresh water in Cambridge Bay. Tobias has been at the helm since 0600hrs, and as instructed, he's following the course I set. But when I set a line to the mouth of the bay I failed to zoom in on the electronic chart to double-check I was inside the buoys marking the beginning of the harbour entrance. The buoys are barely visible when the chart is at a large scale, making it hard to accurately plot a line between them. Tobias, enjoying the bright sunny morning and still learning the ropes of sailing and navigation, doesn't pay attention to the buoys because he's following the course I'd plotted for him. Plotted incorrectly. The first sign of trouble is a thud and gentle bump from the keel. I race up the companionway steps and look to port. All I can see is Simpson Rock, a jumbled island of rocks protruding from the sea.

"Turn to starboard" I shout to Tobias. But he has already looked to starboard and has seen the rocky sea bottom through the clear water. The pilot guide says Simpson Rock is "surrounded by very shallow water, shoal patches extend across the bay south of the rock." We are south of the rock. Moments after the first bump there is another, and then *Silent Sound* grinds to a halt. I slam the boat into reverse and give it full throttle, but she's stuck. We're on a falling tide, which means that with every minute we remain on the reef we have less chance of getting off it. We swing the boom out over the rail and Tobias and I climb on, shimmying to the end of the boom in an attempt to use it as a lever to heel the boat, thereby reducing its draught. No luck. Then we drop the dinghy into the water and Hanns rows out a kedge anchor. We run a line from the anchor to the windlass and try and pull the boat into deeper water using the windlass, but we are stuck fast. It doesn't take long to realize that we will have to wait for Mother Nature to save us with the next tide, more than six hours away. The water around the boat is one to two metres deep with the rocks and seaweed on the bottom clearly visible.

Hanns was still out in the dinghy trying to place the kedge anchor when our radio crackled to life. Inuvik Coast Guard Radio hailed us to ask us to contact the icebreaker *CCGS Sir Wilfrid Laurier*. It was bad timing, but I turned on the single sideband radio and hailed the icebreaker, which was somewhere in Coronation Gulf. They knew we were the first boat into Cambridge Bay, and they wanted us to check on the lateral navigation buoys coming into the harbour. The buoys had been left in the water over winter, and they were worried that the ice had destroyed them. I sheepishly confessed we were aground and it would be a few hours before we could give them a report on the rest of the channel leading into Cambridge Bay. Simpson Rock was well marked on the charts and we had motored far too close to the rocks for common sense, regardless of the buoys, but they respectfully withheld any wisecracks. In my embarrassment I imagined a guffaw in the radio room and every time they called me "Skipper" or "Captain" thereafter, and my ears burned with shame. They graciously offered to stand by on frequency in case we needed help.

So there we sat. Tobias and Drew rowed the dinghy over to Simpson Rock—not a very long trip—for a beach break, while I wrote some letters and baked bread. It was 10°C and sunny. A lumbering Canadian Air Force airplane passed by overhead several times and we heard the crew chatting with Inuvik on VHF, enquiring about the boat below them, heeling at a crazy angle. Yes, we're the fools that ran aground, and no, we don't need help. Other than the roar of the plane it was so quiet my ears began to hum. We could hear the occasional tweet of birds that were too far away to be seen. Any movement from Hanns sounded like the first thunderclap of a summer storm. The low, featureless land trailed off into the distance. There was little for the eye to rest upon, yet it felt like we could see the whole world from here. My eye was drawn to a rock one mile away on the shore. It broke the monotony of the otherwise empty shoreline. An orange marker on the headland could just as well have been a one million watt strobe light in the night. It was a peaceful little spot and would have made a lovely afternoon anchorage, but I'd rather not have been there at that moment.

The quiet was broken by the whine of an approaching outboard engine. A hundred metres out the driver of the aluminum skiff shouted out his version of a greeting. "Cameron, you ran aground!" We were in the middle of the Arctic approaching a town I've never visited before and someone knew my name? It was Colin Dickie, a Cambridge Bay resident who had contacted me by email months earlier and told me to look him up if I came to his town. He just happened to be cruising the coastline on his boat in search of seals to feed his dogs. As soon as he saw the name on *Silent Sound*'s stern he knew I'd arrived. Colin came aboard for a chat and a coffee. And to deliver a gentle ribbing over our misfortune. Before zooming off in his boat again he told us he'd send some help if we weren't at the town dock by 1600hrs.

By 1400hrs *Silent Sound* began rising with the tide. We called Tobias and Drew back from Simpson Rock, where they were building an inukshuk, or Inuit statue, and having a *Lord of the Flies* moment. Once she was floating free we unfurled the genoa to pull her bow towards deeper water, and then gunned the engine. A jump, a bump and we were back on our way into Cambridge Bay, where we would find out just how much trouble we were really in.

# CHAPTER 8
# Cambridge Bay

*There's an element of power and privilege indicated by who 'takes
an interest' in whom. Inuit don't go on ecotours of Montreal.*
—Rick Salutin, 2009

Ikaluktutiak Elks Lodge No 593 could have been in any one of a thousand small towns across Canada. The lodge was part bingo hall, part
bar. Flags and a dartboard hung on the wall beside a trophy case full of
Cambridge Bay pride, all in the clinical glare of florescent lights. A giant
projection screen was showing a football game—the Montreal Alouettes
upset the Winnipeg Blue Bombers 39–12—and the place was filled with
friendly, smiling people eating steaks and drinking beer.

It was the perfect end to the first half of our expedition. When Colin
visited *Silent Sound* as she sat high and dry on Simpson Rock he told us
about the weekly Elks Lodge Friday Night Jamboree and invited us to join
him at the party. Colin also told everyone at the party that he had found
us stranded on a rock that was clearly marked on the charts and well
known to anyone who had ever driven a boat into Cambridge Bay. Our
folly produced endless jokes and soon everyone knew who we were. The
crowd reflected a broad cross-section of the town—off-duty RCMP officers, giggling young women in tight jeans, boot-wearing men and grand-
mothers double-fisting rye and cokes. This was the only Arctic town we
visited where you could buy a drink in a bar setting, and everyone was
making good use of the opportunity.

Severe alcohol problems across the Arctic have led to strict laws con-
trolling the sale, possession and consumption of booze. In many towns
alcohol was either banned outright or heavily controlled, creating a booming market for bootleggers. Regardless of strict laws, alcohol abuse remains
rampant. We were warned not to let people know we had a few bottles of
whiskey on the boat; locals might break into the boat to steal them.

In the Elks Lodge the smiles were getting wider by the hour. I joined
a table of off-duty police officers and the conversation quickly turned to
their attempts to control booze. They explained the arcane and varied

rules of buying alcohol in the Arctic. The rules range from towns being "dry," meaning it is illegal to possess alcohol; "damp," where you can import limited amounts of alcohol for personal use if you have a permit; and "wet," where you can import as much as you want or it is sold within the town. Cambridge Bay is damp; you needed a credit card and a permit to buy alcohol. The permits were issued by a special town council on a case-by-case basis. With credit, the police officers said you could have a bottle of liquor brought into town for about $100, about four times the cost in southern Canada. Once a bottle arrived in Cambridge Bay it was often resold at $200 to $300 cash to those without credit cards and a liquor import permit. Unfortunately, that often meant the consumer had already proven that they couldn't hold their liquor, or did not have the financial stability to hold a credit card or afford over-priced bottles of whiskey. About 75 percent of the police work was alcohol related, varying from drunks passed out in the street during the winter to booze-fuelled domestic violence. Towns with alcohol bans are often able to get by with far fewer police officers. Cambridge Bay sometimes introduces total bans on alcohol when the detachment is short-staffed. Late that night, after we'd left the party, a drunken brawl broke out outside the Elks Lodge, and the organizers worried that it would jeopardize their permit for future jamborees.

Tuktoyaktuk was classed a wet town. There were no rules about how much alcohol you could import for personal use, but you could not buy booze in the town itself unless you were friendly with a bootlegger, of which there were many. A few months before we arrived, the town council implemented a one-week ban on drinking or importing alcohol to coincide with the Beluga Jamboree, their spring festival. Less booze meant less gaiety for some, but it also meant fewer fights and arrests for the police. The community had already been debating if it should hold a plebiscite on whether to restrict alcohol permanently, and the temporary ban during the festival was meant to give people an idea of what dry life would be like. Those caught bringing alcohol into town during the ban could be fined $2,000 or spend 30 days in jail. The town has also debated opening up further to allow liquor to be sold within the town, but elders oppose the plan.

Barrow, Alaska has tried a few different approaches, from outright bans to allowing some alcohol in under a permit system. Despite the steady flow of international scientists, oil workers and tourists visiting the town, none of the hotels sell alcohol, and some display "No Alcohol

Allowed" signs on their doors. Harold Curran, Barrow's chief administration officer, said the town was still struggling to find a workable solution. "We decided to go dry for a year, and it was a very politically volatile time. But the issue of drugs and alcohol have not gone away. Now, the mayor is emphasizing that people need to make healthy lifestyle choices," Harold said.

Over the course of the summer, Arctic newspapers reported on two towns that voted very differently on alcohol control, while other towns met to discuss their options. Pangnirtung, a large town on the east coast of Baffin Island, voted to remain completely dry following a petition from some townsfolk who wanted the laws changed. But even as a dry town, police said the vast majority of crimes committed in the area were alcohol-related due to rampant bootlegging. Some residents said that going dry wasn't effective enough. They argued local government needed to maintain an alcohol education committee to counter the effects of bootlegging. In Rankin Inlet, a wet town on the northwest coast of Hudson Bay, residents voted on whether or not restaurants should be allowed to serve alcohol with meals. The proposal received 52 percent approval, short of the 60 percent majority needed to change liquor laws.

Alcohol has left its mark across the Arctic. In Cambridge Bay, kids ran wild on the streets throughout the night. This despite the nightly wail of a siren marking the town's 10 o'clock curfew for children under 16. Late into the night, far after we'd gone to our bunks, children roamed the town on foot and on bicycle. Many of them were too young to be allowed to cross a city street on their own, but here they had the run of the town. While some of their freedom could be attributed to the midnight sun and warm weather, as well as the Inuit laissez-faire approach to childrearing, some of the kids pointed to a more sinister explanation. One night I climbed up on deck in the wee morning hours to get some fresh air and encountered a group of children playing on the dock. "Why are you kids not at home, in bed?" I asked.

"'Cause Mom and Dad are drinking," a little boy answered.

The children in Cambridge Bay were a constant source of chatter and amusement for us, but they had a wild streak. Each time we returned to the *Silent Sound* after running errands in town we'd find another scattering of gravel on our deck, thrown on in one chubby handful at a time. Sometimes the rocks would be complimented by a mutilated fish or some other bit of rubbish they'd found. The children were fearless in jumping down onto our deck and playing with or trying to pilfer anything not bolted down. The crystal-clear water around the town dock revealed a selection of bicycles at the bottom of the harbour. We began pulling up the various toys that had been given a sea burial over the years, recovering a collection of fishing rods and bicycles. We pulled one bicycle up, still in good condition and ready to ride, but as soon as we'd turned our backs the kids threw it back in the water.

On the afternoon of our arrival we had been docked for about an hour and were still on the boat when a little girl's voice called down to us. "Hey, the pigs are here to see you!" Greg, an off-duty police officer, was standing on the dock. I went up and said hello and had a chat with him, then returned below deck. The kids remained on the dock, hollering at us and throwing pebbles onto our deck. We were trying to ignore them in the hope they'd go away when a little voice piped up. "One of our friends fell off the dock and she's gonna drown if you don't help her." Yeah right, I thought. But the kid wouldn't go away and she kept calling down the companionway to us, so I poked my head out for a look. She was standing beside the boat alone and looked worried. All of her friends were huddled together at the other end of the dock, looking down into the water. Some of them were kneeling and leaning over the edge. I climbed onto the dock and ran to them. Staring up at the children from below was a round face with even rounder eyes. A chubby little girl was hanging onto the edge of the dock by her fingernails, kicking her legs and whimpering. "Help me, help!" she squeaked. I grabbed her arms and pulled her to the dock. She ran off like a startled deer.

It probably won't be the last time she finds herself on the edge. Few Inuit youth complete high school, let alone go on to higher education. Inuit youth are three times more likely to leave high school before graduation than children elsewhere in Canada. We spoke to students at schools in Ulukhaktok and Gjoa Haven and were taken aback by the sullenness and lack of spirit among the children. They stammered out dull, unimaginative questions in stilted sentences, their attention span could be measured in seconds and the teachers were clearly worn out by the daily struggle. It wasn't for lack of facilities. School buildings were far better than the ramshackle facilities I had grown up with in the Manitoba countryside, but a few generations of unemployment, misdirected government programmes and a loss of self-identity had robbed these children of their dreams. The problem with the children was clearly a community concern. Elders clucked their tongues and shook their heads in dismay when they spoke of their youth.

When I met Melynda, a 15-year-old volunteer at the Cambridge Bay tourist centre, I regained some hope. The first time I met her was when I went to her office to ask if I could use the office internet connection. She was on the telephone as I entered. "So this cruise ship will be here on Saturday, and we're looking for guides. You really should do it." She waited in silence as the unwilling candidate tried to talk their way out of the job. "Oh come on, it's only one weekend. And you know you need the money." This went on for several minutes, with her pointing me to a chair to wait. Finally she cajoled a reluctant commitment from the person. "Okay, great, we'll see you Saturday morning then. But don't you dare be late, okay? So don't go off partying on Friday. Do you promise?" When she'd hung up she turned to me, giving me a professional smile and efficient service. I had formed a strong prejudice against Arctic teens, expecting little more than mumbled answers and listless shrugs. Melynda surprised me.

A few days later Melynda and her friends joined us aboard *Baloum Gwen* for the evening. They'd come with Vicki Aitaok, who had thrown open the doors of the visitor centre to us, helped us find tools, parts and supplies, and earlier that evening had hosted a small public meeting for the three yachts visiting Cambridge Bay. I prodded Melynda to tell me her story. She'd been one of 30 children in her kindergarten class. Now there were just seven in her high school class. Most had dropped out. But Melynda and her friends, crowded together in the boat, were brimming with excitement. I asked them who their role models were. The schools we'd visited had their hallways plastered with posters of young Inuit who were being held up as role models for their community involvement, dedication to sports and arts and focus on education. Melynda and her friends didn't think much of the posters, and were hard-pressed to name any role models of their own. Finally Melynda said she respected her sister, only a few years older than herself. "She's a single mom, but she got herself straightened out and now she's doing okay. She's got her own place and everything."

One of Melynda's friends had been on a school trip to Europe a year earlier, and he was still awed by what he had seen. Melynda planned to go on the next trip, and with every city he described she would excitedly outline her own plans. She and a friend planned to stay on and backpack their way through Europe after the rest of the students returned home. Her hunger to experience life outside of Cambridge Bay was her reason for coming to the boat. "It's so exciting," Melynda gushed. "You people are from all over." Her short-term goal was simple: get out of Cambridge

Bay. Asked if she would consider coming back after college in the south, she thought for some time before answering. "Maybe. But there are no opportunities here, so I'm not sure what I'd do."

At one point her cell phone beeped and she turned away for a quiet, earnest conversation. "But Dad, I'm on one of those boats, and Vicki is here too." She turned back and told us she'd convinced her father to extend her curfew by half an hour. This was in sharp contrast to the much younger children running around town all night, and I asked her why her parents were so strict. She replied without pausing: "Because my parents love me and care about me." Melynda was no angel. She admitted that yes, drinking was popular with teens, and that it wasn't hard to buy a bottle of from a bootlegger. She and her friends would save up, pool their money and buy a bottle and then do what rural teenagers do everywhere in North America: hang out, listen to music and cruise around town, albeit often on an ATV rather than in a car. "It's pretty boring," she concluded.

Earlier I had met Logan Nasogaluak in Tuktoyaktuk. Logan was in the youth centre when I met him, playing video games with his friends. He was 17 years old and about to return to school to complete Grade 10. His family had just returned to Tuktoyaktuk after two years in Inuvik, and he was missing the relative sophistication of the bigger town to the south. "It's a lot better than Tuk," he said. "I didn't want to come back but my parents did, so I had to. There are a lot more opportunities there. More chances for education, jobs."

Like all Arctic teens, the decision to stay in school and away from booze and drugs was one Logan had to make every day. "There's a lot of corruption if you're into that. Lot of kids drinking and doing drugs. I'm trying not to," he said. "There's a lot of unemployment among the locals, but a lot of them are hunters and they live off the land. They don't want a job. I'd like to get a government job. Something in an office. Something with good pay and benefits. But there's not much opportunity for me if I don't have an education."

Alcohol and chronic high unemployment kept the police busy. Nunavut, the self-governed territory in which Cambridge Bay is located, had an unemployment rate of 17 percent in August, 2011, versus the national average of 7.3 percent. Its crime rate is seven times that of southern Canada. Suicide rates among Canada's Inuit are more than 11 times the national average, and 83 percent of these are people under 30 years of age. The numbers are all stacked up against them, right from when they're young.

Marg Epp works as an economic advisor to small local businesses, giving her a good view of the clash between the relaxed and unstructured life on the land that the Inuit cherish and the reality of modern day job requirements. She invited us for a driving tour of Cambridge Bay, and while we bounced down potholed lanes across the tundra in her pickup truck she summed up the challenge facing her clients. Unlike in many other parts of rural Canada, a business owner in the Arctic is unable to look to other nearby towns as a possible source of clients because in the Arctic the nearest town is hundreds of miles away and there are no roads connecting communities. "And really, how many small restaurants or snowmobile repair shops do you need in a town this size? There are not many businesses you can run here."

While a hunting guide could make $30,000 or $40,000 in a month of guiding hunting tourists from the south, once the season ended the hunter was again faced with unemployment. "A guy can get a job, and he's a great worker, but then it's hunting season and he can't make it to work at eight o'clock because he came back from a hunt at two in the morning. And it makes sense to him that he shouldn't have to be at work first thing in the morning, but that's not how jobs work. It's really hard to fit the two lifestyles together." For women it's even harder, and some young women see motherhood as their best employment option. The government pays enough child support—the more kids you have the more money you get—to allow many mothers to live off support payments alone.

Cambridge Bay became an important transport and supply centre for the DEW Line during the Cold War. Most of the radar stations have been closed but Cambridge Bay remains part of Canada's Arctic security system. In 2010 Ottawa chose the town as the site of its long-awaited High Arctic Research Station for science and technology, which is to be in operation by 2017. The town is a growing sprawl of fuel tanks, tin-sided buildings and dirt roads.

Cambridge Bay appears naked without winter snow. Summer brings a wild bloom of flowers, birds wheeling across the sky and a welcome break from the cold, but it is just a short interlude from the Arctic's regular state. Winter defines the Arctic and its culture. The rows of waiting snowmobiles and komatiks, the long heavy wooden sleds Inuit hunters tow over the ice, are a reminder that winter is the longest, most dominant season here.

Many Arctic towns are set in stunning locations with scenic backdrops that explain why people are forever "going off" to hunt, fish or just relax at their summer camps outside of town. But in town, on the main street, it's an ugly sight. Roads are gravel and dirt. ATVs and 4×4 trucks kick up a storm of dust as they bounce over the town's potholed streets. Houses, new or old, all appear in need of paint as the blistering cold and tundra winds strip them of colour. The yards reflect the lifestyle of those that live in them, focused on practical needs. ATVs compete for front-yard space with wooden komatiks and the drying hides of various beasts. Broken toys, out-of-season snowmobiles and a few barking dogs normally complete the scene. I imagined what it would look like in winter when there would be a metre of snow on the ground, the rubbish and mud invisible. The mental image was of a much cozier, prettier village.

One of my first tasks upon entering any port was finding out where we could buy fuel, find potable water, make small repairs and do all of the other things that were needed to keep *Silent Sound* in sailing condition. In Cambridge Bay this place was Kitnuna Construction. They ran a fleet of trucks and heavy equipment and had a large and well-stocked shop. I walked in and made arrangements for refuelling. While there I asked if one of the mechanics could come take a look at my engine vibration. Eamon, a tall, gangly and incredibly patient Irishman, came to take a look. He clomped aboard in his giant oil-stained boots and folded his bony frame in half to inspect the engine. The engine sat on four brackets, which in turn were connected to the hull of the boat. Each bracket, or engine mount, had a single steel bolt protruding from it, holding the engine in place. Tobias and I had inspected the engine a few days earlier, trying to find the cause of the vibrations. We'd reached around the engine to feel the mounts, but they'd appeared fine. Now I was in for a humbling lesson.

Eamon ran his fingers underneath the engine mounts, shone a light into the engine compartment to double-check and announced that I'd sheared off all four mounts. The engine had shifted forward half an inch on the stubs of the broken bolts. To blind fingers, it felt like the bolts were still attached to the engine because the stubs were butted solidly against the engine frame, hiding the breaks. Because it was nearly impossible to actually see the mounts, we had mistakenly concluded that they were fine.

We were very lucky. The engine remained almost perfectly in line, held in place by the broken bolts. If it had shifted any farther the driveshaft could have broken. A broken driveshaft thrashing about in the bilge could easily put a hole in the hull. I couldn't remember hitting anything with the propeller, and even our grounding outside of Cambridge Bay had been a fairly gentle experience. Eamon speculated it was metal fatigue, and later inspection of the mounts supported that theory. We didn't have time to order new engine mounts to be flown to Cambridge Bay, and Kitnuna didn't have the same type of bolts in stock. Our only choice was to redrill and rethread the mounts to fit the stainless steel rods Kitnuna did have in stock. But first we had to get the old bolts out, and they were held in place by rusted nuts at the bottom of the bilge. Accessing them required hanging upside down into the engine compartment, reaching around and under a large, greasy diesel engine. In the dark. This would take some time and effort and I couldn't afford Kitnuna's shop rates. I knocked on the office door of the shop manager. Dennis was a short man with a trim grey beard and an efficient air about him. I told him about our voyage, where we'd been and where we hoped to go before winter. It didn't take long to convince him to let me use their shop for free while he would charge me for the materials I used.

I got right to work. Eamon showed me how to run the drill press and where to find the tools I'd need. We borrowed a come-along, a type of jack, as well as some wooden blocks and a heavy steel bar so we could build a frame from which to hang the jack, allowing us to lift the engine and work on the mounts underneath. I got the first engine mount off, took it to the shop, tapped it for a larger steel rod and bored out the bushings to make them fit the new bolts. The first one was fairly easy, but the other three were badly rusted. The only way to get them off would be to cut them off with an angle grinder, but there was not enough room in the engine compartment to work with a grinder. I borrowed a Dremel, a small electric tool used by local artisans to carve whalebone. I stocked up on tiny grinding wheels and started cutting, hanging upside down over the engine to get at the bolts. It wasn't really the right tool for the job, and we broke the tiny grinder discs as fast as we could replace them.

Over the next several days, Hanns and I would spend much of our time working on the engine and getting the boat ready to return to sea. The work was slow and dirty, and it put me in a foul, impatient mood. The boat became a mess of grit and grim, the saloon littered with tools and spare parts. I resented the fact that Tobias and Drew had time to explore the town and meet the locals, although they too were busy running errands and getting shore duties such as laundry and shopping done. In any case, there wasn't enough room for everyone to work on the engine. This was not how I wanted to spend our precious few port days, but I had little choice. Outside of Cambridge Bay the water was ice-free, but who knew for how long those conditions would last? I was seething with impatience and frustration, and the crew did their best to avoid me and my sour mood.

By Tuesday evening, four days after our arrival, the engine was sitting on its new mounts and we started it to charge the batteries. Everything seemed to be working fine. The engine had to be lined up with the drive shaft to within a millimetre or else the shaft would wobble and eventually break. It appeared to be almost perfectly in line despite Eamon's warning that it would take us hours to get it perfectly true. The next morning I called him over to the boat to take a look at our work, and he confirmed that the engine was sitting perfectly true on her new mounts. Hanns and I were grinning from ear to ear and suddenly the stress of the last several days vanished. We took *Silent Sound* for a test drive in the bay, revving the engine hard then throttling down to an idle, all the while watching for a telltale vibration. The engine was more solid than it had ever been. Hanns and I did an oil change and made a few other small repairs. *Silent Sound* was once again ready to set sail.

Most boats transiting the Northwest Passage's southern route stop in Cambridge Bay, and for good reason. It's the biggest town for miles, marks the middle of the passage and you sail right by the entrance of the bay whether you are heading east or west. *Ocean Watch* and *Baloum Gwen*, the yachts we'd met in Barrow and Tuktoyaktuk, joined us a few days after we arrived after their rough crossings of Dolphin and Union Strait. The crews from all three boats had formed a strong bond and it was good to see everyone again. While at sea there was little we could do to help each other, other than share what information we could by email and radio. But once in port together we poured over charts and swapped weather reports and advice. In Cambridge Bay we met our first westbound yacht of the year, *Fleur Astral*, a 60-foot aluminum ketch sailed by the French racing yachtsman Philippe Poupon. Philippe was making a speedy trip through the Arctic with his wife, actress and filmmaker Géraldine Danon, and their four children. They had stopped in Resolute and Gjoa Haven and were now enroute to Nome, Alaska. I met Philippe in the lobby of the Arctic Islands Lodge, where we were both stealing into the hotel's free Wi-Fi connection. He had encountered some very heavy ice sailing south from Resolute, at one point simply letting the boat drift with the pack rather than fighting it.

It wasn't just sailing yachts in harbour. One night while we were tied up at the dock the first barge of the season arrived, carrying fuel and supplies for the nearby DEW Line station. The tug arrived late at night in heavy rain, her decks lit up and crew working the dock lines, shouting instructions over the roar of her giant engines. *Silent Sound* was tied up on the town dock, and the captain of the *Nunakput*, the tug pulling the barge, radioed ahead and asked us to move. We moved *Silent Sound* around to other side of the dock where the water was shallower and we were only a few metres from the menacing rocks on the beach. Even though the barge was carrying little more than fuel and lumber, and none of the community's groceries and long-awaited household items, people gathered on the dock to watch its arrival.

*Ocean Watch*, better funded than we were, rented a hotel room in most towns they stopped in, and always generously invited us to use it. Although their crew slept aboard the boat in port, the hotel room was a place to take a long hot shower, log onto the internet and do laundry. Tobias and Drew spent hours in their room in the grandly named Green Row Executive Suites on the outskirts of Cambridge Bay, uploading photos and videos and connecting with their friends and families back home. We also continued to spend long evenings with *Baloum Gwen*, filling their saloon with a babble of French and English sailing stories. There were only two or three restaurants in town, so we often met for dinner, invariably staying late with our laptops open, comparing notes and impatiently trying to update our blogs and websites using an achingly slow internet connection.

Peter Semotiuk was the one man who kept track of all the boats. A civilian working for the Canadian military in Cambridge Bay, Peter is an avid ham and marine radio operator known to yachtsman by his call sign, XNR79. He runs a daily radio net on single sideband radio to connect with all boats sailing through the Northwest Passage. I got in touch with Peter months before departure and spoke to him by radio nearly every day of our voyage. He and I were both from the Interlake region of Manitoba, so I was eager to meet him in person and hear his Arctic sailing stories. Peter is a large man with heavy-rimmed glasses and a deep rumbling voice. Accustomed to hearing him on the radio, it was strange to see him in person and hear his voice without the background of radio static.

Peter's idea for the Arctic radio net came about in the 1970s when he was helping his friend John Bockstoce, an archaeologist, adventurer and writer. John had built a 32-foot *umiak*, a wood-framed Inuit boat covered in walrus hide, and used it over several seasons to travel through various parts of the Arctic. John was carrying a portable radio, and Peter provided him with weather and ice information as well as passing messages to his friends and family. Later, John would buy a sailing yacht, and in 1988 he sailed it through the Northwest Passage. He had made five previous attempts to sail the passage, but was stopped each time by the ice. When he did finally make it through Peter was aboard. But Peter confessed he was not much of a sailor, was prone to seasickness and preferred dry land.

"This was before GPS and modern digital equipment, so it was awkward to get weather information," Peter said. "You had to listen to the radio but it didn't always pick up very well. So when I came back I noticed that there were one or two yachts coming through who were having trouble getting information. There weren't many yachts sailing here then. I had operated amateur radio, or ham radio, for some time so I got a marine license to make it all official and set up the frequency on single sideband. As word got around I ended up with almost every boat calling in and I was able to pass them weather and ice information. Sometimes they needed parts or to get a message back to the family. It kind of kept growing year to year. I do it to help the sailors. It's an interesting hobby for me. Being up in the Arctic here means the evenings are relatively free, and it feels good to be help them, knowing that when I was in that situation I could have used some of that information.

"The first ones, 15 or 20 years ago, were the sort of people who really wanted to be out on a limb. Those people are still coming through now, but you'll also see other people who are more pleasure orientated. The boats now have a lot of satellite communication, GPS, better communications, digital items. So the boats in one sense should be safer, because they have all this equipment. They can easily get ice charts aboard now, with the satellite connections. Eight or 10 years ago it was much more difficult. Then they had to get it on one of the stations run by the Canadian government, faxes broadcast by radio in black and white. Now they can get colour charts. All of this means less work for me, but there are more people coming through each year. The people with the yachts have all this information but they still don't know if the ice is safe or not. I try not to say whether they should go through or not. This spirit of adventure should be for the people doing it. If they do ask for information or what I think about it, I will tell them, and if I see a glaring danger I'll point it out or at least question it with them. But basically I leave it up to the individuals."

We had trouble hearing Peter on occasion, and I thought it was a fault with our own radio. But he told me that the signals were generally weaker in summer than in winter because of the long days, and that this summer was particularly bad due to sun spots and poor propagation, or

transmission. The 24-hour sunlight during the summer months also inter-
feres with the signal, particularly at higher frequencies. Sunlight affects
the ionosphere, which is the uppermost part of the atmosphere starting
about 50 kilometres above the earth's surface. The ionosphere is used to
"bounce" a transmitted signal down to the ground, and by bouncing the
signal several times it can be made to travel between continents. During
daylight hours the sun heats the ionosphere, splitting it into four separate
layers. Some of these layers absorb the radio waves instead of reflecting
them back to earth. The two lower layers normally absorb signals while
the top ones combine to reflect radio waves, providing better radio propagation in the high frequency spectrum that we use for marine radio communication. During darkness, when there is no sun ionization, the lower
two layers disappear, providing the radio signal a clean reflection off the
upper layers.

Peter has seen everything from small open boats to super yachts sail
through over the years. In recent years the number of boats attempting the
passage has grown, and as we sat chatting in *Silent Sound*'s saloon there
were a total of nine private yachts trying to get through the Canadian
Arctic, a new record. Five of them were transiting east to west, with four of
us attempting it the other way. While the ice was breaking up faster than
it had historically done due to climate change, 2009 was posing more of
a challenge than 2007 and 2008.

"There is a bit of a problem in the central Arctic," Peter said. "It's a
bit late. In the past two years the Northwest Passage has been open for
two months. We're in mid-August now and it will probably start freezing in mid-September under normal conditions. So it hasn't really opened
properly. We had one boat go through [*Fleur Astral*], but that was just
sheer luck that it was able to escape before the ice started to move. But
I think you have a chance because you still have a whole month. One
or two good storms could move the ice around, then if it clears it away
from Boothia Peninsula and through Peel Sound or Prince Regent Inlet
you should be okay."

The Canadian Coast Guard is keenly interested in who is sailing the
passage so they know which foreign boats to expect in Canadian ports
as well as prepare themselves in case a rescue is needed. We were in constant contact with the coast guard. They were always aware of where we
were, partially due to the daily radio chat with Peter, which they were free
to listen in on. "Usually at the beginning of season when the [icebreak-
er] *Wilfrid Laurier* first gets up here I have already been active, so they'll

usually ask for information on where the yachts are and how they're doing, what type of vessel it is or how big it is."

While Peter and his call sign XNR79 have been a fixture for Arctic sailors for decades he may not be on the airwaves much longer. Peter was preparing for a move back south and retirement, giving him more time to pursue his other hobbies, such as guitar-making. "This is not home, although it has been my home for a long time. The next year or two will be my last ones here," Peter said.

One afternoon I was running errands in Cambridge Bay when I passed by the community hall and saw it was busy with a flea market. I wandered in and was soon drawn to table where a man was displaying grainy black and white images of Arctic life and talking to a few old timers. I recognized a book lying on the table, *Arctic Front: Defending Canada in the Far North*. I told the man that I had the same book aboard *Silent Sound*, and he answered that he had written it. He was P. Whitney Lackenbauer, an Arctic historian and expert on Canadian Arctic defence issues. Whitney has travelled extensively across the Arctic on his research trips, much of it with the Canadian Rangers, a part-time reserve unit of the Canadian Forces made up of northern hunters who conduct surveillance and "sovereignty" patrols across the Arctic. I invited Whitney aboard *Silent Sound* for dinner. The next evening he arrived to a rather dark boat. Our engine was still up on jacks and we couldn't charge the batteries, so we were saving as much energy as we could. But we lit some candles, Tobias cooked a stew and the conversation soon turned to Canada's approach to Arctic sovereignty.

Canada has never had a comprehensive approach to protecting its interests in the Arctic and has struggled to address issues of sovereignty, administration and control ever since it first laid claim to this land. The British government ceded the Arctic territory to Canada in 1880 but for years the Canadian government did little to confirm its sovereignty and establish Canadian law in the north. There were already whispers of American explorers claiming the archipelago for their country. Canada had been forced to make a hasty bid to regain control of islands near Ellesmere Island when it found the Norwegian explorer Otto Sverdrup had extensively surveyed the territory. They paid Sverdrup $67,000 for his surveys and maps, giving him the money only two weeks before he died. The islands are now named for him.

The summer of 2009 marked the centennial of the first time Canada proclaimed ownership of its Arctic territory based on the sector principle,

which uses longitudinal lines to extend ownership over the northern archipelago. Canada's claim was made by Joseph-Elzéar Bernier, a Quebec sail-
or. On July 1, 1909 Bernier erected a tablet in Winter Harbour on Melville
Island, officially claiming the Arctic Archipelago for Canada.

Bernier had argued for years that the Canadian government needed
to claim possession of the Arctic but the government focused instead on
settling and developing southern lands. He was an experienced sea captain, making regular crossings of the Atlantic to trade between the Old
and New Worlds, and he decided to take matters in his own hands. In
1904 he bought a German ship on behalf of the government and named
her CGS Arctic. He made 12 trips to the Arctic between 1906 and 1925,
establishing Royal Canadian Mounted Police posts across the region and
surveying each island he visited.

Although Bernier sailed thousands of miles through the Arctic, he
never actually transited the Northwest Passage, although he did have the
opportunity. During his 1908–09 expedition he found himself in M'Clure
Strait, just south of Melville Island, in the more northern of the two popular Northwest Passage routes. The strait leading west to the Beaufort
Sea was free of ice. Bernier would have been the first to sail the northern
route, which is still rarely sailed to this day. However, Bernier's instructions were to confirm Canadian sovereignty in the Arctic, and he decided
to stick to his plans and forgo the passage, proceeding instead to Winter
Harbour to raise the Union Jack as promised. He was bitterly disappointed at not being able to sail the passage, and the chance never presented
itself again. In 1933 Bernier was given a papal knighthood recognizing
his work. The honour entitled him to wear a cape and plumed hat, which
he sported at every formal occasion in his later years.

Few Canadians since Bernier have been so single-minded about sovereignty. For many Canadians, Arctic sovereignty is symbolized by the
Northwest Passage. The US wants the passage to be considered an international seaway, governed by international law, while Canada maintains
that it is an internal waterway, and therefore must fall under Canadian law.

We had our own experience with Arctic sovereignty. A few weeks
earlier we had been in Sachs Harbour as a thick, wet snow was falling. We were trudging down a gravel road when the Royal Canadian
Mounted Police pulled up in a four-wheel drive truck. They had tracked
me down with a message to contact a Canadian immigration official.
When I reached him by telephone Neil Stewart, a border services official
in Yellowknife, told me that US satellite surveillance had shown a yacht

heading into Canadian waters. Neil had heard about *Silent Sound*'s arrival in Sachs Harbour, and since he didn't find our yacht in his clearance records, he gave us a call and told us we were breaking the law by entering Canada without clearing immigration or customs.

Before setting off on my sailing expedition through the Arctic I had had extensive contact with the Canadian Coast Guard, asking their advice on equipment, ice conditions and Nordreg, their voluntary reporting system. As soon as we had entered Canadian Arctic waters we had begun filing daily reports with Nordreg, which included our exact position, weather and ice observations, as well as our plans for the next 24 hours. We'd kept up those reports while at anchor in Sachs Harbour. In addition, I'd supplied the coast guard with the web address of our live tracking site, which showed where *Silent Sound* was at all times. *Silent Sound* had also been in radio and visual contact with coast guard ships on several occasions. They had provided us with printed weather forecasts, and we'd even met some of their crew ashore. We were also regularly on the radio with Peter in Cambridge Bay, and the Coast Guard often listened to these chats. Canadian authorities knew exactly where we were.

*Silent Sound*, which was Canadian-flagged, had left Alaskan waters in late July, making a short stop at Herschel Island before arriving in Tuktoyaktuk, the first major town along Canada's shore. We arrived at the town dock late at night and tied up next to *Baloum Gwen*, which was Belgian-flagged although most of the crew was French. They told us they had visited the RCMP detachment where the officer in charge had cleared them into the country. Thierry, *Baloum Gwen*'s skipper, commented on how friendly and efficient the officer had been. The next morning I gathered my ship's papers, went to the RCMP detachment and told the officer on duty that I wanted to clear my boat into Canada. It was unusual for an RCMP detachment to serve as border services, but in the Arctic the RCMP often play a larger role than in the south, so I thought nothing of it. An officer looked at my Alaskan port clearance, the ship's insurance papers and crew passports. I was surprised when he declined a copy of my port clearance, but didn't pay as much attention to this as I should have. He asked me to send my foreign crewmembers up to the detachment and waved me off with a smile and a welcome home.

It would be another week and several hundred miles of sailing before I realized that we were not cleared into the country, and that the RCMP officer in Tuktoyaktuk had done nothing more than look at my papers. I had made a mistake by not telephoning immigration officials in Inuvik or Yellowknife to clear into Canada. However, the RCMP in Tuktoyaktuk also didn't know that we weren't following correct procedure. Neil, the border services official, later told me that border officials had met with the RCMP to clear up the matter and make sure it didn't happen again.

"Your experience points out that it's right on the ground where these connections are not being made," Whitney said as I told him the story over dinner aboard *Silent Sound*. "With all that goes on in Ottawa setting up work groups and committees, where it really matters is where the boots hit the tundra. It's not the big spending; it's about the training of constables in Tuktoyaktuk, about investing much more in the direct interactions with Canadian sovereignty. One of the biggest issues is that, given how thin on the ground government is in the Arctic, the RCMP have to talk with immigration, with Transport Canada, with Canadian Forces. If the probability of these incursions by other nations were real they would have invested more in these protocols. Ottawa is not using what it already has very efficiently. Instead, it sees this as a safe theatre to accomplish some military spending."

Climate change has come into play because with the rapid melting of Arctic sea ice there is speculation that the Northwest Passage will become a shipping shortcut between Europe and Asia. Voyages between China's main ports and Western Europe using the Northwest Passage would be some 40 percent shorter than they are via the Panama Canal, saving considerable fuel, effort and cost. This is why kings and explorers feverishly searched for the passage for centuries. However, it remains debatable if the passage will ever become reliable enough for commercial shipping traffic. Modern shipping runs like clockwork, and even with less ice the Arctic will remain unpredictable, threatening a ship's schedule. Arctic waters are also notoriously dangerous with reefs and shallows. The northern Northwest Passage route, above Victoria Island, is the more likely shipping route as it is straighter and deeper, but it is rarely ice-free for long. However, it is a fact that traffic is increasing, particularly in the past decade. Only 69 ships made it through in the 100 years following Amundsen's first transit in 1906. In 2011 there were a total of 23 complete transits, including 15 by adventurers, according to the Canadian Coast Guard.

Under the UN Convention on the Law of the Sea (UNCLOS) coastal countries have the right to control waters up to 12 miles offshore. No one disputes that areas within 12 miles offshore are Canada's territorial waters, including those narrower portions of the Northwest Passage where the water is less than 24 miles across. However, the US argues that even though parts of the Northwest Passage fall within Canada's territorial waters, the passage is an international strait because it connects the Atlantic and Arctic oceans, and is used for international navigation. The US says that Canada must grant ships the right to transit through what is otherwise sovereign territory.

Canada claims the Northwest Passage as internal waters, and not territorial waters, given the 12-mile rule. This means that foreign ships may only enter with Canada's permission. Ottawa bases this claim on the fact that through history, in all but two cases, foreign ships sailing through the passage have requested consent. Canada has always been willing to do some horse-trading with countries on a case-by-case basis in order to keep the peace on this front.

In 1969 the US oil tanker *Manhattan* sailed through the passage. The Canadian government, unwilling to risk a confrontation, ordered a Coast Guard icebreaker to escort the ship. Even though the *Manhattan* did not request the assistance it turned out it needed it, as it ran into heavy ice during its transit. That stunt by the Americans inspired the introduction of Canada's Arctic Waters Pollution Prevention Act, with which Canada claimed the right to control traffic up to 100 miles offshore, extended to 200 miles in 2010, for safety purposes. In 1985 the US again challenged Canada's claims to the Northwest Passage when it sent the icebreaker *Polar Sea* through the passage without informing Canada. This incident led to an agreement that has come to define Canada's approach to shipping and sovereignty in the north. The Arctic Co-operation Agreement stipulated that the US would not send any more icebreakers through the passage without Canadian permission, but that Canada would always grant that permission when requested. That didn't solve the problem of whether or not Canada's Arctic waters, including the Northwest Passage, were internal or international, but it meant that Canada could display a semblance of sovereign control while still keeping its southern neighbour happy.

Canada's claims are also based on the "straight baselines" it drew around the Arctic archipelago in 1985 and upon the thousands of years of use by Inuit people, who are now Canadian. Michael Byers, who holds the Canada Research Chair in Global Politics and International Law at the University of British Columbia and has written the book *Who Owns the Arctic,* says the Inuit have a case. Until the Inuit changed from a nomadic to a settled lifestyle in the 1950s and 60s they hunted, fished and travelled on the sea ice for nine to 10 months of the year. In 1993, Inuit negotiators inserted a provision into the Nunavut Land Claims Agreement that affirms "Canada's sovereignty over the waters of the Arctic archipelago is supported by Inuit use and occupancy."

"The provision has a sound basis in international law: In 1975, in a case concerning the Western Sahara, the International Court of Justice held that nomadic peoples can acquire and transfer sovereign rights," Michael wrote in *Up Here Magazine*. "For this reason, the Inuit might be the strongest element in Canada's Northwest Passage claim—and should be treated by the federal government as such."

Michael says Canada's position on the Northwest Passage is identical to Russia's position on the Northern Sea Route, or the Northeast Passage. For almost half a century, Moscow has claimed that the Vil'kitskii, Shokal'skii, Dmitrii Laptev, and Sannikov straits along Russia's northern coast constitute Russian internal waters. In 1965 the US Coastguard icebreaker *Northwind* approached the most western of these straits. Moscow objected, and the US Department of State spokesman at the time said Moscow threatened to "go all the way" if the American ship proceeded into the passage. The *Northwind* turned around. No foreign vessel has sailed the Northern Sea Route without Moscow's permission.

Nordreg, operated by Canada's Marine Communications and Traffic Services, tracks vessels north of 60°N, assisting in potential search and rescue operations and pollution control. In 2008, Prime Minister Stephen Harper promised Nordreg would become compulsory. It finally happened in June, 2010, with the rules becoming compulsory for all vessels over 300 tonnes. The government had already expanded its pollution control area to 200 miles offshore from 100. In announcing the new rules, the government described them as a "measure to protect and defend Canada's northern sovereignty." They are, in other words, about much more than pollution and shipping safety. Ottawa sees that Canada's sovereignty claims are strengthened if vessels submit to Canadian rules in what are for the most part international waters.

Whitney sees it differently. I telephoned him at his home in southern Ontario after the new rules were announced. "If we have 98 percent compliance with voluntary Nordreg it's an impressive record and it is actually a signal of confidence. This leaves Canada some wiggle room in some scenarios if it needs it. It means a building up and accruing of Canadian sovereignty in the Arctic. In Ottawa they know that time is on our side. Every year that goes by it makes it more difficult for outside countries to jeopardize our position."

Ottawa's move to make Nordreg compulsory triggered a flurry of objections from shipping companies, which Whitney said had a negative effect on Canada's claims. "The more letters of protest the government gets on this, the less strength Canada's position has when we say 'generally the world has been compliant'." But while powerful shipping companies could influence their countries' politics, international law is set by nation states, not by corporations.

Ottawa has repeatedly promised to build ships and submarines to patrol the Arctic. In 1985, following *Polar Sea*'s voyage, the government announced plans to build a $500 million icebreaker, but the plans fell victim to cost-cutting. Two years later the government said it was considering the construction of as many as 10 new nuclear-powered submarines, some of which would be used to patrol Arctic waters. Again, nothing came of the plan. In 2007 the government announced it would build six to eight Arctic patrol ships at a cost of $3.1 billion, with another $4.3 billion needed to maintain them. The first ship has been promised for 2014. In 2010 the Arctic Patrol Ship Project was grouped with several other federal government ship procurement projects for the Royal Canadian Navy and Canadian Coast Guard into the National Shipbuilding Procurement Strategy. In October, 2011 the government announced that Irving Shipbuilding would be awarded the $25 billion contract for building eight Arctic patrol ships as well as 15 other warships for the navy over the next two decades.

Inuit communities are understandably concerned about sovereignty issues, and they want a say in the matter. A group of teens in Arctic Bay, an Inuit hamlet on the north end of Baffin Island, launched a "Sovereignty includes me" campaign while we sailed through the Arctic. Inuit leaders have backed Ottawa's new compulsory rules for Arctic shipping, but, as in the past, the government has paid little attention to Inuit interests. Canada says because the waters between most islands in Canada's Arctic are frozen for much to the year, and Inuit often hunt and live on the ice, they should be considered an extension of the land. But while Ottawa has used the Inuit to bolster its claims, it hasn't proactively involved indigenous people in the decision-making.

"It should be about partnership, not about Ottawa saying 'we've made a decision, come to Ottawa to discuss it,' and the minister comes to talk to the indigenous groups for 10 minutes, and then the next day he says that it's all been in consultation with Inuit leaders," Whitney said. "When you call something a crisis you take it out of normal deliberation. You must immediately act on it. They're calling this a crisis, so the first priority is to take action, not to sit down with the Inuit or Gwich'in [a First Nations people living in Alaska and northwestern Canada] to talk about it. The big Achilles heel of Canada's record internationally relates to indigenous relations. We didn't sign the UN Declaration on the Rights of Indigenous Peoples in 2007, and that was a blemish. The more that the northern people are allowed to represent themselves, the more compelling a case Canada has internationally. Not in legal terms, but in moral terms. If the Inuit complain about activities not being favourable for Canada, it's much harder for others to take a position against us."

Canada does not have a great record of including the Inuit in its Arctic sovereignty plans. The most horrendous of many missteps might be the forced relocation of Inuit. A total of 87 Inuit from Inukjuak, a relatively lush community in northern Quebec, were moved to Grise Fiord and Resolute, in the barren and bitterly cold environment of Canada's High Arctic, in 1953 and 1956. An additional three families from Pond Inlet were also moved north. Many of the transplants died from the shock of the move.

A more successful attempt may be the Canadian Rangers, established in 1947 to be the country's eyes and ears in the far north. The Rangers are a force of Inuit, First Nations, Métis and non-Aboriginals who are paid while on operations and are either issued equipment or paid to use their own. They also act as guides when Canadian Forces from the south come to the Arctic, and in that respect have played an important role in establishing good relations between the military and Arctic communities. The role of the Rangers has meant that while northern people are playing a role in implementing Canada's sovereignty strategy, they do not have a voice in forming it.

There is also the issue of Arctic oil. Some analysts speculate the Arctic contains 30 percent of the world's reserves. Most of that oil is in Russian or US waters, with only a small portion of potential reserves located in areas that are under dispute. In 2007 Russia sent two mini-submarines to the sea floor beneath the North Pole in a publicity stunt meant to display its dominance over the Arctic and its natural riches. Artur Chilingarov, the 68-year-old expedition leader, told reporters his mission was to prove "the Arctic is Russian." However, even though the explorers planted a Russian flag on the sea floor, 4,300 metres under the surface, few polar countries took the stunt as a serious challenge for Arctic sovereignty. Every country now controls resources up to 200 miles offshore, and under UNCLOS

Arctic nations can expand this if they can prove that the seabed is connected to the continental shelf. All polar nations are busy mapping the seabed in order to support their claims. Canada must prove any claims it makes by 2013.

"In term of security, there is no doubt that in theory climate change may make the Northwest Passage more attractive to shipping," Whitney said. "It's also real in terms of access of resources, but the whole sovereignty issue really isn't about access to oil or minerals since in most cases the resources are located close enough to shore for it not to be an issue. It's only under debate in a few small areas. At the end of day, the real key, especially politically, is to properly implement what is already there rather than just talk about these broader issues."

By the afternoon of August 19th, five days after arriving in Cambridge Bay, we were preparing to leave port. *Silent Sound* had become a filthy mess due to our work on the engine and the constant tramping of sand on and off the deck. Tobias and Drew offered to give *Silent Sound* a good scrubbing while I went for a walk to get out of their way. I walked to the store, where one of the town's few pay phones was located, and called my father. I tried to call him from every port we stopped in. Speaking with him, and knowing he was following my progress on a giant sea chart pinned to his dining room wall, was encouraging. My 80-year-old father had displayed his own sense of adventure as a young man when he'd moved from an established farming community to the virgin forests of the Interlake region. He and my mother had cut down trees to make room for their first crops, living hand to mouth while enjoying the romance and adventure of their quest. When he questioned my plans to sail the Northwest Passage I pointed out that he had taken significant risks of his own, and that taking a risk didn't have to have a professional or economic reward in order to be a worthy goal. After that he never again questioned my plan, and instead gave me his whole-hearted support.

Dad could hear the fatigue in my voice but I reassured him we were on course. The last few weeks had been tough. I had spent much of that day on the telephone with reporters, trying to sound upbeat and keep people interested in our journey. It was inspiring to see how many people around the globe were following our progress and reading our blog. I didn't want to spoil the spirit by letting on just how difficult I was finding some aspects of the journey, like engine repairs and personality clashes. I was also struggling to find time to interact with people in the communities we visited. Now that we were halfway through the journey I'd begun to think about the end and the bills that were waiting for me. After chatting with my father I wandered down the shore. I could see *Silent Sound* in the distance. It was a warm, windy day, perfect for sailing. Having a few hours alone to decompress helped, and by the time I wandered back to the boat I was in better spirits. The boat was clean and Tobias had dinner waiting.

We had arrived in Cambridge Bay nearly out of propane, our cooking fuel. We assumed that we would be able to buy more, and normally it would not have been a problem to do so. But a leak in the town's gas storage tank had shut it down until an inspector could be flown in from the south. I resorted to desperate measures, knocking on the doors of people I'd met in town, and other people I hadn't met before, asking if they had a full barbeque tank I could buy. Everyone was waiting for fresh supplies and no one was willing to sell what little gas they had left. I had resigned myself to rationing our gas and hoped for better luck in Gjoa Haven, still several days away. But then a man appeared on the dock and asked if we needed assistance of any kind. We had just completed a hellish week of work, cursing and skinning knuckles as we made *Silent Sound* seaworthy again, and my first reaction was to say no thanks, we've got it sorted now. But I mentioned our gas shortage, and he repeated the story about the broken storage tank. I returned to my work, quickly forgetting about our short conversation. Soon he reappeared with a full canister of gas, taken from his company's own private stock of fuel canisters. He waved away my offer to pay for the gas, wishing us good luck before hopping back into his truck. I didn't even know his name.

We left Cambridge Bay early the next afternoon. Just before we cast off our lines Vicki, manager of the town's visitor center, arrived with a large chunk of grizzly bear meat for us. It had taken Drew and Tobias our entire visit to Cambridge Bay to secure the meat. Upon our arrival, delayed by our grounding, I sent Drew up to the post office, double-time as it was nearly closing time on Friday afternoon, to check if they were holding any packages for us. There were no letters from loved ones, but Drew spotted a notice on the post office bulletin board advertising free grizzly bear meat. He and Tobias later investigated and found out that the bear had been killed in a nearby summer camp after it had threatened the hunters. They asked the town committee if we could have some of the meat, but it was only being offered to town elders. Vicki and her husband Jorgan pulled some strings and gave us a large chunk of meat, along with a giant bone from the bear's leg. The bone was too big for the soup pot, but a good conversation piece nonetheless. There was also more meat than we could handle, so we shared it with *Baloum Gwen*, and *Ocean Watch*, relishing the exotic meal to come. Months later we would deeply regret the experience.

I felt a huge sense of relief as we pulled out of Cambridge Bay and turned east into Queen Maud Gulf. I had not enjoyed our stay despite the wonderful people we'd met. But ahead lay thick ice, and we weren't sure if we'd be able to get much beyond Gjoa Haven. Victoria Strait and Larsen Sound still had large areas of 9/10th to 10/10th ice and very little of the 3/10th to 4/10th we could sail through. A few boats had navigated through this area from the west, but with considerable trouble. At one point *Fleur Astral* had been forced to drift with the ice. Another yacht, *Fiona*, put out a distress call to the Canadian Coast Guard when ice threatened their boat in the Franklin Strait area. Everything I'd read and heard told me we were better off to wait in Gjoa Haven rather than try to beat the ice.

During our first night out we started having trouble with the batteries. They weren't holding their charge, and while charging their voltage fluctuated wildly. I tested the batteries' electrolyte with a hydrometer, which seemed fine. I traced the cables from the alternator to the battery, and they appeared in good condition. I pulled the cables off the battery posts, cleaned them and replaced them. The batteries still didn't charge properly. Once they were charged they would run down within a few hours of regular use. I spoke by radio with David Logan, the skilled first mate on *Ocean Watch*, and Thierry aboard *Baloum Gwen*. Both of them had years more yachting experience than I, but none of their suggestions yielded results. I pored over mechanical guides, searching for clues and cursing myself for not being better versed in the workings of my own boat. With battery alarms buzzing and flashing, we had to keep the engine running despite perfect winds blowing from the west. There was little we could do but aim for Gjoa Haven and hope to fix the problem there.

During our second night out of Cambridge Bay the wind picked up to about 25 knots from the northwest as *Silent Sound* carefully followed the recommended route through the maze of islands in Queen Maud Gulf. By now the nights were growing dark, restricting our visibility. We were worried we would encounter ice while in rough seas and heavy winds, surrounded by small islands that gave us little room to run with the wind or manoeuvre around obstacles. It was cold on deck, with the thermometer dropping to 1°C. We looked at possible anchorages where we could wait for daylight. Hat Island was an option, but we calculated that it would be morning by the time we'd get there, giving us little advantage. So we shortened sail and continued on through the night. I'd already learned that my night vision was awful, and sure enough, shortly after I took over the watch *Silent Sound* hit ice. Not a huge piece, and the collision wasn't serious, but it was enough to ensure I spent the next few hours blinking furiously and stretching my eyes wide, desperate to get a glimpse of the next piece in time. It also helped cement my reputation as the most dangerous helmsman aboard, as I was on watch for every collision we had. While the situation on the boat was tense, above us the aurora borealis glowed and danced. This was the first time that the rest of the crew had ever seen northern lights. They crowded into the cockpit, oohing and ahhing at the sight.

We were now approaching King William Island, scene of one of the Arctic's most tragic stories. If there were ever a locked chest of Arctic mystery, this was it. King William Island, and the waters around it, is where Sir John Franklin and his men perished. Late in the summer of 1846 Franklin led his ships south along the west coast of King William Island, a route that even today is not always clear of ice in summer. Franklin's ships, HMS *Erebus* and HMS *Terror*, were caught in the ice of north of the island. The men spent two winters on King William Island, with Franklin dying in June, 1847. Finally they abandoned the ships and those that had not yet died of starvation and scurvy began walking to Back River on the Canadian mainland. The expedition was poorly equipped for land travel, as evidenced by the bizarre and indulgent collection of personal belongings that they carried with them—silk handkerchiefs, scented soaps, slippers and hair combs. The men didn't make it far; most died on the island while some perished on the northern coast of North America. Searchers would comb the Arctic for years before the truth emerged. Inuit told searchers they had seen a group of 35 to 40 white men walking towards the mainland, and that later they had found human remains bearing signs that the men had resorted to cannibalism before perishing.

The eastern portion of Queen Maud Gulf is a nightmare of low-lying islands which are hard to see and are so low that many don't appear on radar. As an extra challenge, they are interspersed with poorly charted reefs and rocks. Government-issued sailing instructions say the area is "encumbered by islands, reefs and shoals; the channels through these, Markham Strait, Palander Strait and Requisite Channel, are among the most difficult to navigate in the western Arctic." On another page the guide warns that "the track through this area is tortuous and abounds in dangerous shoals."

Eventually the hellish night gave way to day, and by midday we had made it through the gulf and entered Simpson Strait. As we entered the strait we spotted *Baloum Gwen* popping out of a small bay where they'd anchored for the night, hiding from the same wretched conditions we'd sailed through all night. Although Simpson Strait is two miles wide at its narrowest point, islands and shoals limit safe waters to less than half a mile wide, making it a tricky passage. However, fair winds and sunny skies made for a pleasant afternoon of sailing. *Baloum Gwen* was faster than *Silent Sound* and had disappeared over the horizon by nightfall.

Late that night Tobias and Drew began making caribou stew, using a battered old pressure cooker I'd salvaged from my mother's pantry. The pot had seen better days, and none of us had used a pressure cooker before. Tobias and Drew loaded the pot with caribou and water and put it on the stove. I was in my bunk, half asleep as they worked. A short time later Tobias decided to open the pot to check on his stew, but he didn't release the pressure first. As he unlocked the lid there was a bang, a scream, a lot of clattering and racket and then gales of laughter. The lid had blown off, and Tobias was lucky to have come away unhurt. The stew was everywhere: in their hair, on our computers, in Tobias's and Hanns's sleeping bags in the main saloon, on the ceiling and floor and on the ship's log book. Tobias and Drew spent the next hour mopping up soup and collecting bits of half-cooked caribou from all corners of the boat. The next morning I found bits of half-cooked caribou that had been blasted all the way into the cockpit.

With that we arrived at Gjoa Haven. CCGS *Sir Wilfrid Laurier* was anchored just outside the harbour, her bridge lit up and night watch silhouetted in the windows. We made a courtesy radio call to say hello, and then slipped into Gjoa Haven through its doglegged entrance, happy to drop anchor and fall into our bunks.

# CHAPTER 9
# The Hunt

*The Eskimo ... have grown so accustomed to white man's food
that if they cannot obtain it they deem it a great hardship.*
—Roald Amundsen, 1908

The sun was shining when I awoke and poked my head above deck. Now I knew what Roald Amundsen meant when he describe this as "the finest little harbour in the world." We were anchored in the middle of a small bay with gentle hills protecting us on three sides. A dogleg in the approach channel kept the weather and waves out. Small aluminum fishing boats were anchored along the beach. On one side of the bay the town of Gjoa Haven came down to the water's edge, with a small concrete dock for unloading barges. On the opposite side were a few scattered houses and a row of abandoned wooden schooners. In 1903 Amundsen and his six-man crew arrived here on the *Gjøa*, an aging wooden schooner rescued from the herring fisheries. They were on their way to completing the first traverse of the Northwest Passage. Amundsen put into this small bay on the southeast coast of King William Island for the winter, and stayed nearly two years.

Amundsen was 17 years old when fellow Norwegian Fridtjof Nansen became the first person to ski across Greenland in 1889. Watching Nansen return to Copenhagen as an Arctic hero fired Amundsen's passion to follow in his tracks and make a name for himself exploring the polar regions. His dream was also inspired by the stories of Franklin and his lost expedition. Amundsen had long been a student of the north, devouring books by Arctic explorers and readying his body for a life of hard travel. Born into a family of ship owners and captains, Amundsen's chances for a life at sea looked good. However, his mother wanted him to stay ashore and become a medical doctor, a course he would pursue until she passed away. Then he began in earnest to prepare for the Arctic. Although Franklin served as an inspiration for his dream, Amundsen took a very different approach to Arctic exploration than the British sea captain took. Amundsen followed Nansen's example, counting on fur clothing and native modes of transport over the ice rather than European clothing and conventional modes of travel.

Amundsen's admiration for Nansen was logical, as Nansen was an exceptional man. He was intelligent; Nansen returned from his first Arctic voyage as a young man to do his dissertation on the central nervous system of certain lower vertebrates. He was also an excellent athlete and relished hardship, being the first man to ski across Greenland, and then in 1893 setting off in the *Fram* to become frozen into the Arctic Ocean to test his theories on ice drift. Nansen and his deputy suffered a horrendous winter huddled in a stone cave, but throughout it all Nansen kept up his lively and learned journal.

Amundsen and Nansen resemble each other in photographs. Both have hangdog faces. As with Nansen, photos of Amundsen never show him smiling. Amundsen appears entirely dispassionate, but his writings reveal him otherwise. He was blond and sometimes sported a beard, and he looked like he meant business.

As he planned his attempt at the Northwest Passage Amundsen realized he needed a scientific mission in order to raise the funding and respect he wanted for the project. He set a goal of finding, and learning more about, the Magnetic North Pole. When he arrived in the tiny bay that would eventually become known as Gjoa Haven the first thing he did was set up his observatories. He built a cluster of huts on the hill overlooking the bay to house his magnetic and astronomical observation equipment, along with shelters for supplies and dwellings for a few of his crew.

Amundsen and his team made numerous expeditions within the surrounding area. Although he did not reach the Magnetic North Pole he discovered that it was not a fixed position but rather one that was constantly on the move due to changes in the earth's molten core, earning himself a place in the books of scientific discovery. (For most of recorded history the magnetic pole has been positioned near Ellesmere Island, at the north end of Greenland. However, the pace of its movement has increased in recent years, and in the last decade it has thrown off compasses by about 1 degree every five years.)

Amundsen didn't isolate himself in his research and life aboard the *Gjøa*, as was the tradition amongst Polar explorers. Instead he spent time with the local Netsilik Inuit, learning as much as he could about Arctic survival. He tried the local foods, learned how to build an igloo and adopted the Inuit way of dress, wearing loose fitting skins instead of the tight woollen suits traditionally favoured by European explorers. This was a radical approach at the time, and learning these skills played a key role in enabling Amundsen to later become the first man to reach the South Pole, beating Briton Robert Scott to the prize. Amundsen lived to tell the tale, while Scott died trying to achieve his goal.

In 2010 a wooden box thought to hold records either from Sir John Franklin's lost expedition or from Amundsen's Northwest Passage voyage was unearthed from under a stone cairn marking Amundsen's camp in Gjoa Haven. The box, which had been unearthed and reburied several times in the past century, was opened in Ottawa by the Canadian Conservation Institute. It proved to be a disappointment. The box contained the remains of a cardboard box and pieces of newspaper and tallow, but no messages from dead Arctic explorers.

Many of the explorers and whalers of that era started families in the Arctic, and then often abandoned them when it came time to sail home. Their dalliances with local women were kept quiet, and Vilhjalmur Stefansson in particular went to great lengths to hide his Arctic family from patrons and family in the south. Women were sometimes hired as "seamstresses," a plausible cover since travelling the Inuit way over the ice and land meant bringing someone along to repair the skin clothing. Today, many of the more prominent families in the Arctic carry the name of trappers, whalers and explorers from the past, and they do so with pride. These include the Gruben family in Tuktoyaktuk, the Carpenters in Sachs Harbour and the Porters in Gjoa Haven. The names of explorers such as Amundsen and Stefansson are not as common since the men didn't stay in the Arctic to raise their families, or even give their names to their offspring. However, while in Gjoa Haven I met several people, such as the artist Danny Aaluk, who proudly said he was a descendent of Amundsen, while in Sachs Harbour we met descendents of Stefansson.

In Cambridge Bay we were repeatedly told that Gjoa Haven was much more traditional than Cambridge Bay or Tuktoyaktuk. The same had been said about Sachs Harbour and Ulukhaktok, but in those communities it seemed that remoteness and isolation were standing in for tradition. While the more remote settlements didn't have all the amenities available in the larger centres, it wasn't immediately obvious that the people were any closer to their roots. Gjoa Haven looked much the same as every other Arctic community we'd visited, but once ashore we heard much more Inuktituk being spoken, by all generations. It was also one of the first towns we visited that had a visible art community, even if much of what it produced was intended for sale to tourists.

I went looking for George Porter, a respected Gjoa Haven elder, to learn more about the struggle to maintain Inuit culture. Neighbours pointed me to George's house near the beach, and told me that he drove a yellow ATV. In case George wasn't at home I could watch for him on the road. George pulled up on his yellow ATV just as I arrived at his house. He shouted out a cheery hello and invited me in for tea.

The Porter family is now spread across the continent, but their story began with George's grandfather, W.P.S. Porter, an American whaler originally from Scotland, and his Alaskan Eskimo wife. George's father moved to Gjoa Haven in 1927 to open a Hudson's Bay Company trading post, and the family has remained ever since. George, at 78, was retired but still looking strong and active.

"I worked for the government for 35 years. Now I'm retired and a full time pensioner. The money keeps coming in, even though I'm just sitting around," George said with a pleased chuckle.

George's wife sat nearby, chatting with a granddaughter. They had family scattered across several summer camps, and they were catching up on gossip. They talked about who had a successful hunt, who left town for the summer camp, who was on their way back and whether the conditions were good for travel. Many of the communities we visited over the course of the summer were quieter than usual because people were at their summer camps. The camps are less remote than they used to be thanks to fast motorboats and snowmobiles, which are used to get to the camp in early spring before the sea ice has melted. It's not uncommon for hunters at the camps to keep in daily contact with families in town using VHF radios, co-ordinating the coming and going of family and freshly dressed game. Summer camps are an important part of passing traditional hunting knowledge on to the younger generations, and have traditionally been seen as a fun, if busy, break from life in town. But camping, and the hunting and fishing that come with it, no longer appeals to everyone.

"Lots of young people don't even know the culture. They don't even go hunting with parents, instead they stay home watching TV," George said. "When you live in a nice warm house, who wants to go out? You have TV to watch. Life is too easy. Even when I was working a job I had to hunt caribou and get fish, get seal meat. Here we have so much food to survive on. We have seals, caribou, whales, polar bear, lots of fish. We won't ever starve, as long as you go after them."

Another key part of maintaining Inuit culture is their language. I had begun hearing more Inuktituk spoken as we entered Canada's eastern

Arctic, and many of the signs around town were written in both English and Inuktituk. There are two basic Inuit writing systems, one using the Roman alphabet and one using an adaptation of the Cree syllabary for a system called titirausiq nutaaq. Moravian missionaries helped develop the first writing system in Greenland in the 1760s, and this is the system used in Greenland, Alaska, Siberia and the western Canadian Arctic. Eastern Canadian Inuit took longer to adopt a writing system, and in the 1860s missionaries introduced the titirausiq nutaaq syllabary, based on the one they had developed for the Cree Indians. Titirausiq nutaaq remains in wide use across the Eastern Canadian Arctic and Gjoa Haven is on the western edge of the area that uses it.

"You go west and there's more people speaking English," George said. "People from Tuk area, they're shy to speak their own language. They tell you they don't speak Inuktituk. Full blooded Inuk! Wish I could punch them. They learned English in school, and they keep speaking it at home. I told them the Chinese, Japanese, French, German, they all speak their own language."

From the loss of culture the topic of conversation quickly moved to the state of the Inuit youth. At first George was defensive, saying that the young people in the Arctic were doing just as well as kids to the south. And indeed, many of the problems he pointed to are common problems. But in the Arctic the mix of boredom, few job opportunities, readily available public assistance and a propensity towards substance abuse has created a particularly destructive cocktail.

"When we were young, once you were five or six, you'd have to go sealing. You didn't want to be called a lazy kid. Now kids don't care if they are called lazy. It's too easy to go on welfare. They say 'Why should I work if can get this assistance for free?' I had to work 35 years to get what I'm getting today.

"Lately it seems there's been a lot of really young families. They like booze and this stuff. But a lot of the places are worse. Gjoa Haven is not bad. We don't have as many suicides here as in some other places. Some other places get their booze so easy. Gjoa Haven is supposed to be dry, but it's not really working. Someone still sells it to them."

Hunting remains one of the most consistent and prevalent ties to the old ways and language. We heard this from Roy Cockney, the hunter in Tuktoyaktuk, as well as from Jean Ekpakohak as she skinned seals on the beach in Ulukhaktok. The amount of hunting being done, together with the degree of scarcity of wage-earning jobs, seemed to be the standard for how traditional a community was. While many Inuit men proudly said they lived off the land it was clear that they lived off government or family support but still spent large amounts of time on the land and that their families' diets consisted largely of wild game. Except for successful guides with international clients it is very difficult for hunting to pay for a modern aluminum boat with powerful twin engines, a new ATV and snowmobile, global positioning systems, radios and satellite telephones and the array of rifles and guns needed to live as a modern hunter. Wage-earning jobs, income from serving on hamlet boards and committees, or simple public assistance pay for the tools of the trade. But yet, the high cost of processed and packaged food in the Arctic does mean that most people do subsist on hunting. Subsistence and sustenance hunting—both terms commonly used to describe Arctic hunters—means hunting for survival, or hunting and gathering for the sole purpose of providing for yourself and your family. Most, if not all, hunters cited the high cost of store-bought food as the main reason that they hunted to feed their families. They also know that eating off the land is healthier and tastier than "white man's food," which is easy to understand when you see what they buy at the stores.

One early morning as I rowed ashore I encountered Yvonne Clark, the manager of the Gjoa Haven Co-op franchise. She was striding across town towards her store with a sense of mission rarely seen in the laid-back North. She'd just received word that the annual barge was due at any time, and her warehouse wasn't ready. "The barge is coming in. This is a big day. We have to really hustle for a few hours to get it all ashore," she told me as I fell into step with her.

I needed to buy a replacement part to make repairs to *Silent Sound*, and Yvonne unlocked the store, turned on the lights and helped me search the shelves for the piece I needed. Our search was in vain, even though Co-op and Northern stores in the Arctic carry everything from bread to bolts. While one end of the store was stuffed with fishing gear and clothes, the other had shelves filled with cookies, bread and jars of jam. As we searched we began talking about what Northerners want to see on the shelves of their general grocers. I'd been struck by the size of the frozen food sections in these small stores. Even the smallest shops had banks of gleaming stainless steel and glass-front refrigerators filled with an array of exotic, ready-to-eat meals wrapped in plastic. Thai curries, fish and chips and pizzas. I could understand the lack of selection in fresh vegetables given the remoteness, but in some towns we even found it difficult to buy basic dry goods for our galley. Instead, shelf after shelf was filled with junk food, instant meals and soft drinks.

"You see people walk in here and buy $500 in groceries without buying vegetables. It's mostly chips, soft drinks and cigarettes," Yvonne said. When she did try to introduce new, healthier options, they often sat on the shelf until they were past their best-before date. "The customers don't really like change too much when it comes to their food. We try to offer some different things, and we try to offer healthy choices, but the most popular thing is still the frozen ready-to-eat meals."

The results were plain to see. The majority of the Inuit we met were overweight. One study by Canadian university researchers and the Nunatsiavut government found that 75 percent of northern Labrador Inuit were either overweight or obese. Inuit in northern Labrador have twice the Canadian average incidence of diabetes, and high blood pressure. Their active, nomadic lifestyles have been replaced by sedentary unemployment, and as rich as whale blubber may be, it sustained them better than potato chips ever will. In 2001, the estimated life expectancy for Inuit was 63 years for men and 72 years for women compared with Canada on average, where men live to 77 and women live to 82 years old. Canadian Inuit life expectancies are similar to those of people living in Bangladesh and Kazakhstan.

Aboard *Silent Sound* our diet had gone native, although not due to our own hunting prowess. We had found that showing intense interest in the various game that hunters spoke about more often than not resulted in them offering us a sample. Their generous gifts gave us a welcome break from the beans and rice diet I had budgeted for, and our method of hunting became a running joke aboard the boat. So far we had eaten seal, whale, goose, beluga, grizzly bear, caribou, muskox, and plenty of Arctic char. But despite our attempts we had not yet managed to participate in a real hunt. In Cambridge Bay I'd asked Tobias and Drew to look for a chance to tag along on a hunt, but they didn't find an opportunity. Now we were in Gjoa Haven and I decided to make another appeal.

Many Arctic towns hold sing-song neighbourhood call-in shows on VHF radio every day. It's as if everyone in town steps onto their front porch at once. Mundane domestic messages were passed on—"Shirley, Bob said he'd be home late" sort of stuff—while gruff hunters sent sweet hellos to their lovers and children and home businesses advertised their wares. The afternoon radio chats were a beautiful thing to listen to.

But most towns also have a real radio station that serves up entertainment while doubling as a community chat room and lost and found
service. I went to Gjoa Haven's hamlet office and knocked on the radio
station door. Taped to the door was the key for a Honda ATV with a note;
"This key was found in the hamlet office."

Behind the door I found Jane, a small, grey-haired woman, and she
was on air. The switchboard and microphone rested on an unpainted ply-
wood table, and above her head ticked a clock set in a shiny frying pan.
On the wall hung a picture of Queen Elizabeth, serenely smiling down
upon the DJs. Jane was busy punching buttons and answering phones, putting one caller after the other on air to send out birthday wishes, advertise
goods for sale and ramble on about a myriad other community concerns.
Some read poems. It was much like the VHF call-in show, only monitored
by a DJ and interspersed with music. The callers spoke mostly in Inuktituk,
with a smattering of English callers.

"Yea ... I've lost one of my Ranger boots. If anyone finds it, call this
number..." requested one man. His voice trailed off as a Stompin' Tom
Connors song picked up momentum. And then Tom developed a stutter
and Jane began fishing around for a fresh CD while fielding a few calls in
the meantime. I thumbed through the station's record collection as I waited for Jane to get off air. Blue Oyster Cult. Krokus. Air Supply. German
Beer Drinking Songs. Jane wrapped up her conversation with a caller and
put on the next song ... the speakers emitted some heavy breathing and
then ... "This is Britney, bitch!" before the bubble gum beats of Britney
Spears filled the room.

Jane didn't speak much English, but a woman sweeping the hallways did, and I told her what I wanted. Before I knew it I was standing
in front of the microphone. I waited for an introduction, a cue. Jane ges-
tured towards the microphone. I nodded and smiled. Yes, I was ready and
I would speak into it when cued. "It's on," she said.

"Er, ah, okay. So ... My name is Cameron Dueck, and I'm on one of
those sailboats you see anchored in the bay. My crew and I would like to
go caribou hunting. Is anyone going out hunting tomorrow? Would you
be willing to take three or four people along? We just want to tag along
and watch. So ... um, once again, my name is Cameron, I'm on the boat
*Silent Sound*, and we monitor VHF CH16. And we're willing to help pay
for the gas if you can take us along."

I was still regaining my breath after my soliloquy when the phone
began to jangle and Jane handed me the receiver. Just as I was weighing

up the call-in offers, she pointed towards the door. A sun-wizened hunter stood in the doorway, also offering to take us on a hunt. In the end, it was a call from Silas Atkichok that won out. I could hear his father Jacob giving him instructions in Inuktituk in the background as Silas and I negotiated. We agreed to check in with each other by 1000hrs the next day. He needed to buy fuel, and the fuel station only opened at 1300hrs, but he would see if he could borrow some gas from a neighbour so we could get an earlier start. When I hung up, I realized I had no idea where we were going for the hunt. All I could remember was that Silas had said something about travelling a few hours by boat.

The next morning I went ashore and waited outside the Northern store for an hour until it opened. The store had one of the few pay phones in town, all of which were kept behind locked doors to prevent vandalism. I dialled the number Silas had given me, and after a long series of rings Jacob picked up and answered in Inuktituk. I ploughed on in English, sure that he'd understand if I just spoke a bit louder. Just as I was repeating who I was and what I wanted, a short, heavyset woman who had been standing beside me in the store entrance elbowed me aside. "You wanna talk to my Dad? Won't work on the phone. Here, I'll talk to him." I stood aside and listened to Josie chat back and forth with her father in Inuktituk, occasionally turning to cast a critical look my way. Finally she hung up and told me to follow her. "Better to come see my Dad, he doesn't like the phone much."

Off we went, Josie's young daughter in tow. Most people in Arctic communities ride their ATVs everywhere, and Josie was no exception. But now she had to walk across town, through a few drainage ditches and over a hill, and it had her gasping for breath. Jacob was waiting for me when we got to the house. He was short and powerful with giant mitts for hands and an open mouth with a scattering of long, yellowed teeth. He filled any breaks in the conversation with his chortling laugh and ear-to-ear grin. He was about 70 and still hunting regularly. He, Silas and a grandson named Rodney would take us out. They had not found any gas, so we would have to wait until the fuel station opened, and then we'd be off. Silas said we would travel about two and a half hours to a place that promised good caribou hunting. They had planned to go on a caribou hunt later in the week anyway, and they were glad for my offer to pay for fuel in exchange for allowing us to tag along.

By early afternoon Drew, Tobias and I were aboard Jacob's fibreglass boat and driving out of the bay. Hanns decided to stay on the boat for the day. Jacob had just bought the boat to replace one that had sunk, but this boat was also well into the latter half of its life, with two mismatched outboards requiring their own unique series of tricks and taps to get started and into gear. Jacob and his family seemed to be living lean compared to some of the hunters we'd met who had four-wheel drive trucks, multiple ATVs and drove new boats with powerful engines. Drew, Tobias and I wore fleece and Gore-Tex jackets while the hunters came dressed in a mix of track pants, flannel shirts and sneakers. This was warm summer weather for them. Under a rough wooden covering over the bow lay a shaggy muskox skin in case we had to wait out a storm, along with a banged up old .30-30 rifle, a steel box full of ammunition, and our own camera gear and extra clothing. In the middle of the open boat sat a row of fuel cans, filled to the brim for the ride home.

The sea was calm and skies sunny, putting everyone in a jovial mood. But the deafening drone of the engines and frigid wind soon ended all chatter and had us huddled on the floor of the open boat while Jacob steered, eyes streaming with tears as he pointed his boat into the wide-open sea. He had a habit of opening his mouth wide and sticking his tongue out into the wind, reminding me of a giant lizard. Behind him, Silas occasionally peered at a GPS hanging from his neck before shouting directions to his father. After about two hours of driving Jacob throttled down the engines and began cruising along a low, rocky shoreline. We had arrived at Hattuq, a hunting area about 35 miles northeast of Gjoa Haven, on the Boothia Peninsula. A bright red, late model snowmobile stood out in stark contrast to the dun-coloured landscape. There were no riders visible. The machine looked lost, surrounded by pebbly beach and emptiness. "My brother-in-law's," shouted Silas. "His chain broke, and he couldn't find it again last winter." Well, there it is.

Minutes later the boat veered to port as Jacob and Silas excitedly pointed at the low hills. They saw caribou where I saw only brown hills. As we came closer to shore I also could see the shapes of several caribou grazing just behind a small hill. It didn't take long to pull the boat into a shallow bay, drag it up on the beach and unload the gun, ammunition, cameras and gear. We stooped low and followed Silas and Jacob as they crept along the beach towards the caribou. Jacob, holding the rifle, moved in an awkward crab crawl as he tried to keep the gun out of the mud while crawling on all fours. Silas followed his father, his track pants sliding down and his jacket creeping up, exposing his ample bottom as he crawled across the beach. Soon they had reached the crest of the hill and settled in to take aim. The caribou were about 75 metres away, oblivious to what was coming. The air, until then deathly still and quiet, was filled with a barrage of gunfire. They fired off a storm of lead before the first caribou dropped, and it took a few more clips full of ammunition to bring down the second one. Precision hunting this was not, and we were amazed at how slow the caribou were to flee the scene. Jacob fired another clip off after the caribou as they loped off into the hills.

The Arctic has up to 30 unique herds of caribou that fall into a few main groups. The animals Silas and Jacob were shooting at belonged to the Porcupine herd, which is part of the larger barren-ground herd. The barren-ground herd lives in the central Canadian Arctic and travels up to 1,000 kilometres between their calving and winter grounds. The smaller Peary's caribou live farther north in the Canadian archipelago, while the Grant's caribou live to the west, in northern Alaska. To the south is a woodland herd, which lives in the taiga forests and migrates only short distances. Reindeer, which are domesticated caribou, live in Canada and Alaska only as an introduced domestic breed.

Caribou make a unique clicking sound when they walk, caused by tendons that roll over a small bone in their shovel-shaped foot. Both male and female caribou carry antlers. They are the most numerous of the large Arctic mammals and their tender, fragrant meat is one of the favourite foods in the north. Caribou soup bubbled on the stoves of most homes we visited.

Jacob was laughing with open-mouthed glee. "Two tuktu!" he shouted, pointing two thick fingers to the sky. One caribou was a fat, sturdy male, the other a slightly smaller female. Jacob pulled a folding knife from his pocket and began skinning the male, starting with slits down the insides of the legs, then slowly peeling the hide back with giant tugs. The naked caribou steamed in the afternoon chill as Silas and his father reached their arms deep under its skin, separating the thick hide from the flesh. Jacob was wearing a bright red T-shirt, matching the blood that was soon smeared over his hands and forearms.

Jacob issued quiet, guttural instructions to Silas. They threw the hide onto the ground, hair down, creating a clean surface on which to stack the meat. Next Jacob slit open the belly, carefully pulling out the stomach and a steaming grey tangle of innards. The head was twisted off with a grisly cracking sound and flipped upside down before Jacob cut out the tongue, throwing it onto the hide. Heart and liver soon joined the tongue in the pile of delicacies, then the kidney. Silas caught the kidney on its second bounce and carefully began pulling the outer layer of tissue off. Soon he was holding a chunk of clean raw meat the size of a hockey puck. It was warm and steam rose from the rose-coloured flesh. Silas took a large bite with relish. "My favourite part," he said. He held it out to me for a bite. I hesitated … when would I next have the chance to eat a still-warm caribou kidney while out on the tundra with a family of Inuit hunters? Not likely, I thought. I took a bite and slowly chewed the flesh, determined to fully appreciate the moment. It tasted tinny and rich at the same time. Its texture was soft and mushy, and the bite-size piece in my mouth balked when I tried to swallow, but it went down at my second attempt.

Jacob, meanwhile, had been preparing his own special treat. He cut open the stomach, exposing a mash of partially digested moss and lichen that steamed and glistened in the sunlight. He hacked off a fist-sized chunk of the liver, and then dipped this into the bright green stomach contents. "You want some?" he asked, green juice and blood dribbling from the corners of his mouth, his teeth clotted with the undigested dinner of the caribou we'd just felled. I declined, my need for prandial exoticism satisfied by the kidney. He went on to nibble at the stomach lining itself, again adding a dollop of green pudding to the raw meat and fat, with his grandson taking a helping as well.

Silas refrained. "Tastes a bit like sour green apple, and I don't like green apple," he confided to me.

Once both caribou were dressed the hunters cut them into quarters and hoisted the meat onto their backs, oblivious to the blood soaking their clothes. Their heads were bent low under the weight of the load, their boots squelching across the soggy tundra as they carried the game to the boat. The carcasses were wrapped up in their own skins and stowed at the bottom of the boat. Jacob was still crowing with delight, a wide grin splitting his face. "Good hunt! Very good hunt!"

The white and blue boat was now smeared with blood, the bright sunshine saturating every colour to a garish degree. The hunters squatted at the edge of the water and washed the blood from their hands, leaving red clouds in the clear shallows. There was a sense of calm and contentment in the air. There was something extremely satisfying in the honesty of this hunt. The animals were killed because they were needed, not because they offered some excitement for an otherwise desk-bound urbanite. Silas and Jacob chatted in Inuktituk, their low tones occasionally lost when our boots set off a harsh rattle of beach stones. The land was brown and empty as far as the eye could see. We were the only things moving, the remaining caribou long gone. We climbed into the boat and squeezed in next to the stiffening carcasses. The boat slowly puttered out of the bay and back into the open sea.

Jacob and Silas kept a sharp eye out for seals as we sped back towards Gjoa Haven. Again, the sea was glassy calm with islands floating on the horizon, stretched into dream shapes by mirages. The seals didn't have a chance of hiding on that surface, and we could spot them surfacing from hundreds of metres away. But seeing the seals didn't mean we could hit them with the rifle. Jacob handed me the wheel and soon I was stopping every half-mile so he could try and get a shot at a seal. After every sighting we would cut the engines and coast through the water, waiting for them to surface again while Jacob rested his rifle on the windscreen, cocked and ready. He opened his mouth and stuck out his tongue, as if tasting the wind for game. Behind him, Silas stood poised with a harpoon. The seals were luckier than the caribou, and we didn't get close enough to them to add to our kill. As the sun dipped and we turned for home the hunters hunkered down in the bottom of the boat and opened several packets of instant noodles, munching the noodles dry as they propped their feet on the caribou carcasses.

That evening we went to Jacob's home to collect our share of the meat and retell the hunting story. By the time we arrived most of the caribou had been cut up and stashed in a freezer. A huge steel pot of meat bubbled and steamed on the stove. The house was full of children and grandchildren. The mix of adults, fat babies in diapers and rowdy teenagers wrestling on the couch made it hard to draw generational lines. Jacob presided over the entire family from a chair in the corner, a plate of raw kidneys, stringy fat and other delicacies before him for him to enjoy and dole out to his family. The respect for each other, and particularly for the elders, was clear and added to the familial setting. Occasionally the door would open, and people would be given packets of meat to take home or they would shuck off their boots and join the feast. Sharing the meat with their neighbours is a key part Inuit culture, and the thought of hording it for oneself unimaginable.

It turned into one of our favourite evenings of the journey as we joined the family, sitting on the floor on sheets of cardboard. Martha, Jacob's smiling, silent wife, served the boiled caribou on a cookie sheet set on the floor. We cut off chunks of meat and added salt and pepper before gnawing at them, the fat running down our chins. If a piece was too big and too tough, we used a knife to hack off the bite we held clenched between our teeth. There was no table or plates. Cups of hot tea were set down on the floor, leaving both hands free for the feast. It was a warm, welcoming family and the house was filled with chatter and laughter.

Once all of the meat had been eaten and we had wiped the grease off our faces the family began teaching us a variety of string games and showed us all the different Inuit strongman competitions. Knuckle hop, finger pulling, high kicks, airplane. As the young men rolled across the floor their sisters and aunties hooted and hollered from around the room. There was as much Inuktituk spoken as English, by both the children and the adults. They told us stories and jokes and teased each other amid gales of laughter. After all the social upheaval we'd seen, the kids running snot-nosed on the streets at midnight and stories of alcohol-fuelled violence, Jacob's home felt like a precious refuge. Maybe the Inuit culture of family, respect for elders and traditional language had a chance of winning out over junk food, television and monotonous hours of cruising dusty town streets on an ATV. It was after midnight by the time we said our farewells, a bag of caribou under our arms and our bellies full of meat and tea.

When we arrived in Gjoa Haven I had yet another repair job ahead of me. I had to sort out why *Silent Sound*'s batteries were not charging properly. Despite cleaning the battery connections and making all the checks I could think of, I had not yet found the problem. On Monday morning, our second day in Gjoa Haven, I set off into town to hunt for new batteries. Bulges on the sides of my batteries suggested they'd come to the end of their life. Neither the Co-op nor Northern store carried suitable batteries, so I went to the hamlet shop, where town workers maintained Gjoa Haven's dump trucks, road graders and other heavy equipment. The mechanics found some new batteries but said they'd have to charge $600 each for what were just normal truck batteries. The price sounded high even to them, and they promised to double-check on it. That night we went aboard *Baloum Gwen* for dinner, something we'd done at nearly every port we'd met them in. When Thierry heard about my problems he offered me a set of spare batteries he was carrying. They were larger than mine, and a different voltage, but with some alterations they would fit.

Two days later I returned to the hamlet garage, and the workers told me the batteries would cost only $150 each, rather than $600. But by then we had Thierry's batteries aboard and Hanns had nearly completed the installation while the rest of us were hunting caribou. But the cables from the old batteries didn't fit the new batteries. Neither of the two stores in

Gjoa Haven sold battery cables or terminals, so once again I had to get creative. Angus, a Newfoundland immigrant who did the maintenance at Northern Inns, gave me a few bits of brass piping which I hammered flat to make my cable ends. He also came aboard to give us some advice, again revealing our woefully inadequate mechanical knowledge. I took the parts he gave me to the power station, where they gave me some heavy copper cable to connect them. Then I trudged over to the town housing department, where they let me use their soldering gear and drill press to turn the bits of copper into cable ends and solder it all together. We connected the new batteries and *Silent Sound* purred to life.

While we worked on *Silent Sound* another sailor came by to ask for help. Uwe was a German sailor who was travelling the seas with his partner Kathrin aboard *Perithia*, a Bavaria 44 sailing boat. They were having trouble with the heat sensor on their engine, so Angus went to their boat to offer advice, with Hanns along as translator. Uwe was a tall, skinny man wearing tattered grimy clothes and long unkempt blond hair. His appearance matched his approach to sailing. He was attempting to sail the Northwest Passage without proper charts, and it had already led him into trouble. He was transiting from east to west, and he had become lost as *Perithia* had approached Gjoa Haven from the north. He had turned into a bay to the north of the town, mistakenly thinking it would lead him to the harbour. Instead, he found himself sailing in circles in a large, shallow bay, with the water depth dropping to two metres at times. It had taken him nearly an entire day to find his way to Gjoa Haven, even though it was only a few miles away. Now he sheepishly asked if he could study our charts and make some copies. I gladly lent him charts and pilot books, aghast at how ill-prepared he was.

It was late in the evening by the time I left the workshop and walked to the beach where the rowing dinghy was pulled up onto the sand. It was a chilly 2°C, but the sky was clear and shining a deep blue, with a rind of orange glow on the horizon. There were no clouds or smog, just a deep pool of colour studded with a few winking stars that were reflected in the smooth bay. I pushed the boat out onto the glassy water and hopped in, sending ripples creeping off into the night. *Silent Sound*, *Baloum Gwen* and *Perithia* hung from their anchors atop perfect reflections, the images of their masts stretching far out into the bay. At first it seemed deathly silent, with only the hollow thud of my oarlocks echoing across the water. But then I began to hear the gentle sounds of an Arctic town at night.

Chained sled dogs yipped and howled in their forlorn way. Somewhere in the hills behind town an ATV droned down a road. The voices of a few children playing on the beach carried across the water, tiny and shrill, but muffled by darkness. As I neared *Silent Sound* I could hear voices coming from her saloon, the warm glow of cabin lights spilling through her portals and onto the deck. Drew was busy in the galley, cooking caribou stew, and the smell reached me while I was still on the water. I drifted for a moment, soaking up the beauty and domestic bliss of the scene. My life in Hong Kong—a rush of jobs, socializing and urban life—seemed a lifetime away. I had travelled extensively around the world, through deserts, mountain ranges and seas in cultures vastly different than mine. But never had I felt as far away from home as I did in the Arctic. Even though I was in my native country, surrounded by people who could speak my language, "home" felt very, very far away. Perhaps it was because aboard a sailing yacht you feel each mile you travel, living it through the waves, wind and weather.

"The white man's customs go the way of the mist," Harold Noice wrote of the Arctic in his book *With Stefansson in the Arctic*. "The world of newspapers, business, telephones, ballot-boxes, and jazz seems in memory no more real than his dream does to the sleeper awakened. Is it possible that somewhere out there are people even now are being ostracized by their kind for eating olives with a fork or peas with a knife? People who judge a man by his grooming, his bank account, or his ancestry? Our new world has stripped us to the fundamentals, and it is salutary, if not a little humbling, to reflect that these fundamentals—intelligence, character, and health—are not peculiarly human, that they are the same with men, with horses, with dogs and with ants."

I was happier than I'd felt in a long time on this journey. Finally, I thought, we've got all of the boat's problems sorted out. I was tired—people told me I looked exhausted—but I felt we'd fallen into an easier rhythm now. Tobias and I were still not getting along, but I'd pushed that problem aside. I couldn't see us solving our problems on this trip so I tried to ignore the friction between us. He and Drew found good company in each other, and they'd spent much of their time in Gjoa Haven wandering the town and making friends with the children on the street. Hanns continued to spend more time on the boat than any of us when we were in port, enjoying the chance for some quiet solitude while making small repairs and looking after much of the maintenance. The voyage had shifted gears now that we were on our way home. We also had the best ice forecasts we'd had in the entire journey, giving us renewed confidence for the next leg of our voyage.

On our first day in Gjoa Haven Captain Mark Taylor of the CCGS *Sir Wilfrid Laurier* invited us aboard for a tour of the ship, ice briefing and Sunday lunch. Bruno Barrick, the ship's ice expert, explained that despite earlier forecasts there was more ice blocking the passage in 2009 than there had been in both 2007 and 2008, but it was still far below historical averages. An exceptionally cold winter in 2008–09 had created thicker first-year ice than in recent years, meaning it was taking longer than usual to melt. Bruno said that with heavy ice remaining in Peel Sound, we would be better off sailing through Bellot Strait, a narrow ribbon of water separating Somerset Island and Boothia Peninsula that is notorious for its vicious currents and crushing ice floes. Although the latest satellite images showed heavy ice towards the western end of the strait Bruno expected it to clear within the next few days. In order to get to Bellot Strait we needed to make our way through James Ross Strait, which was open water, and through Larsen Sound and into Franklin Strait, which both held bits of older ice. As the first-year ice melted it allowed the multi-year ice—thicker and slower to melt—to drift south into our path. However, because there wasn't a heavy concentration of older ice we should be able to sail around it without too much trouble.

Following Bruno's briefing the crew of the icebreaker gave us a tour of the ship and told us about their scramble to assist the sailing yacht *Fiona* a few days earlier. *Fiona*, skippered by Eric Forsyth, a winner of the Blue Water Medal of the Cruising Club of America, was making an east to west transit of the Northwest Passage. She was caught in heavy ice in Larsen Sound, and the tightly packed ice had begun to lift the boat out of the water. The crew had contacted the Coast Guard headquarters, which told *Sir Wilfrid Laurier* to go assist the yacht, about 434 miles to the northeast. The icebreaker quickly wrapped up its work in Cambridge Bay and began steaming towards the yacht at full power on all three main engines, instead of operating on one engine as it normally does. *Sir Wilfrid Laurier* started out for *Fiona* at mid-morning on August 17th. That evening at 1830 hours they listened to Peter Semotiuk's radio net, on which they heard that the yacht was no longer in trouble. Mark, the icebreaker captain, passed this information on to Coast Guard headquarters, which eventually reached *Fiona* to confirm they were no longer in need of help. Just before midnight, some 12 hours after they'd been sent on their mission, *Sir Wilfrid Laurier* stood down. Despite their professionalism the ship's crew struggled to hide their indignation. They said *Fiona* had not contacted the Coast Guard to tell them they were safe, as they should have done. While all mariners are obligated to respond to a mayday, the Coast Guard goes a step further to assess whether the situation could become an emergency and considers pre-emptive action in order to prevent a full-blown emergency. Even though *Fiona* had not issued a mayday, the Coast Guard had scrambled an icebreaker anticipating that the yacht's problems would likely become more serious in the coming hours. With the yacht some 40 hours from the nearest rescue ship at normal cruising speeds they wanted to get help underway as quickly as possible. We felt lucky to have avoided that kind of drama and grateful to know how responsive the Coast Guard was even at these high latitudes.

On the morning of August 27th, after three days in port, we were ready to leave Gjoa Haven. There was just one more thing to do before leaving, and that was to have a hot shower. We had heard that most RCMP detachments had showers attached to their holding cells, so Tobias and I went to the detachment to try our luck. We banged on the heavy steel door, and after a long wait an officer unlocked it. We explained who we were, and asked if we could use their showers. At first the officer who opened the door flatly refused and tried to send us on our way. But we pled our case. I reminded him that policing was about preventing crime as well as catching criminals. "And letting us go another day smelling like this would be a crime," I said. He groaned at my weak joke and ushered us through the door.

After we'd had our showers we asked if we could take a picture with the two officers on duty, one on a full time assignment to Gjoa Haven and the other on a short-term transfer from Toronto. The officer from Toronto refused, explaining that he was an undercover police officer and he didn't want pictures of him in uniform circulating the internet. He was the only black person we'd met anywhere in the Arctic. A black police officer working undercover in the Arctic? After an awkward silence and looks of disbelief on our faces, he quickly explained that he wasn't working undercover in the Arctic, but that he did so in Toronto, and taking photos in uniform could jeopardize his job.

By noon we were underway, and the first 24 hours of sailing were perfect. We reefed the mainsail and genoa and sailed north in a steady northwesterly wind. It was sunny and still 5°C by 2100hrs. In the evening the sky darkened and the northern lights came out, once again creating a magical night on the Arctic seas. Tobias and Drew barbequed grizzly bear steaks with baked potatoes for dinner, and all was well aboard *Silent Sound*. At around midnight we passed a small southbound cargo ship, the first we'd seen in the Arctic so far. We hailed her on radio, and the officer on watch told us to expect 3/10th to 4/10th ice beyond James Ross Strait. We were sailing through Rae Strait, a narrow, protected waterway running between King William Island and the mainland. It is a key point in the passage, as the alternative, Victoria Strait, is often choked with ice. The strait is named after the man who discovered it, John Rae, a Scottish doctor who explored huge swaths of the Canadian Arctic on foot.

Rae is the greatest unsung hero of Arctic exploration. By 19 he had completed medical school and was shipped to Canada to work as a doctor for the Hudson's Bay Company in Moose Factory on the far southern tip of James Bay. He would spend a decade exploring northern Canada from this base, walking hundreds of miles through the forests and tundra in order to survey the Arctic coastline and search for Franklin. He, like many successful Arctic explorers, turned his back on the narrow-minded ways of the xenophobic British establishment and instead asked aboriginals and the Inuit for advice on how to travel the land. He wore fur clothing and learned to make and repair his own equipment. He was renowned even amongst the Indians for his toughness and endurance on the land, and in one trip he snowshoed from Lachine, near Montreal, to Moose Factory—more than 800 kilometres as the crow flies.

Rae solved two of the greatest mysteries of the Arctic. He was the first to reveal the fate of the Franklin expedition, and he found one of the last missing links of the Northwest Passage. In 1853 Rae was travelling on King William Island when Inuit told him a story about a crew of starved and dying white men who were walking south in search of the mainland. Rae proceeded to buy Franklin relics such as silver cutlery, buttons and a gold hatband from the Inuit, and brought the first news of Franklin back to England. He also discovered that King William Land was really an island, separated from the mainland by a stretch of water later named after him. Half a century later Amundsen would prove Rae right when he used this route to make the first transit of the passage, going east of King William Island in order to avoid the heavy ice in Victoria Strait, just as we were doing.

Despite his contributions Rae was never accepted as a hero in Britain. When he returned with the Franklin artefacts and stories of the expedition's demise he also brought the grisly news that the men had succumbed to cannibalism in their last days. The Inuit told him that they had found bodies that had been cut up in ways that could only mean that the dead had been eaten to keep the living on their feet for a little while longer. This was too much for Victorian England to accept, particularly because the story came from the Inuit, who the English still regarded as wild savages. Lady Jane Franklin in particular did whatever she could to discredit Rae and his story, haughtily dismissing that her husband's crew would have succumbed to such measures. She succeeded in taking him off the books as the discoverer of the Northwest Passage, claiming that Franklin had found the route himself before dying. Although Rae eventually did receive credit and a financial reward for discovering the fate of Franklin's expedition, he was never knighted, an honour given to many lesser Arctic explorers.

We had made a special connection with Rae's legacy as we departed from Victoria. Our friends Norman and Trudi Prelypchan had told Robert MacRae about our expedition. Robert is a former rector and the founder of the Clan MacRae Society of Canada. Robert wrote a prayer for our safety, which was read just before we sailed out of harbour, and gave us a Scottish flag to carry through the Rae Strait.

The next morning we encountered a few bergy bits as we entered James Ross Strait between low, unremarkable headlands. We were tacking directly into the wind as we worked our way through the narrow strait, happy for the one-and-a-half knots of current in our favour. Despite our good sailing conditions my mechanical nightmares had returned. Our batteries were still not charging properly. The constant repairs had begun to make me feel vulnerable aboard *Silent Sound*, even though they were to be expected on a voyage of this distance and difficulty.

Once we were through James Ross Strait and in open water we stopped to once again look for the problem. Tobias had earlier suggested that there might be a loose wire somewhere, that perhaps something had come loose when we were working on the engine in Cambridge Bay. I had carefully inspected all the cables I could find and the connections were now all clean and tight. Once again I opened up the engine compartment and hung over the edge. I groped at the cables I was able to see, tugging at them to make sure they were tight. I had already decided the problem did not lie with the alternator because my tests showed that it was producing a charge, but I inspected it once more for good measure. I climbed deep into the engine compartment to get a fresh point of view of the alternator. There, hidden behind and underneath the alternator, I

found the culprit. A small ground wire snaked out the back of the alternator and was screwed to the engine—all hidden from my view until now.
I tugged at it, and it wiggled. I had to remove the alternator in order to
tighten the wire, but once I did the battery charge began to climb.

I was embarrassed. Not only had I failed to find the problem despite
hours of painstaking investigation and reading of shop manuals, but I
hadn't paid enough attention to Tobias's suggestion that something like
this could be the problem. I felt inadequate to be in charge of *Silent
Sound*. First I'd failed to detect the broken engine mounts, and then I'd
passed over the loose wire dozens of times. And those were only two of
my biggest mistakes. Being humbled my own mistakes had become a
daily occurrence aboard *Silent Sound*. I'd set off for the Arctic with very
little mechanical knowledge or experience, and I'd leave with not much
more than I'd had when I set out. But I had learned a lot about humility.

# CHAPTER 10
# Zenith Point

*We're as far North as I want to come,*
*But Larsen's got us under his thumb,*
*And I signed up for the whole damned run,*
*I can't get off half way.*
*But when I get back onto the shore,*
*I'm going South where it stays warm,*
*And there'll be someone on my arm*
*To help me spend my pay,*
*So I'll take it from day to day.*
—Stan Rogers, "Take it From Day to Day," 1999 (posthumous)

The fog that rolled in on the night of August 29th left us feeling our way forward like blind men. Even worse, we had re-entered the ice. The entire Boothia Peninsula coastline was a maze of 1/10th to 3/10th multi-year ice. Drew joined me on deck as an extra lookout, shouting warnings from the bow. The fog muffled his voice.

We slowed the boat to a crawl, barely making two knots as we edged our way forward. The ice materialized from the darkness as a dull grey smudge on the water. It was hard to see how large the floes were until we were within a few metres of them. Eddies of fog swirled over the surface of the sea and every small break in the gloom raised our hopes that we were finally clear. But then another cloud would swallow *Silent Sound* and the ice that surrounded us. Adding to my discomfort was the knowledge that somewhere in this area, underneath the sea, were Franklin's ships, the HMS *Erebus* and HMS *Terror*.

Summer was nearly over and a thin skin of new ice was starting to form on the sea at night. It crackled and snapped as *Silent Sound* pushed her way north. The temperature of the water in our tanks fell to -1°C at night and we worried that the water lines would freeze. The fog began to clear shortly after midnight. Sunrise brought a sense of freedom and relief. The sky turned orange, illuminating the ice, and the warmth of the sun soon raised the air temperature from near freezing to 5°C. The ice that covered *Silent Sound*'s deck at night quickly melted in the morning sunshine.

By noon we were passing the red rock of the Tasmania Islands, which rise 170 metres above the sea. The islands are surrounded by small bays and channels, and with sunny skies overhead it was tempting to stop and explore the outcropping. But we were eager to get to the mouth of Bellot Strait, promised to be one of the most difficult parts of our journey.

By afternoon we were in Franklin Strait, with Prince of Wales Island to port. The land was rising higher from the sea with each mile sailed north. Sharp clefts in the mountains created narrow fjords. Raised beaches, created by the slow rebound of the land after the downward pressure of the last ice age, formed terraces along the shore.

It was nearly midnight as we approached the mouth of False Strait, just to the north of Bellot Strait. Our plan was to drop anchor for the night and leave with the next day's tide in order to get a push through the strait. The land here rose almost vertically from the water, hemming us in. We entered False Strait in darkness and tried anchoring near its mouth, but the water was too deep and the bottom too rocky for the anchor to hold. Slowly we pushed farther up False Strait, which is actually an inlet (hence its name). The bottom began to shoal and we could see a rocky beach ahead. The bottom here was good holding, but several large pans of ice threatened to drift down on us from upwind. I was worried the ice might catch our anchor chain, so I manoeuvred *Silent Sound* to the side of the inlet, so close to the rocky walls we had to crane our necks to see their tops. The anchor chain rattled through the hawser, echoing off the hills and we were stopped for the night.

While Tobias and I guided *Silent Sound* into the anchorage, Drew was busy in the galley cooking caribou bolognese. We shucked off our oilskins, lit the heater and got ready for another Saturday night in the Arctic. Soon the saloon was warm and cozy and filled with the smell of dinner. We turned on the stereo and opened a bottle of wine given to us in Cambridge Bay. Spirits were high, although Hanns was a little groggy with a cold and flu. We were about to tackle one of the last big challenges of our journey.

Our plans for a morning hike were dashed by a cold, grey drizzle. Instead, I cooked a large breakfast and we had a quiet morning aboard *Silent Sound* reading, writing and doing chores. After almost three months of sailing we were tired and needed quiet mornings like this to relax and refocus. Boots and socks hung above the heater to dry as the crew climbed into their bunks with books and journals, seeking privacy.

We raised anchor at about 1300 hours and headed for the mouth of the strait, our eyes peeled for polar bears. We had yet to spot one, and I'd begun to worry I would sail the entire Northwest Passage without seeing one. Other boats, including *Baloum Gwen*, had seen bears in this area in recent days, and they predicted we would see one as well.

Just as we entered Bellot Strait we met David Crowley aboard *Polar Bound*, a rugged motor yacht, making his third transit of the passage (and second solo one). Meeting another vessel in the lonely Arctic is cause for excitement. "We have company!" I shouted to Tobias and Drew, who were below deck. After all the talk and anticipation of bears they assumed the company was big and furry. Tobias came hurtling up the companionway, all elbows and camera lenses.

Drew, busy in the head, called through the door for clarification. Tobias shouted that it was the *Polar Bound*. To Drew's eager ears it sounded like "polar bear." Drew is not a man to miss a good photo opportunity and he was on deck in a surprisingly short time, looking a bit flushed and hard-pressed but clutching his usual jumble of cameras. He was visibly disappointed to see a small yellow ship beside us. He half-heartedly snapped a few photos and then slipped back into the cabin without a word. When he returned to the deck a few minutes later he confessed that he'd been in a bit of a rush to finish his task in the head when he'd heard the word "bear." After learning the truth, he thought he'd better go back for a second cleanup. "I don't have many pairs of clean underwear left," he explained sheepishly.

Seeing David wasn't as exciting as spotting a bear, but we hailed him on the VHF radio anyway. He told us he was seeing less ice in the Arctic than in any of his previous voyages. We chatted about weather and ice conditions as our boats wallowed in the swell. I had his book *Northwest Passage Solo* aboard and wished I could get him to sign it, but handing it from boat to boat at sea would have been more trouble than it was worth. Soon his yacht was chugging west, thousands of miles to go on his planned circumnavigation of North America.

And then we were alone, facing Bellot Strait, an 18-mile long channel connecting the Gulf of Boothia and Prince Regent Inlet with Peel Sound and Franklin Strait. The strait was discovered in 1852 by a ship searching for Franklin and named for Lieutenant Joseph René Bellot, a French Navy officer aboard the British ship. The strait was first crossed by the Hudson's Bay Company ship *Aklavik* in 1937 and by our count only eight private sailing yachts, including *Baloum Gwen* and *Ocean Watch* days earlier, had made it through since. Fast currents and unpredictable ice conditions have given the strait a sinister reputation.

Entering Bellot Strait is like jumping onto a waterslide at an amusement park. Once you have started, there's no turning back. The land on either side of the strait towers as much as 300 metres above the sea. Because the strait is less than half a mile wide at points, the currents can reach eight knots, faster than our engine could push us if we needed to retreat. To complicate matters, the strait is rarely ice-free from end to end. Ice conditions change within minutes, and you're likely to run into ice at the eastern end even if the western end is clear.

Magpie Rock is one of the strait's greatest dangers. It sits smack in the middle of the eastern entrance, awash at low water, but because of the current it is rarely visible, making it a constant navigational danger. The rock is surrounded by violent rip tides and eddies, and a large shoal reaches out into the navigable channel. Ice floating in the strait during the eastbound stream can get caught on the rocks and shoals, creating the equivalent of a brick wall at the end of your waterslide.

The pilot guide offers detailed, if daunting, instructions on how to approach the channel. It warns that "mariners should exercise extreme caution in this area. Passage … should be timed to pass Magpie Rock near slack water [to] permit a reduction of speed to avoid damage if ice is struck…"

It goes on to describe a westward attempt by survey ship *Baffin* in 1977. A reconnaissance helicopter sent by the *Baffin* found only open water. However, when the *Baffin* had entered the strait three hours later it encountered 9/10th ice, and soon the ship was stuck in solid older (and harder) ice that was under extreme pressure due to the current. The *Baffin* had to run its engines at full power for two hours to keep up with the tide and avoid being crushed by the ice. The account ends with this cheerful advice: "From this experience it appears the ice reports cannot be relied on unless they are less than 30 minutes old…"

Our ice reports were several days old. But we knew that *Baloum Gwen* had made it through a day earlier, and we crossed our fingers that conditions had not changed much since.

Despite the dire warnings, Bellot Strait turned out to be much less dramatic than advertised. Perhaps it was because it was cold, rainy and foggy, and the weather hid the impressive cliffs on either side of the strait. Or, maybe it went smoothly because we took careful precautions as advised. The current swept us along at 9.5 knots at one point and, as promised, there were some large chunks of multi-year ice grounded on the rocks at the eastern end. But we were able to steer around the ice and out of the channel.

The day's highlight was passing Zenith Point, the most northerly point of the North American continent, at exactly 72°N. But the landmark wasn't much more dramatic than the rest of the strait—it looked like any other part of the foggy shoreline. We took pictures anyway, because it was there, and because we were some of the few people to have made the trip. We toasted it with mugs of steaming tea as we huddled in the cockpit, trying to drum up some excitement for this pivotal point in our journey.

Although Bellot Strait turned out to be a pleasant disappointment, our exploration of Fort Ross, an abandoned trading post at the eastern end of the strait, more than made up for it. This was where Francis Leopold M'Clintock sought shelter for his ship the *Fox* in the winter of 1858–1859, as he combed the Arctic for signs of Franklin.

Lady Jane Franklin, frustrated by the Admiralty's waning interest in the search for her husband, bought the *Fox,* a three-masted schooner with auxiliary steam power, and asked M'Clintock to continue the search. M'Clintock had gained considerable Arctic experience over three earlier searches of Franklin, and had earned a reputation as an expert on human-hauled sleds, the favoured form of ice travel for the Royal Navy despite the obvious drawbacks over dogsled.

M'Clintock sailed into the Arctic via Lancaster Sound, spending the first winter being swept back into Baffin Bay by the ice. In the spring the *Fox* retraced her route, making it as far as Beechey Island. There, at Lady Franklin's request, M'Clintock raised a memorial to her husband. He then sailed south down Prince Regent Inlet to the mouth of Bellot Strait. He set up camp at the site of Fort Ross, preparing to send sledging teams across the ice looking for Franklin. M'Clintock built a cairn on the top of a hill overlooking the small bay. The cairn remains there today, holding bottled messages left by more recent visitors. M'Clintock went on to explore the surrounding coastline all the way south to King William Island. He found a cairn near Point Victory containing the only written record left by Franklin and his men. The letter documented Franklin's death and the attempts of the remaining crew to escape the Arctic.

Eighty years later, the British returned to the eastern end of Bellot Strait. This time they were searching for profits. The Hudson's Bay Company build Fort Ross in 1937 to link the company's eastern and western fur trading regions. Even though the nomadic Inuit in the area constituted a trading market, the location proved to be a logistical nightmare. Ice continually choked Bellot Strait and its approaches and made it hard to supply the fort and its traders. At one point the fort had to be evacuated by airplane after being blocked by ice for two years. As a result, Fort Ross was abandoned only 11 years after it was built.

It was early evening when *Silent Sound* dropped her anchor in Depot Bay, the harbour in front of Fort Ross. A blanket of low cloud gave the entire place a dreary, forlorn look. There was no one home, and no one else within hundreds of miles of the fort. Drew and I lowered the kayak into the water and paddled ashore while Tobias and Hanns remained aboard, with Tobias starting a batch of bread. *Baloum Gwen* had passed this way a day earlier and sent us a message that they had left a "present" for us in one of the cabins.

The fort reminded me of an English garden, with a sense of orderliness out of place in the Arctic wilderness. Neat footpaths lined with rocks run between the cabins and the flagpole and throughout the grounds of the small settlement. The cozy cabins stand in stark contrast to their bleak environment. The manager's house, however, is dilapidated and overrun by wildlife. Polar bears have left their claw marks on the wall while a dead Arctic fox lies rotting on the kitchen floor. But in other parts of the house it was not hard to imagine the life of a 19th century fur trader. Two ratty, over-stuffed armchairs remain in the parlour, pulled up next to a small stove and wooden bookshelves. An old kettle sits atop of the stove, ready for afternoon tea. This is where the traders would have spent long evenings, reading, smoking and looking out of the window at the barren landscape. Flowery wallpaper hangs in tatters from the walls and rusty bedframes stand abandoned in the tiny bedrooms.

The second building was once the Hudson's Bay Company trading house. Today, it is a hunting and expedition cabin. The white paint on the walls, with green and red trim, is faded and peeling, but the walls and ridge line are still straight. The windows and doors are blocked by heavy boards to keep bears out. I was carrying the hunting rifle slung across my back just in case we ran into one of those bears. While that was a frightful prospect, we were secretly hoping to see one.

Drew and I dragged an empty 45-gallon oil drum to the doorway and I clambered up to pull away the boards. Once we uncovered the door we saw a message scrawled in marker pen: "The key is under the southeast corner of the cabin." Bears, after all, can't read. The magnetic pull of the North Pole had affected not only *Silent Sound*'s compass, but also Drew's sense of direction, and he began digging under the northwest corner of the cabin. After some remedial navigation we found the key and threw open the door. The first thing we saw was a plastic bucket containing three huge Arctic char left by the crew of *Baloum Gwen*.

The cabin is well equipped for hiding from winter storms. In the middle of the main room sits an oil-burning heater, connected to a drum outside. Bunks line one wall, with a tidy kitchen in the corner. The shelves are stocked with tea, sugar, jam and other staples. Candles and a box of matches ensure we're not left in the dark. A stack of bear bangers, similar to firecrackers, lay at the ready, as polar bear researches often use the cabin. Travellers have scrawled graffiti on the walls to mark their passing, and each visiting yacht has drawn a small picture of their ship. *Silent Sound* joined the list, looking a bit stubby and slow, but on the record books all the same.

At the back of the cabin a set of stairs lead to the second floor, which once would have been used to store furs. Now it holds a camp toilet, a small library of pulp fiction within easy reach. The "throne" is open to the rest of the room, with the window next to it offering a lovely view of the approaches to Bellot Strait.

After exploring the cabin Drew and I collected our fish and returned to *Silent Sound* for dinner.

The next day we pack a lunch, shoulder the rifle and row ashore for a hike. From the small area of level ground along the beach, where the cabins stand, the land folds into a maze of hills and valleys as we walk inland. The land is a dull orange and appears barren at a distance. But at our feet there is an explosion of coloured lichens. White, orange, red and brilliant green lichen clings to the rocks and spreads across the land. In the valleys and along the small creeks grass grows in thick hummocks. Walking on the hummocks is like hopping across a river on stepping stones. If you miss, or your boot slips off one of the round wobbly knobs of soil, you will plunge into a soupy bog.

We examine M'Clintock's cairn, then head off across the hills, Hanns in the lead with the rifle across his shoulder and GPS in his hand. Living at sea has weakened our legs, and it feels good to climb the hills and feel a burn in our thighs. Hanns, who has discovered a love for hiking on the few excursions we've taken on this journey, leads us up a narrow gully and to a hilltop shrouded in clouds. Up here the rock is bald and unforgiving, with only the occasional sprout of grass or moss breaking the greyness. Small round caribou droppings nestle in the hollows of the rock, with bits of fur clinging to the few plants that manage to survive.

It's a cold and blustery day and as soon as we stop hiking the chill sets in. Hanns is still fighting the flu and is keen to get back to the shelter of the cabin. We stop for a drink and snack and then Hanns leads the way back. I follow him, while Tobias and Drew wander off to take their own route back.

Once back at the cabin Hanns and I wait for some time and then grow worried. We have not seen any bears, but we know they're in the area, and Tobias and Drew are unarmed. I grab the rifle and retrace our steps, but I can't find them. I call out their names and my voice echoes across the empty land. As I turn back towards the cabin I spot movement along a hilltop. It's Drew, scrambling over a ridge. They have wandered along the seashore, looking for the cabin in the wrong direction. Soon we're all back in the cabin, enjoying hot drinks and the leftovers from our char barbeque the night before.

August 30, 1745 hrs

We have just raised anchor and are motoring into the Prince Regent Inlet. The sea is covered with a suffocating blanket of fog, leaving me blind at the helm. I watch the chart plotter carefully as I steer *Silent Sound* through the jumble of rocks and islands that block our way to the sea. At first, I feel fairly confident in my navigation, putting my blind trust in the GPS. But soon I realize that something is badly wrong. The position shown on the chart plotter doesn't match with what I can see, or can't see, in the heavy fog.

It looks like my position on the electronic chart is off by up to one mile, but I'm not sure in which direction the mistake lies. The compass is at a 90° variance from the chart plotter. The pull of the magnetic North Pole, which is more than 500 miles to our northeast, has rendered it useless. The electronic compass, which finds its direction from satellite signals, is inaccurate because satellite coverage in the Arctic is spotty. The electronic compass is not tracking my movement as I change the heading of the boat, and the movement of the two compasses do not match.

My hands tighten on the wheel as my eyes try to bore through the fog. I am surrounded by unbroken white, with only a few meters of grey seas to be seen around the yacht. The chart shows there should be an island just off to port, which matches with what I remember seeing when we came into this bay, so I edge in that direction, determined to locate it and confirm my location. *Silent Sound* sails ever closer to the island until the electronic chart shows we've sailed right over it. I cannot see the island. I have little choice but to follow my instinct and steer towards where I think I'll find open water, but by now my internal compass is as confused as all the other compasses aboard the boat. After another nervous 10 minutes of blind navigation *Silent Sound* breaks out of the thick fog. I eagerly point her towards the open sea, relieved that we didn't run aground.

I set a course for Creswell Bay, about 45 miles to the north, where we're told there's a good chance we will see belugas and narwhales.

The weather was not on our side. As September 1st dawned visibility remained less than 100 metres and a light rain began to fall. The wind built from the northeast until we were forced to put a second reef in the main and switch to our storm jib. *Silent Sound* began to wallow in the waves and our progress rapidly deteriorated.

Creswell Bay was a mess of steep grey waves, rain and fog when we arrived. We quickly realized that our whale-watching idea was not going to pan out. The 20 to 25 knots of northeasterly wind made it easy to sail into the bay, which opens to the east, but then we had to claw our way upwind and into growing seas to get back out. The long, narrow bay funnelled the wind and waves until it felt like we were sailing up a fire hose. There was also a strong tide running against us. At one point it swept us south—the opposite direction of where we wanted to go.

The wind held steady in both strength and direction, giving us no relief. We tried different sail combinations to work *Silent Sound* upwind, but she was a heavy boat with full keel and not designed to beat into the wind. We even dropped the sails to motor upwind, but it didn't improve our progress. All of September 1st was spent slowly working our way out of the bay and across Prince Regent Inlet. Our plan was to hug the coast of Brodeur Peninsula to get some shelter from the northeasterly wind and waves, making it easier to make miles to the north.

Finally, a day and a half later, we were clear of the bay and the northeasterly blow died to less than 20 knots. We took down the storm jib and unfurled some of the genoa, leaving the mainsail with two reefs. We remained within five to 10 miles of the steep coastline, where the seas were much flatter, and sailed north towards Lancaster Sound.

*Silent Sound* had been hard-pressed for the past two days, and everyone was cold, wet and tired. The outside temperatures hovered just above freezing, and with the heavy seas and constant heel of the boat we couldn't light the saloon heater. The cabin became a clammy cave. It stank of wet boots and dirty pots. Drew had huddled in his bunk for much of the past few days. It was too rough to cook or edit video and photos, and he struggled with seasickness. Tobias and I were still in no mood to chat with one another, and Hanns wasn't a big talker at the best of times. *Silent Sound*'s crew fell silent, quietly changing watches and pushing the boat into the wind hour after hour. I spent my long solo watches thinking of home.

The weather forecast didn't offer much comfort. The wind was predicted to hold for at least another day and we needed to watch for icebergs, which were hard to see in the fog. We spotted a few in the distance and turned the radar on for good measure, but we had plenty of open water to keep us safe. Icebergs posed less of a threat to us than the ice floes we had seen so much of in the past few months because the icebergs were easier to see. But we still had to watch for the smaller chunks of ice that broke off the iceberg because they were too small to be detected by the radar and hard to spot with the naked eye.

Most of the icebergs in eastern Arctic waters are from the Greenland ice sheet, and are made of fresh water, versus ice floes, which are frozen seawater. Icebergs began as snow on land. As the depth of the snow increases the lower layers are crushed by the weight of the new snow until it becomes dense and hard. The snow becomes ice. The ice in icebergs contains tiny bubbles of air created by the air trapped between the snowflakes. If you put a chunk of iceberg in water it will fizz as it melts and the air is released.

On September 3rd, at 1525 hours, we hit 73.55°N, the furthest north we'd make on this voyage. Our journey was a long way from over, but from here on we would be sailing south, towards home. *Silent Sound* seemed to understand this as she picked up her skirts and sped along in the steady breeze blowing through Lancaster Sound. Soon we were turning into Navy Board Inlet, skirting Bylot Island towards Pond Inlet, our next port of call. After days of heavy sailing and poor visibility we revelled in the favourable winds and stunning scenery. *Silent Sound* gybed back and forth down the winding channel, with the mountains of Borden Peninsula and Bylot Island on either side.

Huge icebergs floated in the centre of the inlet. They glowed an ethereal blue and white, with their massive underwater hulks shining a brilliant aqua. Their features varied radically from face to face, with one side showing the vertical wall where they broke free from the glacier, while the waves had carved other sides into swooping lines and curves. The harder ice protruded from the surface where it had resisted erosion, like a giant piece of old driftwood. Small hollows in the ice held pools of electric blue water.

Along the shore we could see glaciers creeping down the mountains, with massive ice faces where they met the water. Their sheer size, and the lack of anything—cars, houses, even a road—that could provide a sense of scale, made me think that the glaciers were close by. When I looked at the radar and chart I saw that they were still five miles away. The fan of silt and runoff below a mountain stream stretched a mile wide even though the stream was barely visible from where we sailed.

It began to snow as we approached Pond Inlet. The weather reminded us that winter was rapidly approaching, and knowing that made me anxious to run for home, chasing the migratory birds that had left the Arctic weeks earlier.

*Baloum Gwen* was also in Pond Inlet, having arrived only hours before us. It was the last port we would share with them before they sailed to Greenland and we turned south. *Ocean Watch* had already crossed the Arctic Circle as they sailed south on their long journey around the Americas. We went aboard *Baloum Gwen* for a final dinner with our friends, toasting our success with a bottle of gin. Although we had sailed through the heart of the Northwest Passage, we had decided that aboard *Silent Sound* we would not consider the passage completed until we had once again crossed the Arctic Circle. But there was still a sense of celebration, and after a long evening of sailing stories we agreed to meet the following day to visit a glacier on Bylot Island.

The next morning we clambered aboard Thierry's yacht and set off across the inlet while Drew and Tobias made themselves at home in *Baloum Gwen*'s galley, producing a steady stream of pancakes as we sailed. Once we reached the bottom of the glacier, Thierry, ever the daring lifeboat captain, nosed *Baloum Gwen* into the shore until we started bumping the sandy bottom. Finally we got the anchor set and hiked up the dirty mountain of ice. The glacier was breathtaking in scale even with the dramatic melting in recent years. Rivers of runoff had carved deep caves and tunnels through the ice.

After a picnic on the ice we turned back toward Pond Inlet, where the new Sauniq Inns North Hotel had just been built. So far only the restaurant was open for business. The hotel lobby was soon a mess of sailing gear and bags of dirty laundry as we made ourselves at home. We found the hotel's laundry room unlocked, and quietly helped ourselves to the facilities, careful not to let the employees catch us in the act. We sat in a conference room, patiently tapping into the slow, but free, Wi-Fi connection. After several hours a sympathetic hotel employee handed us a key to a large suite, and we took turns soaking in the hot shower and enjoying the thick fluffy towels. We complimented the staff on the comforts of their new hotel, but wondered how it would make money with such generous employees.

The waves were crashing onto the beach when we returned to the dinghy that night. Hanns, still our best and strongest oarsman, put the boat into position and Drew clambered in. Drew was wearing a giant waterproof backpack filled with our clean laundry as well as computers and cameras. I gave the dinghy a good push off the beach and they made it over the first wave with a few strong strokes.

Soon Hanns returned to pick me up, surfing the tiny boat onto the beach. I was carrying more computer and camera equipment and by now the waves had grown even larger. We attempted to launch the dinghy, but it turned broadside to the waves and was soon swamped. Hanns and I stood in knee-deep seas, bailing water out of the dinghy before we made another attempt. We made a half-dozen attempts to get past the breakers, and each time the waves threw us back onto the beach. We were soaking wet, but the water was a warm 6°C and the physical work kept the chill at bay. It was a beautiful night, with a bright moon and warm breeze, and soon we stopped worrying about getting wet as we worked to get the boat launched.

A few young Inuit men passed by and advised us to drag the dinghy down the beach to a more sheltered area, but large rocks along the shore threatened to break the boat apart, so we returned to the original launch site. Finally we spotted a break in the waves and pushed off with a few strong strokes. As soon as we made it through the surf the tension was broken, and we burst out laughing as we rowed towards *Silent Sound*.

The next day was Labour Day and Pond Inlet was closed for business. Aboard *Silent Sound* we celebrated by rising late in the morning. I changed the engine oil and the rest of the day was spent in a leisurely fashion, pecking out emails to family and friends and going for a long walk. I wandered aimlessly through the town until I found myself looking down at the sea from the top of a small cliff.

I was in Marvin Killiktee's backyard, where he was hard at work getting ready for the first snowfall. "If I don't pick this stuff up now, I'll never find it once there's snow," he said, carrying tools and bits of lumber to his house. "I'm looking forward to winter. Can't wait for the snow," he added with a grin. His snowmobile stood at the ready next to his house, also waiting for winter.

Marvin's home had a stunning view. It backed against Pond Inlet, and I could see where the channel cut through the mountainous land and led to the sea. Across the expanse of glittering blue water stood the snow-capped mountains of Bylot Island. Glaciers slid down the mountainsides in a swirl of white, blue and grey ice. It was the perfect lookout for a hunter and Marvin told me about the whales he had seen from this vantage point.

Marvin had just returned from a hunting trip in the interior of Baffin Island. Baffin is the biggest island in Canada, ranging 1,600 kilometres from end to end, filled with mountains, fjords and glaciers. Pond Inlet perches on its northern edge. Marvin pointed at a glacier across the inlet. "That glacier has really been disappearing in the past three years. It used to be a lot bigger, now it gets smaller every year." Marvin told me he recently saw a type of brown eagle that he didn't normally see at these latitudes. He interpreted the changes as a sign of rising temperatures.

Marvin had a job with the hamlet's housing department, but he still hunted to feed his family. "I'm worried that we could go hungry if the animals are hurt by all this," he said. "What can we do though, way up here? I know it's not just people down south causing it. We're to blame too, 'cause we have trucks and snowmobiles and we use a lot of energy. I guess we could go without electricity," he said. We both knew that solution was as impractical here as it was in the south.

As we stopped in different communities across the Arctic I asked many people for their views on climate change. Few had used the term climate change, and few spoke about it in the political, economic and theoretical language I'd become accustomed to hearing in the south. Here, people spoke of change in terms of the land and the wildlife and their survival within it. And they discussed it as just one more challenge facing their communities. Sunken building foundations, political wrangling over Arctic waterways, unpredictable sea ice: these were just the most recent challenges facing communities that were still struggling with the shift from nomadic hunting to suburban life that had occurred decades ago. Improving their schools, finding jobs for their children and hanging onto the remains of their culture were more important to them than a discussion about world climate patterns.

The people I had met over the course of my journey had also blurred the line in my mind between Arctic and suburban life in the south. Most of the romantic notions I had when I set sail were already dashed. Everything I'd seen told me that Northerners were living in a different place, but not in a different time. Their communities were isolated and set in a unique landscape and climate, but most aspects of their lives varied little from life in rural southern Canada.

That meant that, like in so many other places, the communities were looking to a new generation of leaders to take them forward. In Pond Inlet that responsibility had fallen on the shoulders of Abraham Kublu, the hamlet's 30-year-old mayor, and Colin Saunders, the 37-year-old economic development officer. Their elders knew what it had once meant to be an Inuit, living the "old life." It was Colin and Abraham's job to lead the community to understand who the Inuit were now, and who they could be in the future. Abraham was short and stocky, a messy head of dark hair falling into his eyes. He spoke little, and when he did the words fell out in a thick jumble. Colin was the more aggressive, energetic of the two, emphatically arguing his points and shifting restlessly in his chair.

"We're in a culture of transition here," Colin said. "Younger people are taking the initiative. There are a lot of great things the elders can teach us about the old ways, but we're not living the old way. There's always that [romantic] allure to the Arctic, and I always want to tell people before they come that I hope you find what you're looking for. You might not find it but I hope you do. I've slept in an igloo before and it's pretty damn cold. I like room temperature."

This was more than just a theory for the two young leaders. Baffinland Iron Mines was planning to develop its Mary River iron ore deposits, about 160 kilometres south of Pond Inlet. The Canadian company had taken bulk samples of iron ore and was doing its environmental assessments and other preparations. It could be Pond Inlet's greatest opportunity, bringing new jobs and investment, or it could deliver the final blow to the surviving traditional culture.

"We're looking for more support from people who have a lot more experience in these areas like dealing with environmental impacts with mines," Colin said. "We're more or less on the edge of Canada here, and there are not a lot of people up here with that experience. So we're looking to build relationships with other regional organizations who might be able to help us out, help scope it out and look at potential impacts that this project may have."

Colin was philosophical on the pros and cons of the mine, and what it could mean for life in Pond Inlet. He described the difficulty of convincing teenagers to stay in school when there was a scarcity of jobs for them when they graduated. Development of the mine could mean more jobs and offer some hope to youth who saw few options.

"A lot of the economy up here now is government-based," Colin said. "We have a lot of federal government employees with the schools and health centre as well as some with the regional government. We're trying to increase other means of getting money into the community."

Colin and Abraham also worried that unless they could improve the opportunities and activities available in town, any cash created by the new development would be misspent on booze, and the town's existing social problems would only become worse.

"[With the mine] there's the potential for a lot of jobs, but we're gonna have to look at a lot of socio-economic impacts as well," Colin said. "There may be more social problems, but hopefully more positive social things as well, and more infrastructure development. We'll need more recreational facilities, more stores. There's the potential for a lot of growth. We just have to make sure we're ready to manage it when it comes, if it comes."

Some of Pond Inlet's hunters were more concerned about putting food on the table than economic development. They said the helicopter traffic at the Mary River site had already disturbed caribou herds, which calve in the area. Others were concerned that Baffinland's access road, built alongside the Mary River, would cause the river to be ruined by silt and pollution. The river flows into a narwhal calving area and the mouth of the river is also an important fishing area.

"There are a lot of people who don't want to work and would rather just go out and hunt, and that's how they provide for their families," Colin said. "That area out there is sort of like their grocery store." He understands their concerns, but feels that some sort of change is inevitable.

"Losing any culture is a disaster. But you have to look at the big picture. Yes, we are moving to a monetary culture and society, and you have to try and embrace and hold onto what you have. Although you have to keep your culture, it's also important to learn a new one so you can maintain a balance and be able to survive in both."

Colin's words were still ringing in my ears as we prepared to sail home. Without the effects of climate change this voyage would have been much harder, maybe even impossible, especially on an ordinary fibreglass yacht like *Silent Sound*. We were not the first to make this voyage, and we were still far from home, but I felt a strong sense of accomplishment. I was proud at how *Silent Sound* had carried us through the seas and the teamwork and dedication of the crew and our friends ashore.

But most importantly we had met the people who were watching the changes, from day to day and year to year. Climate change meant far more than a sailing adventure for the people living in the Arctic. Economic development, sovereignty issues, social upheaval and the hunt for resources had once again put these fragile communities at a crossroads. There was change in the Arctic, and it threatened the Inuit ways of hunting, their culture and their food supply. Some of it was due to climate change, but their challenge was far more complex than that. I had begun my journey full of questions and preconceptions, and I had found a few answers. But more significantly, I had experienced some of the Arctic's beauty and harshness, and seen the bewildering conflicts between a traditional culture and modern reality.

# POSTSCRIPT

By September 8th we were ready to sail for home. We were still 2,500 miles from Halifax, with winter fast approaching. I had set October 10th as the date of our arrival, and friends and family from around the world were flying to Halifax to meet us. We would have to push hard to make it back in time, stopping only for fuel, short rests and to seek shelter from the worst of the autumn gales raking across the Labrador Sea.

Drew was flying home from Pond Inlet, leaving *Silent Sound* in the hands of her original crew. I knew when he joined that he would not be able to stay aboard for the voyage home, but I was sorry to see him go all the same. We lugged his gear ashore and he found a home to stay in until he could catch a flight south. Hanns, Tobias and I said goodbye to him on the beach and prepared to board the yacht for our departure.

*Silent Sound* was anchored a few hundred metres offshore, with a steady current sucking past the shore and out to sea. The waves had been building throughout the day and were rolling onto the beach in a crash of white foam. Hanns and Tobias crawled into the dinghy for the first trip to the yacht. I pushed them off from the beach, and Hanns got through the surf with a few strong strokes. Soon they were a hundred metres from shore, but instead of rowing towards *Silent Sound* the current swept them away from the yacht and towards the open sea.

Soon Hanns stopped rowing. The dinghy had suffered a hard summer of work, and now the second of its oarlocks had broken. The dinghy was insufficient from the start of the expedition, but I had kept it in order to save money. Tobias had complained bitterly about it all summer, rightly pointing out that a larger motorized one would have been better. We'd had some fun rowing the dinghy, and in most anchorages we had been able to make do with it, but it wasn't up to this task. Now the tiny fibreglass cockleshell bobbed in the cold grey seas as Hanns jury-rigged a new oarlock with a piece of rope, matching the other makeshift oarlock. Meanwhile the wind and current were pushing them farther and farther away from their goal. *Silent Sound* looked very far away indeed.

For 15 minutes Hanns and Tobias struggled against the current without making gains. I watched from the beach, becoming more worried by the minute. I checked the motorized fishing skiffs on the beach to see if I could use one of them to help them back to shore if it came to that. I called them on my handheld VHF radio and they responded that they were fine, but unable to get to the yacht. Eventually Hanns turned the dinghy back towards the shore, landing on the rocks about 50 metres down the beach from where they started.

Tobias was in a rage. He threw the oars ashore and spat out a stream of German curses as he climbed up the beach. Hanns sat silently on a rock, catching his breath. Hanns reassured me that he had not feared for his safety but that he was unable to make any progress into the current and wind. As soon as he stopped struggling against the tide and turned back to shore he'd regained control of the dinghy. Still, it had been a close call, and it was clearly not worth a second attempt. I reached Thierry on the VHF and soon he came puttering through the waves on his motorized dinghy. He gave us a lift to *Silent Sound*, towing our dinghy behind. We climbed aboard, wet, tired and quiet.

Tobias finally broke the silence with the announcement that he was thinking of getting off the boat and flying home from Pond Inlet. He didn't feel safe and thought I was putting his life in danger. It was the last thing I wanted to hear, but there was little I could do. Hanns and I could sail the boat home by ourselves if we had to, but it would be very difficult, and I did not want Tobias to abandon the trip this close to the end. I needed him to stay aboard, and I thought he would regret not finishing the voyage. I was confident that we were as safe as could be expected under the circumstances, and Hanns shared my view. But I couldn't make any promises to Tobias. He had to have his own faith in the boat and our skills. If he was afraid for his safety, the journey home would be even harder for him.

I asked Tobias to think about it until we'd had our dinner. If he still felt the same way, I'd get him ashore and we'd have to leave without him. It was the quietest dinner ever eaten aboard *Silent Sound*. When the dishes were done I asked Tobias for his verdict. He had decided to stay aboard.

It was dusk by the time we sailed into Baffin Bay and turned south. Forecasts called for strong northwesterly winds to give us a good push down the Baffin Island coast, and within 36 hours of leaving Pond Inlet we were running before a 30 knot wind and building seas. We soon furled the genoa, raised our storm jib and put an extra reef in the mainsail. The wind climbed to 40 knots and *Silent Sound* careened down the steep waves. We dropped the mainsail entirely, flying only the small, blaze-orange storm jib and continued running with the wind. The six to eight metre seas were steep and tightly packed, with the top metre curling and foaming as the waves bore down on our stern. The wind varied drastically in both strength and direction between the troughs and the peaks. It was hard work keeping the boat's stern into the growing seas, and occasionally a wave caught her broadside, filling the cockpit with water as it swept over the deck.

We no longer had to worry about sea ice, but now there was a new danger: icebergs. The massive bergs glowed in the darkness, rising high out of the sea and visible for miles. There was little chance of running into an iceberg. But the icebergs were calving, or breaking apart, and the smaller pieces, called growlers, were too small to be seen by radar and they often floated low in the water. By this late in the year the Arctic nights had once again turned dark, and with breaking seas it was nearly impossible to see the growlers. Occasionally as I steered *Silent Sound* down the back of a wave I would catch a glimpse of a growler, awash and nearly hidden from view. They terrified me. Hitting one could be catastrophic, but all we could do was hope we'd miss them and continue steering for home.

The sea finally took its toll on the afternoon of our second day out of Pond Inlet. I was nearing the end of my watch, and my shoulders burned with the effort of keeping *Silent Sound*'s stern to the seas. Hanns took over the last of my watch and I went below to get some rest. I sat at the navigation station, bracing myself with my legs as the boat rolled and pitched in the waves. Without warning a wave slammed into her port side and *Silent Sound* was thrown onto her beam ends. The impact launched me from my seat, and it was all I could do to hang on to the navigation station to avoid being thrown clear across the boat. The wave swamped the cockpit and carried off one of our fuel jugs, and Hanns, soaking wet, wrestled with the helm to regain control.

I returned to the navigation station, bracing myself as best as I could, to fill in the log book and look at the charts. We were sailing over an underwater ridge that was piling up the seas even worse than they had been earlier. Moments after I'd returned to my seat, once again bracing myself against the cabinetry, another wave caught us broadside, again throwing *Silent Sound* onto her side. This time I couldn't hang on, and I was thrown across the cabin and into the galley, where I cracked my head on the wall. I fell to the floor, dazed.

It didn't take long for Tobias to see that I had suffered a concussion. I was talking nonsense and feeling groggy, and sat on the cabin floor for a long time, trying to collect myself. Tobias cajoled me into my bunk, where I rested, dazed. Now Hanns was in charge, and he and Tobias took over my watch and steered us towards Clyde River, the nearest safe harbour while I lay in my bunk, tired, confused and with a pounding headache. At 0100hrs the chain rattled through the hawser and Hanns and Tobias fell exhausted into their bunks.

After about 36 hours of rest, refuelling and a trip ashore for showers, we were once again heading to sea. My head was still pounding with pain, and Tobias advised I stay in my bunk, so he and Hanns did the sailing and work aboard the boat. It would be more than a week before I was able to take over my watch again.

On September 15 we crossed the Arctic Circle. We had entered the Arctic via the Bering Sea two months earlier, and had sailed some 3,400 miles since. There are several definitions for the start and end of the Northwest Passage, but we had now completed it by the most encompassing of definitions. Tobias cooked up our last jar of Mennonite farmer sausage with some pasta, and we toasted the occasion with a few bottles of German beer he had kept tucked away the entire summer. It was sunny and clear, but chilly on deck with temperatures hovering between 0°C and 5°C.

The next day a drama unfolded unbeknownst to us, even though we were at the centre of it. Throughout the summer we had filed daily reports to the Coast Guard's Nordreg programme, giving them our location and sailing plans. The day we crossed the Arctic Circle I added a note that this would be our last message as we were sailing out of their monitoring zone.

There was a miscommunication, and when the Coast Guard didn't receive a position report from us the following day they contacted Tricia Schers, our media contact person in Winnipeg. The Coast Guard told her if they didn't receive word from us within a few hours they would be obliged to send out a search and rescue aircraft to check on us.

Tricia imagined the worst, and she was soon on the telephone to Troy Dunkley, who was managing the expedition website from Hong Kong, where he was still asleep in the wee morning hours. Troy was out of bed in a flash and checking *Silent Sound*'s live tracker. The tracker showed we were still underway. He sent me a message, asking if we were okay, and then tried to calm Tricia down. It was several hours before I saw the email, but when I did it took only a few quick messages back to my friends on land to reassure everyone we were still making steady progress towards home. All was well aboard *Silent Sound*. It was humbling to know how many people were looking out for safe return.

We watched the rugged Baffin Island coastline glide by day after day. Much of the time we were 15 or 20 miles offshore, and the coast was just a dark shape on the horizon, but occasionally we would sail towards it for a closer look. Each fjord and harbour tempted us to drop anchor and investigate, but we were in a rush to get to Halifax. The steady northwesterly winds were holding and giving us good average speeds. We needed to keep up the pace.

The nights were cold and crisp, the sky lit by stars and *aurora borealis*. I stood at the helm, neck craned skyward and mouth agape. I had grown up seeing northern lights on the Canadian Prairies, but these were more spectacular than anything I'd seen before. We were sailing through the Aurora Zone, roughly between 60° North and 72° North, where the lights are the most spectacular because it is the portion of the earth that traverses the midnight portion of the Auroral oval. This zone is centered around the magnetic North Pole and extends from northern Scandinavia to the southern tip of Greenland, southern Hudson Bay, central Alaska and the coast of Siberia.

Long whips of lights undulated across the sky, dissolving into darkness and reappearing in new colours. The colours changed from lime green to pink and then they would fade to white. At times the show reached such a crescendo that a shout would well up in my throat, only to be swallowed with the realization that a shout would probably wake my sleeping crew and bring them, startled, on deck. These were some of the most memorable night watches in my life, with the combination of natural beauty, exhaustion and bittersweet joy leaving me emotional. As eager as I was to get home the thrill of those nights made me sad that my adventure was nearing its end.

Icebergs glowed in the darkness, so big we would watch their approach for hours, then look astern to see them slowly sink beneath the horizon again. They were aliens, suddenly filling so much of the otherwise empty sea. Giants lost in the empty sea, slowly riding towards their death. One of the icebergs, several stories high, was home to a pod of harp seals. Harp seals are the parents of the famous white coats, who are deserted by their mothers when about two weeks old and were once clubbed to death for their furs on the east coast. They are now protected by law. As we approached, the seals began diving off the iceberg, somersaulting through the air and landing in the sea with a splash.

The seals would be the last Arctic animals we would see on the journey. But we had unwittingly carried a little bit of the Arctic wilderness south with us. The deep, pervading exhaustion we felt was accompanied by muscle cramps and soreness. My eyeballs ached, and I felt as if I was running a fever. Every time I awoke in my bunk my arms were cramped and painful to straighten. I thought I had caught a flu bug. But then an email arrived, hinting at something far more sinister.

In Cambridge Bay we had received a large chunk of grizzly bear meat, and we had shared it with the crews of *Baloum Gwen* and *Ocean Watch*. *Baloum Gwen* sailed from Canada to Greenland, and from there the crew flew to France. Several of them fell ill and were hospitalized in France, where doctors quickly diagnosed them with trichinosis, a type of roundworm infection acquired by eating larvae in meat. Trichinosis occurs primarily among carnivores, and humans contract it by eating the undercooked meat of carnivores. The larvae mature into adult worms in the intestine over several weeks, and the adults then produce larvae that migrate through various tissues, including muscle. The cramps, fever and aches I was feeling were caused by the larvae in my muscles.

French health authorities were alarmed. Although the disease is endemic in northern Canada due to the high meat consumption—rates are 200 times higher there than the national average—it rarely surfaces in Europe. Patrick Reader, a crewmember aboard *Baloum Gwen*, lay deathly ill in a Belgian hospital bed for weeks before an email from a fellow crewmember, sick in France, tipped doctors off to what he was suffering from. French researchers soon contacted the Canadian authorities, and the case was written about in medical journals and national newspapers.

The crews on *Silent Sound*, *Baloum Gwen* and *Ocean Watch* had all cooked the meat differently, and to different degrees. The French became the sickest of us all, indicating they had cooked their meat the least. I showed the most symptoms aboard *Silent Sound* while no one on *Ocean Watch* became ill. Although Tobias was sure that our exhaustion and illness was due to trichinosis, there wasn't much we could do while at sea. We decided to push on to Halifax and seek treatment there.

But the conditions were not ideal for a sick and tired crew. It was cold and damp, nearly as bad below decks as above. *Silent Sound*'s diesel burning heater had aged considerably over the course of the summer and developed a nasty habit of back-winding. This filled the entire cabin with acrid smoke and forced us to open hatches and turn the stove off, allowing all the heat to escape with the smoke. We had stopped using the heater while at sea, turning the cabin into a clammy cave. The bulkheads and portals dripped with condensation and our sleeping bags became dank refuges from the cold.

Early on the morning of September 17th we pulled into Brevoort Harbour, the site of a small radar station on a small island near the southern tip of Baffin Island, for a rest. It was a tiny harbour with only a single light showing at the top of the hill. It had been nearly a week since our last stop, and *Silent Sound* was due for maintenance.

It was a dark, overcast night as we pulled into the harbour. Usually we avoided entering unfamiliar new ports at night, but we were tired and eager to drop anchor. The charts showed a long narrow bay on one side, hemmed in by steep stone walls, with a small, exposed beach to the other side. There was a swell coming into the bay, and the entire harbour was exposed to the southeast, so we decided to anchor as deep in the narrow bay as we could, where the protection from the waves was the best. However, the chart showed a large rock just below the surface of the water in the middle of the bay we had chosen. We were blinded by darkness as we motored in, relying on our GPS to tell us where we were. I turned on the radar, but the inlet was too narrow and stone walls to close for the radar to be of any help. We steered *Silent Sound* into the bay and watched the depth sounder, searching for shallow water to drop our anchor. The entire bay was 20 to 30 metres deep, even when we crept so close to the stone walls that we had to crane our necks to see the tops. We carefully circled the inlet, watching our track on the chart plotter and staying clear of the submerged rock, before abandoning our plan. Instead we turned for the beach, and anchored just off the steep shore, ignoring the swell and floating ice that could potentially drag us ashore.

We spent the next day sleeping, eating and resting up for our next leg at sea. We didn't bother going ashore, opting instead to spend as much time resting as possible. *Silent Sound*'s fuel system had developed a leak, filling the boat with the stench of diesel fuel, so Hanns and I spent several hours trying to fix the leak. Tobias baked a cake and then jumped into the 1°C sea for a bath, his teeth chattering as he clambered back aboard and ran, naked and dripping into the heated cabin. Hanns and I opted for a deck shower, shivering in the 4°C air as we dumped buckets of frigid water over ourselves.

As I restarted the electronic navigation system to plan the next stage of the voyage, I realized there was one risk we had not been aware of as we entered Breevort Harbour. The electronic chart plotter showed us 100 metres ashore. I rebooted the system, but it continued to show us on the beach. The satellite coverage in this area, combined with the steep stone walls that were blocking our signal, were confusing our

GPS. It wasn't serious, now that it was daylight and we were safely at anchor, but if our signal had been scrambled a few hours earlier as we manoeuvred through the bay in the dark we could have torn the bottom out of *Silent Sound*.

After a 24-hour break we set off for Nain, Labrador, about 480 miles to the south. By now we were well clear of the ice and we were riding a favourable current. Still, *Silent Sound* was a slow boat, and we rarely averaged better than 5.5 knots of speed. It was a case of grinding on, day after day and mile after mile. I continued to struggle with bad headaches and dizziness from my concussion, and after attempting a return to the watch cycle I was forced to once again hand the boat over to Tobias and Hanns and retreat to my bunk. Tobias kept a close eye on me, instructing me to stay away from my computer and rest my brain. I tried to follow his instructions, but would sneak a little bit of time on the computer to send emails every day when he wasn't looking.

The first thing we noticed approaching Nain was the smell of trees. We had not seen trees since leaving Prince Rupert three months earlier, and seeing them again made me realize how much I'd missed them. We sailed through a long passage that wound between rocky islands before tying up at the town dock. I climbed up the ladder and onto dry land, relieved to be ashore for the first time since Clyde River, 11 days and nearly a thousand miles back.

We spent four days resting in Nain and waiting for a passing storm to blow itself out. Once again we found ourselves soaking up the kindness of strangers. Sarah Webb at the Atsanik Lodge fed us, handed over the keys to a room so we could enjoy a hot shower, and plied us with cold beers as we tapped into her Wi-Fi connection. We met Charley and Virtue Sims, pastors to a small, struggling church. We may not have spent much time in their pews, but they opened their home to us, feeding us and letting us do our laundry.

I was still feeling weak from the effects of my concussion and the trichinosis, but I spent several afternoons wandering into the nearby hills and shuffling down the gravel roads that led out of town. On one walk I found a hunter feeding his sled dogs. He had a box of frozen meat on the back of his ATV, and as he slung the ragged chunks to the ground the dogs erupted with a snarl. There was something distinctly wolfish about all the dogs I'd seen in the Arctic. They were working animals, not pets, and most of them were chained, for which I was glad. I watched the dogs sink their fangs into the meat, wolfing it down while a low whine rumbled in their broad chests. Soon their muzzles and paws were matted with blood. I felt no urge to pet them.

Nain felt like a border town, caught between the isolation and social problems associated with the Arctic and the accessibility and conveniences of the south. It had the first proper bar we'd seen since Dutch Harbor, and the trees and hills gave Nain a beauty that was missing in most northern towns. Goose Bay was only two days away by ferry, and Nain received a regular sprinkling of tourists on their way to the nearby Torngate Mountains National Park. Many of the men in town worked at the Voisey's Bay nickel mine, and there was talk of a new uranium mine in the future. But despite the job prospects and idyllic setting, Nain suffered from high rates of suicide, substance abuse and domestic violence, fuelled by the same issues of disenfranchisement we'd heard of in towns farther north.

But there was also hope. Matthew, a young Inuit man, and his friends had revived the community's interest in drum dance, scrounging up what little knowledge they could find and writing some of their own chants. Drum dances are one of the most important and communal of Inuit art forms, and Matthew was proud of the return to his roots. He and his troupe put on a show in an empty office on our last night in town. The setting was anything but traditional—neon strip-lighting overhead and the audience reclining in leather boardroom chairs—but the enthusiasm of the dancers, the deafening beat of the drums and the pride in their culture sent us on our way with a feeling of optimism.

We set of from Nain on September 26th with ringing ears, clean socks and about 1,000 miles left to sail. We returned to sea to beat into southerly winds, which soon built to 20 and 30 knots from the southeast, meaning we had to beat into the wind and a two-metre sea to make any progress. Every mile was made with the boat heeled hard over as we drove through fog and rain. The boat was once again a sodden mess below decks, and our oilskins were tattered and worn after living in them all summer, leaving us cold and wet to the bone. Cooking a solid meal in these conditions was out of the question, so we ate macaroni and cheese and instant soups.

After four days of this we were once again ready for a break and steered *Silent Sound* into Domino Harbour to wait for the wind to swing to the north. Domino Harbour is a tiny fishing village on Island of Ponds, just off the south eastern tip of Labrador. We entered the long, narrow bay in heavy wind, rain and fog, nervously watching the depth gauge as we worked our way deeper into its shelter. About a dozen houses and red-painted sheds were huddled around the bay, and the surrounding rocky hills had a thin covering of dead, yellow grass. A dilapidated old cannery was slowly slipping into the bay along one shore. We saw a few people peering at us through the fog from the shore, and an aluminum fishing boat buzzed by us late in the night, but other than that the land was silent and unmoving. The charts showed a small town named Black Tickle just over the hill, but we were content to stay aboard and rest.

The next 18 hours were spent sleeping, drying out the boat and our clothing and cooking hot meals. As we slept the wind swung to the north as forecast, and when we awoke the rain was replaced by a bright sunny sky. Once again we raised anchor, snagging a large rotten log in the process, and steered back out into the Labrador Sea. The voyage had become a dogged fight to get home, with no time to explore the shores or harbours along the way. We had only 700 miles left to sail, but with forecasts calling for continued strong winds and heavy seas we knew that the challenge was far from over. One more week and we'll be home, I told myself.

The wind was blowing 30 knots on our port quarter as we slipped through the Strait of Belle Isle and into the more sheltered waters of the Gulf of St Lawrence. A pod of dolphins and a few whales escorted us in, raising my hopes that the last few days of sailing would be more pleasant than the trip south so far.

But my hopes were soon dashed when the radio began to crackle with gale warnings. The wind swung east and started to build towards the forecasted 50 knots. We were 20 miles downwind from the shelter of the Newfoundland coast, and even farther from a port of any kind. The race was on to get to shelter. Our charts showed Lark Harbour was the nearest port and we trimmed in the sails and turned into the wind. *Silent Sound* pounded into the growing seas, and soon we started the engine to give us extra speed. All afternoon we pushed towards the land, rising dark and rocky on the horizon. We were in a race against the storm, and we checked the forecast and our location constantly, worried we'd be the last across the line.

We slipped into Little Port just as darkness fell and the storm hit with its full vengeance. Nestled in between the steep stone walls was a small fishing dock, busy with brightly lit trawlers unloading their catch. Soon we were tied up, with more boats streaming into the port in search of shelter as 50 knot winds slammed into the land.

For the last time of the trip we hitched a ride into town, made new friends, and were welcomed into a home. This time it was Bill and Brenda

Larkin, the owners of the neighbourhood pub, who took us in, fed us and let us use their showers. We waited 36 hours for the storm to blow itself out, anxiously recalculating the 450 miles left to sail against our fast approaching deadline. It was still dark on the morning of our second day in Little Port as we pushed off from the dock and resumed our voyage south.

The glow of Halifax city lights became visible as night fell on October 9th. We slowly ticked off the lights and landmarks that led us into port, leaving Devil's Island to port and slipping through the narrow Eastern Passage. It was past midnight by the time *Silent Sound* was tied up to a dock at Fisherman's Wharf.

We were just outside Halifax harbour itself. Tricia Schers and Jennifer Chan had ensured that Bishop's Landing had a berth waiting for us and the Maritime Museum of the Atlantic was hosting our arrival, with an after-party in the Alexander Keith's brewery. More importantly, I knew our families, girlfriends and friends were probably asleep or preparing to meet us in the morning. My father had cashed in some of my mother's retirement funds and was flying my whole family to Halifax to welcome me ashore. Tobias and Hanns were expecting family from Germany, my girlfriend had flown in from Hong Kong, and friends I had not seen in years would be there to greet me.

But now we had a few hours to ourselves. What to do? The docks were quiet and empty, but I was desperate to see some new faces, to mark our arrival in some way. We walked up and down the quiet dock, startling an amorous couple in their parked car. We asked them if there were any pubs nearby, and were disappointed when they said everything was closed for the night. I was too restless to sleep, or to remain on the boat, so I trudged up the pier, still wearing my oilskins, sea boots and harness. As I came up to the top of the pier and rounded a corner I heard the tinkle of glass and laughter of women. A few more metres and there it was, a pub with lights and laughter spilling from its windows. I ran back to the boat to tell the others.

"There's a pub! It's open! Let's go, beers on me!"

Soon we were bellied up to the bar ordering our first round. The bartender studied our faces. We were unshaven, wind chapped and greasy-faced with exhaustion. But this was a port town, and he'd seen it all before.

"Just get in?" he enquired.

I tried to keep a steady voice and straight face.

"Yep."

There was no further question from him. I couldn't resist.

"From Victoria. Victoria, BC."

He didn't flinch, but carried on polishing and putting away his pint glasses. But I could see he was thinking, drawing a mental map.

"Just sailed through the Northwest Passage on a sailboat," I offered, disappointed at the reaction I was getting. If this journey hadn't given me a pub story to beat all, I didn't know what I would do next.

"Hmm," he said, pursing his lips and raising his eyebrows just enough to show that he understood.

We sat at the bar, unsure of what to say or do. We raised our glasses for repeated toasts to our success, the sea and *Silent Sound*. We watched a few drunken patrons play pool. Soon a woman came to the bar, giving us a lopsided boozy smile.

"Hiya."

"Hello," I responded, preparing myself for another attempt at soliciting some admiration for the journey we'd just made.

She ordered a drink, and cast a sideways glance at us, studying our dishevelled appearance. Before I could say anything she spoke up.

"Something smells funny," she said to no one in particular. "Smells like diesel. Like a boat. Is that you guys?"

Before I could pitch into my tale she'd turned and walked back to her friends, and the three of us were once again left staring at each other, with nothing left to say.

# IN GRATITUDE

After all the miles sailed and months spent writing, this journey is remembered most for the people I met along the way. In every town we visited we met complete strangers who offered us help, welcomed us into their homes and provided us with hot showers and food. Countless people showed genuine interest in our journey and generously told us about their lives, and we left nearly every town with a few fish or other wild game in our refrigerator. And then there were the many friends who believed in my dream and made it their own and my family who held their tongue and supported me. Their support made me want to complete this journey, and this book, regardless of how difficult it became.

The crew of *Silent Sound* poured an exceptional amount of hard work and dedication into this expedition. Hanns Bergmann joined to take charge of the boat, and he did an excellent job of keeping her and the rest of us safe even when we had our noses in our notebooks and eyes glued to the viewfinder. His turns at unplugging the head, maintaining the engine and repairing the rigging proved his dedication not only to the success of the project but to the art of sailing. Tobias Neuberger came aboard a landlubber and over the course of the summer became a very competent sailor. He also became the head chef, keeping bellies full during the stormiest of crossings. His pictures made the website a work of art, and I thank him for his contribution and insights. Drew Fellman joined us for only one month, but he breathed fresh life into the crew and project when we were lagging after some hard miles of sailing. His humour, stunning photos and crafty galley work with wild beasts of the Arctic made the Northwest Passage immeasurably more enjoyable.

Troy Dunkley was there for me from the very start of this dream and once we'd left the dock he continued emailing us encouragement, weather updates, news and the occasional concerned message from the Coast Guard. His countless hours designing and maintaining the expedition website were largely responsible for the following we attracted over the course of the voyage. Most importantly, I thank him for listening as I planned aloud in the months leading up to our departure.

Thank you Tricia Schers for getting the media interested and making sure people heard our story and for planning both our departure and arrival. Thanks to Jennifer Chan for keeping track of everything when I lost the plot, and I am grateful to Dr Chris Pielou for her colourful advice explaining the science behind all we saw along the way.

I am lucky to have friends such as Tom Mitchell, Erin Prelypchan, Nicole Huang, Jackie Ng, Sai-Min Man, Jessie Hui, Torben Kristensen and the rest of the *Authority* crew for pushing me forward when I was ready to ditch my plans. I am also fortunate to have a family who believed I could pull this off, helped me do it, and were there to see it happen. Extra thanks to my brothers Rod, Terry and Bryan for making sure I had a boat that floated and to my sisters Connie and Cheryl for their love and the food they put in my larder. Thank you to my Mother and Father for sharing their spirit of adventure.

Victoria was a foreign city for me until I arrived to buy *Silent Sound*, but over the following months I met some of the most generous and true people in my life. Norman and Trudi Prelypchan provided meals and wheels and made Victoria our home, becoming the de facto expedition parents. Adrian Blunt generously shared his knowledge of yachts and his network of suppliers; Ian and Jo Hansen inspired us with their courage and convinced me that today is always the best time to make a dream come true; Captain Duke Snider exemplified the warm and friendly professionalism of the Canadian Coast Guard; Charles Pike and Joann Rickert listened to our dreams and showed us their own; Jordan and Judy Mills offered mechanical advice while they were swamped with their own preparations to set sail for foreign seas.

I wish to expressly thank the people we met in various ports who shared their stories and welcomed us ashore wherever we went: Curt aboard *Sans Souci*; Dan Richard, Frank Oxereok Jr., Ruben Ozenna in Wales; David and Brenda Lucas in Tuktoyaktuk; Joey and Margaret Carpenter in Sachs Harbour; John Sr. and John John Lucas in Sachs Harbour; Vicki and Jorgen Aitaok in Cambridge Bay; Dennis and the shop crew at Kitnuna Construction in Cambridge Bay; Jacob and Silas Atkichok and their family in Gjoa Haven; Amie Qaqasiq and his mates in Clyde River; Sarah Webb in Nain; Charley and Virtue Simms in Nain; Bill and Brenda Larkin in Lark Harbour; John Owen and Jan Evans in Halifax; Donal Power in Halifax, who lent me his spiffy '88 Oldsmobile when I arrived; and Steven, the guy in Alaska who telephoned our Halifax arrival party to buy the crew a few pitchers of beer. There are many more who I have forgotten to thank.

We were lucky to share this voyage with a group of sailors and passionate adventurers. Thank you to Captain Mark Schrader and the crew of *Ocean Watch* for your friendship, advice, tools and showing us how these expeditions are meant to run. Captain Thierry Fabing and the crew of *Baloum Gwen* shared many dinners, outings and evenings with us, along with generous loans of batteries and dinghy rides. Sharing the seas with these yachts was an honour.

Peter Semotiuk (XNR79) was a constant source of company, support and advice on the airwaves. Patrick Gomes-Leal, whom I have never actually met, sent us great weather advice and kept track of our progress. You were both a huge part of our daily lives at sea.

Thank you to my many friends around the globe who helped raise the money I didn't have. I am grateful to Doreen Steidle, Consul General of Canada to Hong Kong, for her enthusiastic support and introductions. Thank you to our sponsors: Direct Energy, Canadian North, WWF, UK Halsey Sailmakers, Chlorophylle, Mustang Survival, Eco-Sys Action, RC Outfitters and Discovery.com.

I must acknowledge those who guided me through the messy process of writing my first book. Thank you Tom Mitchell for bravely tackling the first draft and the other friends who helped me sift through the chaff for the bits that were interesting.

Thank you Gregg Shilliday and all those at Great Plains Publications for taking a punt on a new writer and seeing a worthy story where others didn't, and for their patient editing and advice.

Lastly, I must thank *Silent Sound*, who safely carried us through the Arctic. Boats will treat you as well as you treat them, and she proved to have a particularly kind heart because I was often unkind to her. She was never going to be the prettiest or fastest, but she was my first and she did what was asked of her. She's now with another man, but I hope she'll always remember the Arctic adventure we shared.

*Hong Kong*
*December, 2011*

# SAILING GLOSSARY

**Abeam**  The direction of an object visible from the port or starboard side of a ship when it is perpendicular to the centerline of the vessel.

**Aft**  Towards the stern of the boat or behind it.

**Aloft**  The direction/area above the boat; in the rigging.

**Beam**  A ship's breadth at its widest.

**Beam reach**  Sailing at 90 degrees to the wind's direction.

**Beating**  Tacking back and forth, zigzagging upwind, as close to the wind as possible.

**Chartplotter**  A computer with a digital map and global positioning system that shows the boat's location, heading, speed, course, etc.

**Close hauled**  Sailing as high into the wind as the boat is capable, which is roughly 45 degrees to the wind direction.

**Companionway**  The stairs and entrance way down into the cabin of the boat.

**Dinghy**  A little open boat, rowed or powered by a small outboard engine.

**Genoa/jib**  A triangular foresail in front of the foremast.

**Gybe**  Turning the stern of the boat through the wind, causing the sails to move to the other side of the boat.

**Halyard**  The line used to lift a sail up the mast.

**Head**  The toilet/shower on a boat. Also the upper corner of a triangular sail.

**Heel**  The leaning of a boat to one side, due to wind.

**Kedge**  To set an anchor and move a boat by hauling on the anchor line.

**Knot**  The measure of speed and distance at sea or in the air. One nautical mile equals 1.852 kilometres, or 1.151 statutory miles. One knot of speed is 1.852 km/hr.

**Lee/Leeward**  The direction away from the wind; opposite of windward.

**Lifelines**  Steel cables set in stanchions, or posts, around the perimeter of the deck for safety.

**Mainsail**  A triangular sail set on the mainmast. On a sloop it is the aft sail.

**Masthead**  The top of the mast.

**Port**  The left side of a boat when looking forward. That side remains port side regardless of which way you are facing.

**Quarter (port/starboard)**  The direction/area in the quadrant between the beam of a vessel and its stern, creating a port quarter and a starboard quarter.

**Reach** Sailing with the wind coming over the beam of the boat.

**Reefing** Reducing the amount of sail to avoid being overpowered.

**Rigging** The general term for all the lines of a vessel.

**Run** Sailing with the wind coming over the stern.

**Sheets** Lines used to trim the sails.

**SSB** A marine single sideband radio operates on a marine radio spectrum called 'shortwave', medium frequency and high frequency, all at between 2 MHz and 26 MHz. This radio spectrum is shared with shortwave, Ham radio and long-range aircraft. It is used to transmit voice and data over long distances.

**Starboard** The right side of a boat when looking forward. That side remains starboard side regardless of which way you are facing.

**Stern** The back end of a boat, usually the square end.

**Tack** A boat's heading as determined by the side that its sails are on. To change tacks one has to move the bow through the eye of the wind. Also the forward and lower corner of a sail.

**VHF** A marine VHF radio operates at between 156 MHz and 174 MHz, and is used for short-distance communication between vessels.

**Winch** A hand-powered machine used for hauling, having a drum around which is wound a rope attached to a sail or other load.

**Windlass** A heavy winch on the bow of the boat used to raise and lower the anchor.

**Windward** Toward the direction from which the wind is coming; opposite of leeward.

# BIBLIOGRAPHY

Online References

www.arctic-council.org, The Arctic Council

www.alaska.boemre.gov, Bureau of Ocean Energy Management, Regulation and Enforcement

www.cbc.ca, Canadian Broadcasting Corporation

www.ec.gc.ca, The Canadian Ice Service (CIS), a division of the Meteorological Service of Canada (MSC)

www.polarcom.gc.ca, Canadian Polar Commission

www.theglobeandmail.com, The Globe and Mail

www.thecanadianencyclopedia.com, Historica Foundation

www.inuitcircumpolar.com, Inuit Circumpolar Council

www.itk.ca, Inuit Tapiriit Kanatami

www.nsidc.org, National Snow and Ice Data Center

www.nytimes.com, The New York Times

www.nnsl.com, Northern News Services

www.nunatsiaqonline.ca, Nunatsiaq News

www.eia.gov.nu.ca/stats/, Nunavut Bureau of Statistics

Reference Books

Amundsen, Roald and Ellsworth, Lincoln, *First Crossing of the Polar Sea.* Honolulu: University Press of the Pacific, 1928 (reprinted in 2001).

Amundsen, Roald, *The North-West Passage: Being the Record of a Voyage of Exploration of the Ship Gjöa, 1903–1907 Vol I,* London: Archibald Constable & Co., 1908 (reprinted in 2005 by Adamant Media).

Amundsen, Roald, *The North-West Passage: Being the Record of a Voyage of Exploration of the Ship Gjöa, 1903–1907 Vol II,* New York: E.P. Dutton and Co. 1908.

Bennet, John and Rowley, Susan (eds.), *Uqalurait: An Oral History of Nunavut.* Montreal: McGill-Queen's University Press, 2004.

Beattie, Owen and Geiger, John, *Frozen in Time: The Fate of the Franklin Expedition.* Vancouver: Douglas & McIntyre, 1987.

Berton, Pierre, *The Arctic Grail: The Quest for the North West Passage and the North Pole, 1818–1909.* New York: Viking Penguin Inc., 1988.

Brody, Hugh, *Living Arctic: Hunters of the Canadian North.* Vancouver/ Seattle, Douglas & McIntyre and University of Washington Press, 1987.

Brown, Kathan, *The North Pole*. San Francisco: Crown Point Press, 2004.

Brower, Charles D., *Fifty Years Below Zero: A Lifetime of Adventure in the Far North*. Fairbanks: University of Alaska Press, 1994.

Coates, Ken S.; Lackenbauer, P. Whitney; Morrison, William R.; Poelzer, Greg, *Arctic Front: Defending Canada in the Far North*. Toronto: Thomas Allen, 2008.

Coates, Kenneth and Powell, Judith, *The Modern North: People, Politics and the Rejection of Colonialism*. Toronto: James Lorimer & Co, 1989.

Collinson, Richard, *Journal of H.M.S. Enterprise: On the Expedition in Search of Sir John Franklin's Ships by Behring Strait, 1850–55*. London: Sampson Low, Marston, Searle, & Rivington, 1889.

Cowper, David Scott, *Northwest Passage Solo*. London: Seafarer Books, 1993.

De Poncins, Gonthran, *Kabloona*. New York: Carrol & Graf, 1941.

De Roos, Willy, *North-West Passage*. London: Hollis & Carter, 1979.

Elliot-Meisel, Elizabeth B., *Arctic Diplomacy: Canada and the United States in the Northwest Passage*. New York: Peter Lang, 1998.

Fredston, Jill, *Rowing to Latitude: Journeys Along the Arctic's Edge*. New York: North Point Press, 2001.

Griffiths, Franklyn (ed.), *Politics of the Northwest Passage*, Kingston: McGill-Queen's University Press, 1987.

Hanbury-Tenison, Robin (ed.), *The Seventy Great Journeys in History*, London: Thames & Hudson, 2006.

Harper, Kenn, *Give Me My Father's Body: The Life of Minik, The New York Eskimo*. New York: Washington Square Press, 1986.

Hayes, Derek, *Historical Atlas of the Arctic*. Vancouver: Douglas & McIntyre, 2003.

Huntford, Roland, *Nansen*. London: Abacus, 1997.

Jason, Victoria, *Kabloona in the Yellow Kayak: One Woman's Journey through the Northwest Passage*. Winnipeg: Turnstone Press, 1995.

Krupnik, Igor and Jolly, Dyanna (eds.), *The Earth is Faster Now: Indigenous Observations of Arctic Environmental Change*. Fairbanks: Arctic Research Consortium of the United States, 2002.

Loomis, Chauncey, *Weird and Tragic Shores: The Story of Charles Francis Hall, Explorer*. New York: Random House, 2000.

Lopez, Barry, *Arctic Dreams: Imagination and Desire in a Northern Landscape*. New York: Charles Scribner's Sons, 1986.

Loukacheva, Natalia, *The Arctic Promise: Legal and Political Autonomy of Greenland and Nunavut*. Toronto: University of Toronto Press, 2007.

McGoogan, Ken, *Ancient Mariner: The Amazing Adventures of Samuel Hearne, the Sailor Who Walked to the Arctic Ocean*. Toronto: HarperCollins, 2005.

McGoogan, Ken, *Fatal Passage: The Untold Story of John Rae, the Arctic Adventurer Who Discovered the Fate of Franklin*. Toronto: HarperCollins, 2001.

Nevin, Jennifer, *Ada Blackjack: A True Story of Survival in the Arctic*. New York: Hyperion, 2003.

Noice, Harold, *With Stefansson in the Arctic*. London: George G Harrap, 1924

Pálsson, Gísli, *Travelling Passions: The Hidden Life of Vilhjalmur Stefansson*. Winnipeg: The University of Manitoba Press, 2003.

Pielou, E.C., *A Naturalist's Guide to the Arctic*. Chicago: The University of Chicago Press, 1994.

Pryde, Duncan, *Nunaga: Ten Years of Eskimo Life*. New York: Walker and Co.,1971.

Raban, Jonathan, *Passage to Juneau: A Sea and its Meanings*. New York: Random House, 1999.

Sherman, Len, *Arctic Odyssey: Dove III Masters the Northwest Passage*. Anacortes: Fine Edge, 1999.

Simon, Alvah, *North to the Night: A Spiritual Odyssey in the Arctic*. New York: Broadway Books, 1998.

Standlea, David M., *Oil, Globalization, and the War for the Arctic Refuge*. Albany: State University of New York Press, 2006.

Starkell, Don, *Paddle to the Arctic*, Toronto: McClelland & Stewart, 1995.

Struzik, Ed, *The Big Thaw: Travels in the Melting North*. Mississauga: John Wiley & Sons Canada, 2009.

Waterman, Jonathan, *Arctic Crossing: A Journey Through the Northwest Passage and Inuit Culture*. New York: Alfred A. Knopf, 2001.

Wohlfoth, Charles, *The Whale and the Supercomputer: On the Northern Front of Climate Change*. New York: North Point Press, 2004.

### Pilot Books

*Sailing Directions: Arctic Canada, Volume II (Eastern Part)*. Ottawa, Canada: Department of Fisheries and Oceans, 1985.

*Sailing Directions: Arctic Canada, Volume III*. Ottawa, Canada: Department of Fisheries and Oceans, 1994.

*Sailing Directions: General Information, Northern Canada (ARC 400)*. Ottawa, Canada: Department of Fisheries and Oceans, 2009.

*Marine Environment Handbook, Arctic, Northwest Passage*. Ottawa, Canada: Department of Fisheries and Oceans, 1999.